Move Ahead Plus

Student's Book

KEN WILSON

JAMES TAYLOR

MARY TOMALIN

DEIRDRE HOWARD-WILLIAMS

CONTENTS

VOCABULARY	READING	WRITING
School subjects	Gordonstoun School	Formal letter
Dates and events	Civilisations of the Mediterranean	A day in the life
Everyday items – glass, paper; what things are made of and from	The history of pens	Summary
Pastimes	Marathon running	Essay – advantages and disadvantages
Occupations – scientist, lawyer, engineer, architect, doctor	Studying in another country	Conversation
Film styles; film people – director, producer, cameraman, actor/actress	Steven Spielberg	Film review
Gifts, birthdays, traditions	Cultural differences	Opinion essay
Geographical locations	The coldest place on earth	Descriptive essay
Types of writing; book vocabulary	Extracts from novels	Article about a famous writer
Travel	*My Year of Meat* by Ruth Ozeki	Letter of application
Marine geography	Swimming with sphinxes	Opinion essay
Personal information	Seb Clover; Operations Drake and Raleigh	Dialogue
News media and news gathering	Newspaper reports	Newspaper article
Film special effects	*The Adventures of Sindbad the Sailor*	Narrative
Languages	News item about languages in danger	For and Against essay

EVERYBODY'S AT SCHOOL

INTRODUCTION AND VOCABULARY

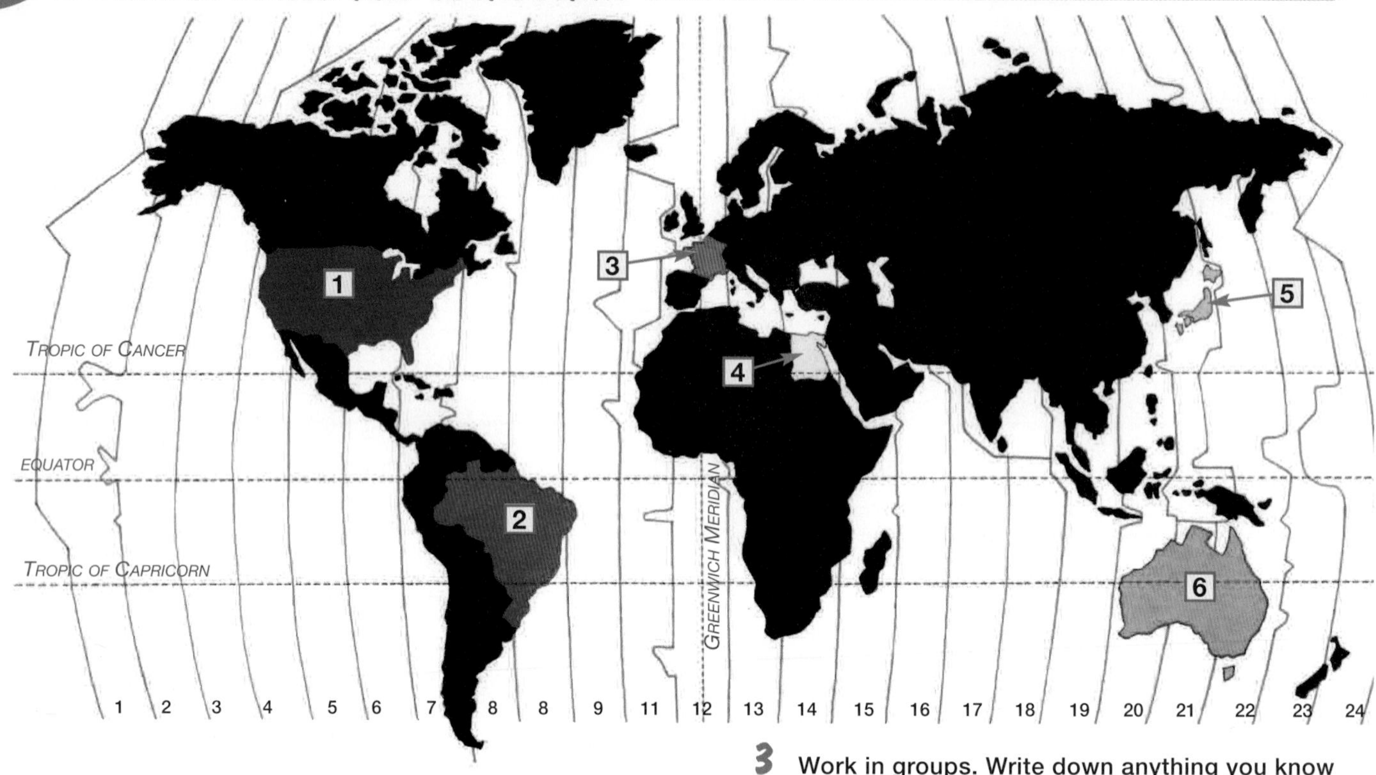

1 **Look at the map of the world. Can you name countries 1-6? Choose from this list.**

Argentina Australia Brazil
Canada China Egypt
France Japan New Zealand
the United Kingdom the United States

Check your answers at the bottom of page 11.

2 **Work in pairs. Insert the name of the country in place of the number.**

1 What time is it on the west coast of (1)?
2 What do you think someone your age is doing there now?
3 What time is it in the middle of (2)?
4 What do you think the weather is like there?
5 What time is it in (3)?
6 What do you think the weather is like in (4)?
7 What is the capital city of (5)?
8 What time is it there?
9 What time is it on the east coast of (6)?
10 What do you think someone of your age is doing there now?

3 **Work in groups. Write down anything you know about countries 1–6. Share your information with other people in the class. Try to write information about the following:**

- the capital cities
- other famous cities or places
- the language(s) that people speak there
- famous people from there
- a famous historical event which took place there.

4 **Discuss these questions. Don't worry if you can't answer them at this point.**

- Do you know anyone from the countries you've been discussing?
- Do you know anything about the education system in these countries?
- Do you think studying languages is important in these countries?

5 **You are going to read about education in three of the countries highlighted on the map. Make sure you understand the meaning of the following words and expressions.**

primary school secondary school
private school school term school semester
school subject school timetable assessment
compulsory subjects examinations

My school is a private primary and secondary school called Colégio Kerigma in Fortaleza, which is in the north east of Brazil. In Brazil, the school year is divided into two semesters. The first semester usually starts in February and ends in June, and the second starts in August and ends in December.

My father usually drives me to school and the maid comes to pick me up at the end of the day. Most schools offer two timetable options. We can either choose to study from 7.15 to 12.15 or from 13.15 to 18.15. Compulsory subjects in our school are Mathematics, Art, World History, Geography, Portuguese, English or Spanish, Chemistry, Physics and Biology. Maths, Art and Biology are the most popular among my age group.

There are two sets of examinations every semester, one in the middle and one at the end. Assessment is based on these examinations, plus your work during the semester. After school, there are music and drama activities and lots of sports teams, with football, volleyball and basketball being the most popular ones.

Larissa Gueiros, aged 16, Colégio Kerigma, Fortaleza Brazil

My school is called Riverview, and it's a private school in Sydney, Australia. There are four terms in a year, running from February to April, April to June, July to September, and October to November. December and January is our summer holiday. We start school at 8.45 and finish at 3.30. I managed to pass my driving test last month, so now I drive to school in my car.

We have to study English, Maths and Science, and after that we can choose from a series of subjects, including languages, Art and Commerce. The last two are the most popular subjects in my year. There are examinations at the end of the year but that is only a small part of our assessment, the rest being based on our homework during the year. We have sport, music and drama clubs after school. We also study Aboriginal Reconciliation, which means that we learn about the history of the original inhabitants of our country.

Brian Malone, aged 17, Riverview School, Sydney Australia

My school is called The Madeira School and it's an all-girls private High School. The school year is divided into two semesters, the first of which is September through December, and the second January through May. We have a LONG summer vacation!

We start school at 7.50am and we finish at 3pm. I take the school bus to and from school, although my mother sometimes picks me up on her way home from work.

We have the usual compulsory subjects and everyone has to do a foreign language, with French, Spanish or Latin the possible choices. We also do Performing Arts, and this year we're writing and performing our own version of a Shakespeare play.

My friends and I don't agree about a favorite subject. My best friend likes Spanish but I prefer Performing Arts. There are mid-semester and end-of-semester exams, which count for 30% of your grade. We have a lot of clubs and teams – soccer, lacrosse, cross-country, track, basketball, softball, volleyball, swimming, squash and theatre club. And I play in a chamber ensemble.

Julia Davies, aged 16, Madeira School, Washington DC USA

6 **Look at the reading texts on this page. They were written by school pupils in Australia, Brazil and the United States. Read the texts quickly and find at least ten school subjects. Then answer these questions.**

1 How many of the subjects are languages?
2 Where in the world do people speak these languages?
3 In which of the other subjects do you learn about …
- arithmetic?
- plants?
- business and economics?
- painting pictures?
- events in the past?

7 **Read the questions in the chart. Answer the questions about your school in the left hand column. Write in note form.**

	You	Brian	Julia	Larissa
What time do you start and finish school?				
How do you usually get to school?				
What are the most popular school subjects among your age group?				
Do you have any clubs or other after-school activities?				

8 **Now work in groups of three. Read the three texts more carefully. Each student should read just one text. Complete the chart with answers from the text you read. Write your answers in note form.**

9 **Now cover the texts (but not the chart). Tell the other students in your group what you learnt about the student you read about.**

10 **Discuss the following questions.**

- Which school is most similar to yours?
- what do you like about the three schools?
- what don't you like?
- which school would you like to visit?

1

Where do princes go to school?

There are two types of schools in the UK: state schools, where education is free, and private schools, where you have to pay. About 7% of students in England and 4% of students in Scotland attend private schools.

Prince William and Prince Harry, the sons of Prince Charles, attended Eton College, one of the oldest and most famous private schools in England. Their father and grandfather attended a very different private school, Gordonstoun in Scotland.

Both Eton and Gordonstoun are boarding schools, which means that pupils live at the school and only see their parents during the school holidays. Pupils board at Eton and Gordonstoun from the age of 12 or 13, but there are some boarding schools where the pupils are only five years old.

Eton College – some interesting facts

- It costs £20,000 (US$30,000) a year to send a child to Eton.
- The waiting list is so long that parents register their children's names as soon as they are born.
- Nineteen British Prime Ministers went to Eton.
- An impressive list of writers went to Eton, including Ian Fleming, who wrote the James Bond novels.

SCHOOL UNIFORM

- Pupils at Eton wear very old-fashioned uniforms. Eton boys wear tailcoats, waistcoats, pinstripe trousers and they used to wear top hats.
- Eton pupils play a strange game called the Wall Game, which nobody outside the school understands. It is extremely difficult to score a goal in this game – the last one was scored in 1909!
- Old Etonians, a team consisting entirely of former pupils at Eton, won the soccer FA Cup in 1882. They also appeared in the Cup Final the following year.

WALL GAME

OLD ETONIANS TEAM

1 **Look at the people in the photographs. What do you know about them? How are they related to each other?**

2 **Before you read part 1 of the reading text, answer these questions.**

1 Which word means *go to* school?
a attend **b** absent **c** attempt **c** allow

2 Which adjective indicates that pupils *spend all their time* at a school?
a breeding **b** bedding **c** boarding **d** bouncing

3 Which word means that you think something is *very good*?
a impossible **b** impressive **c** improved **d** impulsive

4 Which of these means *not modern*?
a old-fashioned **b** old boy **c** old school **d** old master

3 **Now read part 1 and answer these questions.**

1 What percentage of pupils attend state schools in England?
2 Did Prince Charles attend the same school as his father?
3 How often do boarding school pupils see their families?
4 When do parents register their children for Eton College?
5 What unusual facts are there about Eton?

4 **Close your books and see how many facts about Eton you can remember.**

5 **Before you read parts 2 and 3 about Gordonstoun School, find the words in bold and match them with these definitions.**

1 someone who decides what to do in an independent way has this quality
2 this means the ability to do something without practising or rehearsing
3 someone who tells the truth all the time has this quality
4 someone who can work hard for a long time has this quality
5 someone who has original ideas has this quality

6 **Now read *The school with a difference* and decide which of these is the best summary.**

1 Gordonstoun was founded by a German teacher who didn't like the German education system.
2 The founder of Gordonstoun was forced to leave his home country because he criticised the government.
3 The German government forced the head teacher of Gordonstoun to leave because they didn't like his educational methods.

7 **Read the text about the Gordonstoun Challenge and answer these questions.**

1 What kind of activity did participants have on the first morning?
2 Was Andrew's team successful in this activity?
3 What did participants have to do on the first afternoon?
4 Was Andrew's team better than the others in this activity?
5 What was the surprise challenge on the first evening?
6 Did Andrew's team come first in this activity?
7 Where did the activities on the second morning take place?
8 Did Andrew's team win?
9 What kind of activities took place on the second afternoon?
10 Was Andrew excited about doing these activities?

2

The school with a difference ...

Gordonstoun, the school that Prince Charles attended, is situated in the Scottish mountains and was founded in 1933 by a German teacher called Doctor Kurt Hahn. Doctor Hahn had been head teacher of a school in Germany but he left the country after being threatened by the Nazi government, who were not happy with his progressive methods of education. He went to Scotland and continued his work there. He wanted to encourage young people to show **honesty**, **initiative** and service to others, but most of all, he wanted them to have adventures while they studied.

3

Are you good enough for the Gordonstoun challenge?

Every year Gordonstoun invites teams of pupils from different schools to attend the *Gordonstoun Challenge*, where they find out about the unique atmosphere in the school.

Here is the diary of a pupil who attended the weekend.

Gordonstoun Challenge diary
WRITTEN BY ANDREW CURTIS

DAY ONE

There were five teams from different schools and we all watched each other when we weren't involved in the activities ourselves.

In the morning, we were tested on ball skills in the gymnasium – throwing, catching and kicking. My team scored top marks in this test! Then in the fitness room, there was another series of challenges which really tested our strength and ***stamina****, so that we were ready for our lunch after this exhausting session!*

In the afternoon, we found ourselves in the computer room, where we were asked to use our ***imagination*** *to solve problems on a computer. I found it very interesting and all the teams did very well in these tasks.*

In the evening, there was a surprise challenge that involved moving an egg from three metres in the air to ground level without damaging the shell. We had two eggs, straws, string, scissors, coloured paper, glue and a big plastic rubbish bag.

We used the string and the plastic bag to create a slope. We made some padding with the coloured paper to stop the egg, but while this worked well during practice, during the real test, the egg missed the padding and broke. Unsurprisingly, we came last in this activity.

DAY TWO

In the morning, we had to cross a swamp, using stepping stones and three planks. Crossing it was difficult, but the biggest problem was getting the planks out of the swamp when we finished. Then we had to complete an army obstacle course, which was very tough, climbing up poles, over walls and along nets and swinging on ropes. We had to work as a team to complete this, pushing, pulling and encouraging each other, and I'm pleased to say that we did very well in this activity, coming second.

The afternoon drama session was really fun! It was led by two Gordonstoun sixth-form drama students. We started with some relaxation activities, then played some ***improvisation*** *games.*

Overall impression – absolutely fantastic! If this is the way they study at Gordonstoun, I want to go there!

Present tenses

1 Which tense do you use to do the following?

A To talk about the present moment.
B To talk about a longer (but still temporary) present situation.
C To talk about things becoming different.
D With general truths.
E With routines.
F Verbs which do not have continuous forms.

Now read these sentences. Which use of the present tense do the sentences illustrate?

1-2 What do you think someone of your age is doing there now? ....
3 The first semester usually starts and ends in June. ....
4 Do Eton boys wear tailcoats? ....
5 But things are changing. ....
6 I passed my driving test last month, so now I drive to school. ....
7 This year we're writing and performing our own version. ....

2 Write out the conversation below correctly (including negatives). Explain your tense choices.

A: Hello, John. (What - do) these days?
B: (I - study) French at the university.
A: Oh, really? And (you - like) the classes?
B: Well, I didn't at first, but (they - slowly - get) better.
A: Good. (you - have - classes) every day?
B: Four days a week. (I - go) on Fridays.
A: But today's Wednesday. Why (you - study) today?
B: Because (I - go) to the dentist. His office is here on this street.
A: Oh. Perhaps that's why (you - smile) much today!
B: That's right. Well, (I - imagine) that (most people - enjoy) going to the dentist!

3 Explain the tense uses in these sentences. (Help? Grammar Reference, section 1.)

1 You're wasting my time!
2 The referee blows his whistle. Beckham takes the free kick and the ball is in the net!
3 I name this ship *Stella Maris*.
4 My sister's always wearing my clothes!
5 We promise to pay the sum of £100 on December 31, 2010.

Important – read this!

Both common nouns and proper nouns may be used as compounds (to modify other nouns). Examples from the unit include: *state* schools and *James Bond* novels. They may even be used in a series: *sixth-form drama students* (students who are in the sixth form and who study drama). As with other modifiers in English, the form is the same for singular and plural: *state schools* ('schools' is the main noun, so it can be plural), but *school holidays* ('school' is the modifier so does not change form even though 'holidays' is plural).

4 Find eight examples of this structure in Gordonstoun Challenge diary, p 7. At least one should be a 'series'.

5 Explain the difference between what Helmut and Ali say about the key. What does 'key' mean in the last sentence?

My Dad's lost his key car.
No, he hasn't, Helmut.
Of course he has, Ali. That's why he's looking for it.
No, Helmut. He's lost his car key.
That's what I said.
No, you didn't. There's a key difference!

1 **Letters can be formal or informal in style. For each of the statements below, write F (formal) or I (Informal).**

1. A letter written to someone you do not know, for example, a possible employer or a shop manager.
2. A letter written to a friend or relative.
3. A letter with the name and address of the recipient on the left-hand side and the name and address of the sender on the right-hand side.
4. A letter with only one address (the sender's address), on the right-hand side.
5. A letter with colloquial expressions (eg *How's life?*) and contractions (eg *I'll*).
6. A letter with complex sentences, and no colloquial expressions or contractions.
7. A letter that begins *Dear Sir/Madam*, and ends *Yours faithfully,* + full name.
8. A letter that begins *Dear Mr/Mrs (Jones)* and ends *Yours sincerely*, + full name.
9. A letter that begins *Dear Mike* and ends *Best wishes,* + first name.
10. A letter that begins *Dear Sarah* and ends *(With) love* + first name.

2 **Read the letter below. Answer these questions.**

1. Is the letter formal or informal? How do you know?
2. Who is the letter to?
3. What is the reason for the letter?
4. Why is Teresa sorry to be leaving?

26 Wimbourne Road
London W13 2BY

Notting School,
West Place,
London W11

14 March 2004

Dear Mr Green,

In August of this year, the company that employs me will be moving offices from London to Bristol. I shall therefore be moving to Bristol with my family. Consequently, our daughter Teresa, currently in the lower sixth form at your school, will not be returning to your school in September. As you request, I am giving you a full term's notice.

Teresa regrets leaving your school, as she has greatly enjoyed her time with you. We have been delighted by her progress and the fact that she has done so well in her exams. Encouraged by her teachers, Teresa has developed many interests, and has become an excellent pianist. She has made a lot of good friends, and we hope that she will be able to stay in touch with them.

With many thanks for all your efforts. I feel certain that your school will continue to produce students who are both happy and successful.

Yours sincerely,

Michael Broadbent

Michael Broadbent

3 **Find words and phrases in the letter that mean the same as the following:**

this August | I work for | so | at present | ask | letting you know a term before she leaves | is sorry to be | because | a lot | continue seeing | are very pleased with | thank you | I am sure

4 **Rewrite these formal phrases using informal language.**

1. I am writing with regard to your letter of 14 March.
2. Thank you so much for your invitation.
3. I would be grateful if you would enclose this information.
4. I regret to inform you that your application has been turned down.
5. I wish you every success.
6. Please give my regards to your family.
7. I look forward to hearing from you in the near future.

5 **Write Mr Green's reply to Mr Broadbent's letter. Use the notes below to help you.**

- Remember to write the date below the address of the school on the right-hand side.
- **Paragraph 1:** This should contain the main reason for writing.
- **Paragraph 2:** This should develop the letter.
- **Final paragraph:** This should end the letter with one or two final remarks.

Notes

PARAGRAPH 1
Thank you/letter   giving notice well in advance
very sorry/losing Teresa

PARAGRAPH 2
Teresa/popular   excellent student
many conversations with her
interesting, lively, hardworking   do well/new school

FINAL PARAGRAPH
happy/new home   hope Teresa/ in contact with/school   always happy to see her

6 **Optional writing task. Imagine that you and your family have moved to a new town and that you have started at a new school. Write a letter to a friend in your old school describing your new school and how you feel about it.**

Here are some phrases to help you:
It all feels very new and strange.
I've met three or four people I really get on well with.
I miss you and all my old friends.
I'm really looking forward to seeing you.
Give my love to everyone.

QUICK QUIZ

1. What is the population of France?
a) 70 million b) 45 million c) 59 million

2. Which river is Paris on?
a) The River Seine b) The River Thames
c) The River Rhône

3. The Alps is a mountain range. Where are they?
a) In the east of France b) In the west of France
c) In the south of France

4. Which of these famous Frenchmen was executed?
a) Charles de Gaulle b) Napoleon Bonaparte
c) King Louis XVI

5. When did the French Revolution begin?
a) 1814 b) 1789 c) 1792

1 Complete this short quiz about France and famous French people.

2 Now listen and check your answers.

3 Read the following statements about the French education system. Some of them are true and some of them are false. Then listen to the tape and write T (True) or F (False) beside each statement.

1. Education is compulsory from the age of six to eighteen.
2. Most parents send their children to a state school, which is free.
3. Many schoolchildren have lessons on Saturday afternoon.
4. All children, whether at private or state school, learn from the same national curriculum.
5. There are end-of-year exams and students must repeat the year if they do not pass these exams.
6. In both state and private schools, all textbooks, exercise books and pens are free.
7. All children at state schools wear school uniform.
8. Literature is considered more important than Mathematics.
9. If you pass the school-leaving exam, you can go to university.

4 Answer the following questions about the French education system. The answers are in the listening passage you have just heard.

1. At what age do most students leave school?
a Sixteen **b** Eighteen
2. Which is considered to provide the best education?
a State schools **b** Private schools
3. Which day is often a free half-day for schoolchildren?
a Wednesday **b** Friday
4. When does the school year end? **a** June **b** July
5. What is considered more important?
a Logical thinking **b** Creativity
6. Which subject is compulsory in upper secondary school? **a** Drama **b** Philosophy

5 Are the statements in activity 3 true or false about your country's educational system? Write the correct answers if they are false.

6 Where is the stress in these words from the listening passage in activity 3?

education compulsory curriculum equipment
exercise literature mathematics logical
creativity philosophy secondary university

7 Listen and check your answers.

Listen again and repeat the words.

8 Discuss the following questions. Work in groups and then tell the rest of the class what you talked about.

- In this unit, you have learnt about schools in Australia, Brazil, England, France and the United States. Which information impressed you most?
- Is there anything more you would like to know about schools in these countries?

9 Find an internet site for a school in one of the countries and write an email with your questions.

Word watch – Compounds

A compound is a unit of vocabulary made from two separate words that is usually written as a single word, though it can also be hyphenated or written as two separate words (if you are unsure, check in a dictionary).

Choose one word from list A and one word from list B to make 10 compounds.

	A		B	
1	water	ice	speed	fall
2	hand	door	size	way
3	death	life	more	less
4	pipe	light	water	line
5	car	motor	road	way
6	over	under	water	shine
7	leg	foot	side	step
8	day	week	end	side
9	garden	farm	earth	yard
10	friend	home	hood	ship

Lessons in logic

You will have to read carefully to solve this logic problem:

Five people, a man, a woman, a teenager, a boy and a girl, are waiting in a queue to buy cinema tickets. The girl is behind the teenager but in front of the boy. The man is in front of the woman and she is one before the last. The girl is behind the man but he is not the first.

So, who is first …? second …? third …? fourth …? fifth …?

You might like to make up a problem like this for your friends – see if they can solve it, but be sure of the answer yourself!

Focus on reading

The order of words in an English sentence gives us the meaning and it is very important to get it right. In the following sentences two words need to change places for the sentence to make sense. Underline both words.

1. It is unusual to a able to see be fox in a city.
2. There in one thousand metres are a kilometre.
3. Michael was unable and sick to attend school this week.
4. Tropical cattle are being cut down to raise forests.
5. There to no solution was the problem.
6. Was department store the very busy every Saturday.
7. Chatting not the lesson is in allowed.
8. Do by think he will come you bus?

The writing system

The 26-letter alphabet used to write English dates from the late Middle Ages. Do you know what the most commonly used letter is in English?

> **word** word word word *word*
> *word* word WORD

There is a specialised vocabulary to talk about typing – label the features shown with the correct term. Choose from these anagrams (the letters are mixed up) :

litaic ewrol seac noft lobd purep ecas

Look at this sentence:
The quick brown fox jumps over the lazy dog.
It contains all the letters of the alphabet. Invent your own sentence using all 26 letters of the English alphabet.

Did you know? Surprising statistics

The average Briton has 14 close friends.

Is this more or fewer than you would have expected? Does it depend on how the word 'close' is defined? You need to spend time with a friend, so is the number naturally limited by the time you have available for social life? Is there an ideal number? Can you ever have too many friends? Do you think people in your country would have about the same number?

It's time to say what you think.

ANSWERS TO ACTIVITY 1 PAGE 4
The countries are:
1 The United States *2 Brazil* *3 France*
4 Egypt *5 Japan* *6 Australia*

2 WHEN DID IT HAPPEN?

INTRODUCTION AND VOCABULARY

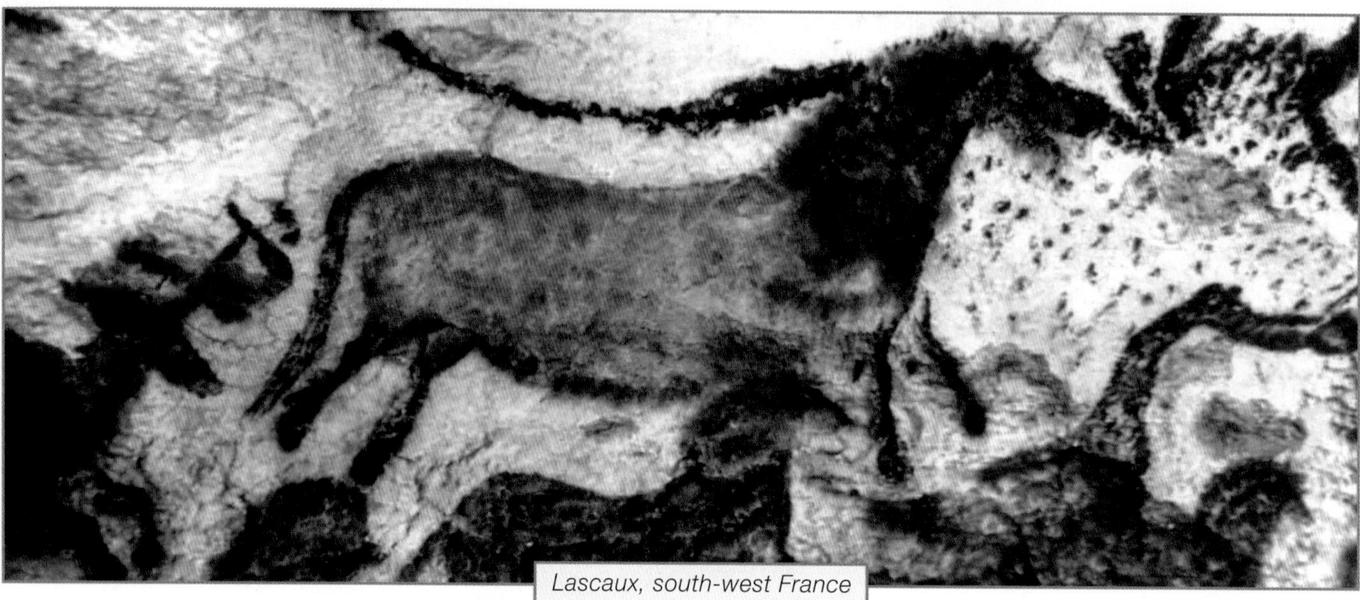
Lascaux, south-west France

1 **Practise saying the dates in this list. The examples are all dates when an interesting event happened, one from each decade of the twentieth century.**

December 17th 1903	December 14th 1911
January 26th 1926	May 25th 1935
September 12th 1940	February 22nd 1956
July 20th 1969	June 26th 1976
August 1st 1981	July 16th 1994

Note that there are different ways that you can say dates.

EXAMPLES: December 17th 1903
December the seventeenth, 1903 (nineteen-o-three)
OR
The seventeenth of December 1903

2 **Look at the photograph on this page and try to answer these questions.**

1 What do you think the photograph shows?
  a a cave painting
  b a painting by a famous artist
  c a painting on the wall of a house

2 How old do you think is it?
  a more than a thousand years old
  b more than ten thousand years old
  c more than twenty thousand years old

3 Who do you think discovered the painting?
  a children
  b professional archaeologists
  c amateur archaeologists

One of the dates in activity 1 is the date when the painting in the illustration was found. Write down the date that you think the event took place. You will find out later if you were right. Don't worry if you are completely wrong!

3 **There are photographs of five of the other twentieth-century events on the next page. Guess or work out the following:**

- which event is referred to?
- which people were involved in the event?
- when did it take place?

4 **Four events left! They have something to do with the following people and topics. Try to match the people and the topics.**

PEOPLE	TOPICS
• Elvis Presley • Roald Amundsen • Bjorn Borg • John Logie Baird	• polar exploration • the first television broadcast • the start of a record-breaking sequence of sporting victories • the first hit of a major pop star

The Wright Brothers

The first moon landing

American athlete Jessie Owen

MTV

The Brazilian soccer team

5 **Here are the 10 events from the twentieth century. Some names and all the dates have been removed. Fill in as much information as you can.**

1 Neil Armstrong became the first person to set foot on the moon on __________.

2 __________, the first all-music TV channel, was broadcast for the first time on __________.

3 __________, a Norwegian explorer, was the first person to reach the South Pole on __________.

4 American athlete Jesse Owen set three world records and equalled a fourth (all in 70 minutes!) at Ann Arbor, Michigan on __________. One year later, he won four gold medals at the Olympics Games in Berlin.

5 The 17,000-year-old cave paintings at Lascaux in the south west of France were found by four children on __________. The children were looking for their dog.

6 __________'s first recording *Heartbreak Hotel*, entered the US pop charts on __________.

7 Orville and Wilbur Wright made the first aeroplane flight in North Carolina, USA on __________.

8 __________ won the Wimbledon Men's Singles Tennis Championship for the first time on __________. He is the only modern player to win the Wimbledon title five times in a row.

9 __________ demonstrated television for the first time in his workshop in London on __________.

10 __________ won the soccer World Cup for a record fourth time in front of 94,000 spectators at the Rose Bowl, Los Angeles, California on __________. They won it for the fifth time eight years later.

Now check your answers on page 19.

It's the last time our local soccer team won the championship.
1934

6 **Work in groups and do the following.**

- Think of an important event that took place during the twentieth century. Don't worry if you don't know the exact date.
- Tell the rest of the class the year of the event you have written down.
- Try to guess the events that other groups are referring to.
- Tell the class events which they can't guess.

7 **Write down dates that are important in your personal history. Choose from this list, or choose other events, if you prefer.**

- the day you were born
- the day you started school
- the day you travelled to another country for the first time
- the day you had your biggest academic success
- an important day in your country's history
- the day you had your biggest sporting success
- the day your country had a big sporting success

8 **Work in pairs. Tell your partner the dates you have written down, but not in the same order. Try to guess what the date(s) refer to. Give your partner three guesses for each date, and then tell him/her what the dates refer to.**

The amazing civilizations of the Mediterranean

Some of the greatest civilizations in the history of the world developed on the shores of the Mediterranean Sea, in particular the civilizations known as Ancient Egypt, Ancient Greece and Ancient Rome.

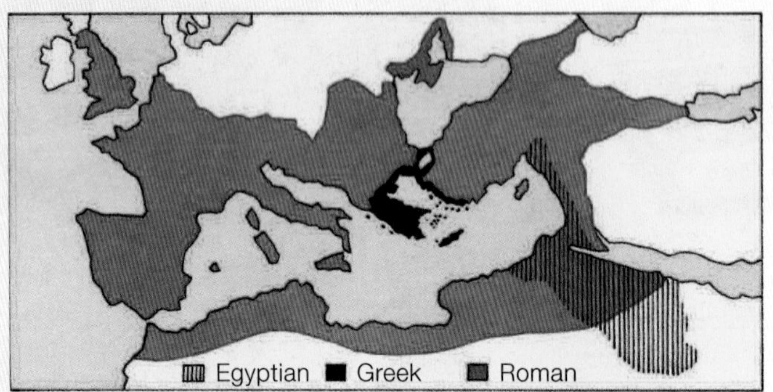

1 Ancient Egypt

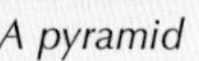

A pyramid

The Egyptians told me that 341 generations separate the first King of Egypt from the last. If we think of three generations lasting for a century, this means a total of 11,340 years. Herodotus (Greek historian who lived 2,500 years ago)

Egypt was the **birthplace** of one of the world's first civilizations. It developed about 5,000 years ago in the valley of the River Nile and lasted for over 2,000 years, one of the most **durable** civilizations in history.

The River Nile was the lifeblood of ancient Egypt, **overflowing** every year and depositing a strip of rich, black soil along each bank, so that farmers were able to produce a large supply of food from the **fertile** soil. The Nile also provided water for irrigation and was Egypt's main transportation route. The ancient Greek historian Herodotus called Egypt 'the gift of the Nile'.

The Ancient Egyptians achieved some amazing things, creating the world's first national government, developing a 365-day calendar, and inventing hieroglyphics, the world's first system of writing. They also built great cities where **skilled** architects, doctors, engineers, painters and sculptors worked, and they invented papyrus (see Unit 3, page 21).

The best-known achievements of the Ancient Egyptians, however, are the pyramids, the tombs of their rulers. The dry climate has **preserved** these magnificent and gigantic stone structures for about 4,500 years.

2 Ancient Greece

The Acropolis, Greece

The ancient Greeks invented democratic government, politics, economics, history, geography, philosophy, physics and biology; they also made revolutionary advances in architecture, sculpture, painting, music, mathematics and astronomy.
F J Lucas, historian

Ancient Greece was the birthplace of Western civilization about 2,500 years ago, and its **magnificent** achievements in government, science, philosophy and the arts still influence our lives today.

Greek civilization developed **first and foremost** in the form of small city-states, consisting of a city and the **surrounding** villages and farmland. These city-states were fiercely **independent** and often fought each other, but the most advanced of them established the world's first democratic governments, and gave their citizens the opportunity to take part in public affairs. The best-known city-states were Athens and Sparta.

The Ancient Greek civilisation provided the foundations of modern science and philosophy, reaching its height in Athens around 2,400 years ago, a period of outstanding achievement known as the Golden Age. Greek writers created new ways of expressing ideas and **explored** human emotions in their writing. You can still see the work of Ancient Greek architects in monuments such as the Acropolis in Athens.

3 Ancient Rome

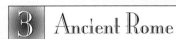

The Coliseum, Rome

The great achievements of the Greeks were in the areas of democracy, philosophy, literature etc. The Romans, on the other hand, were good at making war, conquering and controlling.
Eric Kondratieff, historian

A small community of shepherds in central Italy grew to become one of the greatest empires in history, before collapsing in spectacular fashion. The city of Rome was founded about 2,750 years ago. A thousand years later, the Roman Empire covered half of Europe, much of the Middle East and the north coast of Africa. The empire then began to **crumble** because it was too big to control. Fifteen hundred years ago, the last Roman Emperor was **overthrown** by **warlike** tribes from the north.

Ancient Rome had enormous influence on the development of Western civilization because the empire was so **vast** and lasted so long. The language of the ancient Romans was Latin, and this is the basis of French, Italian, Spanish and many other languages. In addition, Roman law provided the **foundation** for the legal systems of most of the countries in Western Europe and Latin America. There are Roman roads, bridges and aqueducts which are still in use in Europe today.

At the **height** of its success, Rome, the capital of the Roman Empire and its largest city, had almost a million inhabitants. Alexandria in Egypt was the empire's second largest city, with a population of 750,000 people. The Coliseum in Rome is an example of the genius of Roman architects.

1 Work in groups of three.

STUDENT A: You will focus on Text 1, Ancient Egypt. Do activities 2 and 3.
STUDENT B: You will focus on Text 2, Ancient Greece. Do activities 4 and 5.
STUDENT C: You will focus on Text 3, Ancient Rome. Do activities 6 and 7.

If you have any problems with the activities or the reading texts, ask your teacher for help.

2 Look at the words in bold in the text about Ancient Egypt. Match them with these definitions.

1 an adjective meaning lasting for a long time
2 an adjective meaning capable of producing good crops or plants
3 a noun meaning the place where something started
4 a verb meaning to keep in good condition
5 an adjective meaning talented
6 a verb meaning what happens when there is too much water in a river

3 Now read the complete text and write answers to these questions.

1 What three contributions did the River Nile make to the success of Ancient Egypt?
2 What two contributions did Ancient Egypt make to the history of writing?
3 What architectural achievements of the Ancient Egyptians are still visible?

4 Read the text about Ancient Greece and match the words in bold with the following definitions.

1 not controlled by another state or power
2 near or around a place
3 wonderful, fantastic
4 examined or discussed
5 mainly

5 Now read the complete text and write answers to these questions.

1 What did an Ancient Greek city-state consist of?
2 Were the city-states friendly with each other?
3 What architectural achievements of the Ancient Greeks are still visible?

6 Look at the words in bold in the text about Ancient Rome. Decide which of the definitions is correct.

1 crumble – (a) break into small pieces or (b) become stronger?
2 overthrown – (a) helped or (b) defeated?
3 warlike – (a) hostile or (b) friendly?
4 vast – (a) very large or (b) very small?
5 foundation – (a) the basic part or (b) destruction?
6 height – (a) the top or (b) the bottom?

7 Now read the complete text and answer these questions.

1 Why did the Roman Empire start to fall apart?
2 What is Ancient Rome's contribution to language?
3 What architectural achievements of the Ancient Romans are still visible?

8 Work in threes and do the following:

- Take turns to tell your partners what you learnt from the text that you read.
- List the main achievements of each of the civilisations that you read about.

9 Discuss the importance of the three ancient civilizations in the modern world. Which one has contributed most? Consider the following areas where contributions were made:

- the spread of ideas
- communications
- law
- architecture
- roads

2 GRAMMAR PRACTICE

1 Past tenses, including past perfect
2 *Would* and *used to*

1 Underline the correct form of the verb.

1 A month after Amundsen reached the South Pole in December 1911, an English explorer, Robert Scott, *had arrived/was arriving/arrived* there.
2 Some children found the Lascaux caves when they *had looked/were looking/looked* for a dog which they had lost/were losing/lost.
3 Men *tried/had been trying/were trying* to fly for centuries when the Wright brothers finally succeeded in 1903.
4 Brazil *had won/had been winning/were winning* the World Cup four times before when they *had triumphed/triumphed/had been triumphing* in 2002 in Japan.
5 When Buzz Aldrin *had stepped/had been stepping/stepped* on to the moon, Neil Armstrong *had already left/had already been leaving/already left* his famous footprint on the surface.

2 Write out the complete conversation.

TOM: Hi, Will. You look good!
WILL: Hello, Tom. Well I recently got back from a great holiday.
TOM: Really? .... ?
WILL: To Italy.
TOM: .... your first visit?
WILL: No, it .... I .... there once before.
TOM: And .... this time?
WILL: We .... a lot in the sea and .... great food and .... some museums. And we .... to Pompeii.
TOM: Pompeii! ....?
WILL: I loved it. You can see what people .... at the very moment the poisonous cloud from the volcanic eruption .... For example, some .... bread and others .... in their beds. And you can read personal messages on the walls that people .... only a few days earlier.
TOM: Volcanic eruption? When ....?
WILL: About 2,000 years ago. In the year 79, I think.
TOM: Then why are these things still there?
WILL: Well, apparently the whole town .... with six metres of dust and earth for over a thousand years. It .... again about 250 years ago.

Important – read this!

Read these two sentences.

There ***used to*** *be an enormous statue of Hercules on the island of Rhodes.*
People ***would come*** *from far away to see it.*

Both *used to* and *would* can be used to talk about the past. Both indicate that the present situation is different. But *would* can only be used in this way if there is an indication that you are talking about the past. And *would* relates to habits; it cannot be used in this way with stative verbs (See section 5 of the Grammar Reference.)

3 Complete these sentences with *would*, if possible, or *used to*. Explain your choices.

We .... live in the country. When we were children, we .... have a pony and we .... ride it almost every day during our holidays. In the summer we .... swim in the local river and we .... know all the children who lived in the area. Now I'm over 80 and live in the city. I don't know any of my neighbours.

4 Explain why Helmut has a problem (well, *two* problems).

1 Look at the picture of the fresco. How long ago do you think it was painted?

2 Read the text below to find out. Were you right?

The island of Crete

A palace fresco (wall painting)

The island of Crete, in the Mediterranean Sea, was the home of the Minoan civilisation, a great civilisation that lasted from 2600 to 1100 BC. This tiny island had a large population with about 90 cities, good roads, harbours, and well-organised agriculture and trade. We know that there were at least four palaces, decorated with beautiful frescoes. One of the frescoes is shown in the picture above.

3 Read the imaginary narrative below of 'a day in the life' of the seventeen-year-old son of a Minoan fresco painter. Put the verbs in brackets into the correct form.

4 Write 150 words about a day in the life of a boy or girl in your own country 2000 years ago. Make notes about these things:

How much money does the boy/girl's family have?
Does the boy/girl work or go to school?
If he/she works, what kind of work does he/she do?
Does he/she live in a town, city or village?

PARAGRAPH 1
Say something about the boy/girl's family. Write about how his/her day began, for example, what he/she had for breakfast.

PARAGRAPH 2
Describe what happened during the middle of the day.

PARAGRAPH 3
Write about what happened in the evening, for example, where he/she went, what he/she ate.

5 Optional writing task. Think about a typical day in your life, and of one or two small but interesting things that might happen to you during such a day. Write a short narrative of 150 words entitled 'A day in my life'.

I got up just as it (*to get*) **1**_______ light. I ate with my family – cheese and bread that my mother (*to make*) **2**_______ the previous day. Then I went with my father to the palace, where he is employed painting frescoes. When we (*to reach*) **3**_______ the palace, the guards immediately opened the great doors for us. They know my father well because he (*to work*) **4**_______ there for ten years now.

We went to the room where we (*to work*) **5**_______ for the last three months. We have almost finished a beautiful fresco, a landscape with monkeys and wild cats. While my father (*to work*) **6**_______ on the centre of the fresco, I worked in one small corner, (*to paint*) **7**_______ flowers and grass. I am a good painter and one day I hope to be as good as my father.

We (*to leave*) **8**_______ in the early evening and I went to the town square with my friends. There was a crowd (*to watch*) **9**_______ two boys jumping over the head of a black bull. My father (*to give*) **10**_______ me some money earlier in the day, and I ate in the square. Then I went home to bed, tired but happy.

17-YEAR OLD GIRL DEFEATS THE ENGLISH ARMY!

22-YEAR-OLD LEADS A CONQUERING ARMY AND BUILDS AN EMPIRE

A MULTI-RACIAL GOVERNMENT IN SOUTH AFRICA AT LAST!

1 **Look at the newspaper headlines.**

1 Can you connect the headlines with the people in the illustrations on this page?
2 Try to think of one more fact that you know about each of the people in the pictures above.

2 **Read the information below. In one or two sentences, explain how each of these people did something that changed history.a**

Alexander the Great, 356–323 BC

Alexander the Great became King of Macedonia, a state in northern Greece, at the age of 20. Over the next twelve years, Alexander took his army east, conquering the countries now known as Turkey, Northern Syria, Afghanistan, Iran and Pakistan. In 323, he died suddenly of a fever at the age of 33.

Joan of Arc, 1412–1431

In 1429, the English army had invaded Northern France. A 17-year-old girl called Joan of Arc persuaded the French king to allow her to lead his army against the English. She succeeded in defeating the English. However, she was eventually captured by them, and burnt as a witch.

Nelson Mandela, born 1918

In the early 1950s, the all-white government of South Africa established apartheid, a system that separated white people from black people. Nelson Mandela, a black South African lawyer, became deputy president of an organisation that resisted apartheid. In 1964, he was imprisoned for life. When he came out of prison in 1990, Mandela reached an agreement with the white government to end apartheid peacefully. In 1994, Mandela became president of a multi-racial government. Mandela's presidency ended in June 1999.

3 **Look at the list of qualities below. Which of these qualities do you think each of the people above had?**

high intelligence (adj. intelligent)
the quality of goodness (adj. good)
the quality of courage (adj. courageous)
leadership skills – the ability to lead people
drive – a strong desire to succeed
political skills
vision – a clear idea of how you want to change things

4 **Make notes about the three people.**

EXAMPLE: I think Mandela is a very good man. When he came out of prison, he was able to forgive white people.

5 **Listen to a discussion about the following question: *What makes a man or woman 'great'?* Tick the qualities in activity 3 that are mentioned.**

6 **Listen again. Answer these questions. Who says the following, Peter or Barbara?**

1 I think it means that they've changed the world in some way.
2 Nelson Mandela's another good example.
3 I think all great people share some of the same qualities.
4 But they also have different qualities that make them great.
5 After twenty-five years in prison, he was able to forgive white people for what they did to him!

7 **Work in groups.**

1 Discuss this question: *What is the one most important quality that a great person must have?*
2 Choose two people who you think are 'great'. Decide what their qualities are.
3 Tell the rest of the class what you decided.

8 **Research project**

- Choose one of the famous people described in activity 2.
- Find out more about this person using reference books and/or the internet.
- Make notes for a short presentation.
- Prepare one or two visual aids to use in your presentation.
- Give your presentation to the class.

Word watch – Prefixes

A prefix is placed at the beginning of a word to change the meaning of that word. Match each prefix with its meaning and then try to think of a word that starts with that prefix.

One of them means 'before'; two of them mean 'not' or indicate the opposite of a word; one of them means '(do) again'; one of them means 'against'.

Prefix	Meaning	Examples
pre-		
anti-		
re-		
dis-		
un-		

Lessons in logic

1 Five boys took a Maths test. George scored higher than Bill who didn't have the lowest score. Paul had the highest score and Andrew scored more than Michael but less than George.
Who had the lowest score? ______________

2 Girls voted for their favourite school subject. Science had fewer votes than History. Technology had more votes than Literature and Geography but fewer than Science.
Which subject was the most popular?
____

3 There were six cars parked side by side in the teachers' car park – two black cars and four white cars. Each black car had a white car parked on either side.
What colour were the two cars at the ends?
______________ and ______________

Singular and plural

Most English nouns have a regular plural form (adding an s) but a few hundred have irregular plurals that need to be studied and learned. Test your knowledge with the following exercises:

1 Put these words into the plural.

quiz __________ fly __________
half __________ goose __________
radio __________ bus __________
potato __________ youth __________
spoonful __________ still life __________
ear-ring __________

2 Underline the words that have the same form in the singular and the plural.

deer pound ox Swiss solo German
sheep pence rabbit loaf

3 Separate these nouns into two groups: those that are singular-only nouns (always used with a singular verb) and those that are plural-only nouns (always used with a plural verb).

news physics police outskirts
music trousers scissors jeans cattle
folk maths homework remains

Can you add any more to these two categories?

Did you know? Surprising statistics

25% of Britons have physically attacked their computers.

Why do you think this is true? Have you any first-hand experience of people attacking their computers?

What do you think?,

ANSWERS TO ACTIVITY 5 PAGE 13

1 *Neil Armstrong became the first person to set foot on the moon on July 20th 1969.*
2 *MTV, the first all-music TV channel, was broadcast for the first time on August 1st 1981.*
3 *Roald Amundsen, a Norwegian explorer, was the first person to reach the South Pole on December 14th 1911.*
4 *American athlete Jesse Owen set three world records and equalled a fourth (all in 70 minutes!) at Ann Arbor, Michigan on May 25th 1935. One year later, he won four gold medals at the Olympics Games in Berlin.*
5 *The 17,000-year-old cave paintings at Lascaux in the south west of France were found by four children on September 12th 1940. The children were looking for their dog.*
6 *Elvis Presley's first recording, Heartbreak Hotel, entered the US pop charts on February 22nd 1956.*
7 *Orville and Wilbur Wright made the first aeroplane flight in North Carolina, USA on December 17th 1903.*
8 *Bjorn Borg won the Wimbledon Men's Singles Tennis Championship for the first time on June 26th 1976. He is the only modern player to win the Wimbledon title five times in a row.*
9 *John Logie Baird demonstrated television for the first time in his workshop in London on January 26th 1926.*
10 *Brazil won the soccer World Cup for a record fourth time in front of 94,000 spectators at the Rose Bowl, Los Angeles, California on July 16th 1994. They won it for the fifth time eight years later.*

3 WHO INVENTED THAT?

INTRODUCTION AND VOCABULARY

1 Work in groups. Make a list of at least 30 manufactured items. Choose at least one from each of the following categories:

- personal possessions
- clothing
- electrical or electronic items
- furniture
- telecommunication equipment

2 Vocabulary game. Tell the rest of the class the items your group wrote in each category. Get a point for items which other groups haven't got in their lists.

3 Whole class. Answer these questions.

1 What are the items in your lists made of? Choose from this list of materials:
paper wood plastic metal leather wool cotton clay glass man-made fibre
2 What shape and size are the items? Use these words to describe them:
long short narrow wide round square sharp pointed circular tubular oblong rectangular box-shaped
3 Which of the items are made of more than one material?
4 What other adjectives can you use to describe the items? Here are some examples to help:
modern old-fashioned high-tech electrical electronic
5 Where do you think the items are made?

4 Write a short description of one of the items in your list. Choose one which is made of more than one material. Don't say what the item is.

EXAMPLE: It's rectangular and box-shaped, and it's made of metal and plastic.

5 Read the description to the students in your group. Can they guess what it is?

6 Read and try to answer the questions. Don't worry if you don't know the answers. You will find out everything in this unit!

1 Who were the first people to use glass?
2 Who invented plastic?
3 Who were the first people to use paper?
4 Who invented ball-point pens?

Paper – the most important invention in history?

Six thousand years ago ...
Two thousand years ago ...
Fifteen hundred years ago ...
A thousand years ago ...

7 Look at the cartoon story. Try to explain what is happening in each part. These words may help.

army to dry paper mill papyrus reeds

8 Now read the information about the history of paper. The sections are in the wrong order. Complete the time expressions and indicate the order of the sections.

9 Read the text again and answer these questions.

1 Where does the English word *paper* come from?
2 Which part of a tree did Ts'ai Lun use to make paper?
3 What was the importance of the defeat of the Chinese army by the Arab army?
4 Where was the first European paper mill and who built it?

10 Groups or whole class. Discuss the following questions.

- Could you imagine a paper-free day in your classroom?
- Apart from paper, which is the most important material in the list in activity 3 question 1, both inside and outside the classroom?
- Do you agree that paper is the most important invention in history? Suggest other inventions that might be more important.

A

__________________ ago, in Samarkand, on the Silk Route to China, the Chinese and Arab armies clashed after decades of peaceful trading. The Chinese were defeated and many were taken prisoner. Among the prisoners were paper makers who then taught the Arabs the secrets of paper making.

B

__________________ ago, the Ancient Egyptians invented papyrus, the first substance that resembled paper as we know it. Papyrus was a woven mat of reeds, pounded together into a thin sheet. The word 'paper' actually comes from the word 'papyrus'.

C

__________________ ago, paper finally arrived in Europe. The first paper mill in Europe was built by the Arabs in Xativa, Spain. Gradually, paper-making spread across the rest of Europe and the rest of the world.

D

__________________ ago, paper was invented by Ts'ai Lun, a Chinese court official. It is believed that Ts'ai Lun mixed mulberry bark, hemp and rags with water, mashed it into a pulp, pressed out the liquid and hung the thin mat to dry in the sun. This strange mixture started one of the greatest communication revolutions in history. Ts'ai Lun can claim to be the most influential inventor of all time.

1 Quills, leaks and smudges

'No man was more foolish when he had no pen in his hand, or more wise when he had.' Samuel Johnson.

Have you ever stopped to think what the first pens were like?

Quill pens, which were made from birds' feathers, were the most important writing instruments for nearly two thousand years. The best quills were made from feathers on the left wing, which were better because the feathers curved away when a right-handed writer used the quill.

Goose feathers were the most common quills, while swan feathers were scarcer and more expensive. For making fine lines, crow feathers were the best, and the feathers of the eagle, owl, hawk and turkey were also used.

A quill

Quill pens lasted for only a week before it was necessary to replace them. To sharpen the quill, the writer needed a special knife, which is the origin of the word pen-knife. Writers would dip their quills into a small container of ink called an inkwell. Until the 1960s, school desks in England were designed with a hole in the top-right corner for the inkwell, even though pupils had **given up** dipping their pens in ink twenty years before!

The next development was the fountain pen, a pen which contained its own ink. However, early designs of fountain pens were disastrous, as ink would leak onto the writers' fingers and, more important, onto the paper they were writing on.

In 1884, an insurance salesman called Lewis Waterman developed the first practical fountain pen. Waterman had a good reason for wanting to improve the early fountain pen designs, having destroyed a valuable sales contract when ink leaked from his pen.

A fountain pen

2 The incredible Mr Biro

The ball-point pen was first developed in 1935 by the most famous Hungarian inventor of all time, Ladislas Biro.

Biro was an unusual character, who had studied a variety of things, including medicine, art and hypnotism. In 1935, when he was working as the editor of a small newspaper, he began to get annoyed by the amount of time he wasted filling fountain pens and cleaning up ink smudges. In addition, the sharp tip of his fountain pen often scratched the paper. Ladislas and his brother Georg, who was a chemist, were determined to develop a better pen and better ink to use in it.

One summer, while they were on holiday on the beach on the Black Sea coast, the Biro brothers **bumped into** an old man, Augustine Justo. After talking to him for a few minutes, they were astonished to discover that he was the president of Argentina! The brothers showed him a model of a ball-point pen, and President Justo urged them to **set up** a factory in Argentina.

Unfortunately, the original Biro pens were a disaster, only working when they were held more or less vertically, and sometimes not even then. The Biro brothers returned to their laboratory and improved the design, with the result that, one year later, they were selling their new, improved ball-point pen in Argentina. However, it still was not a success, and the Biro brothers **ran out of** money.

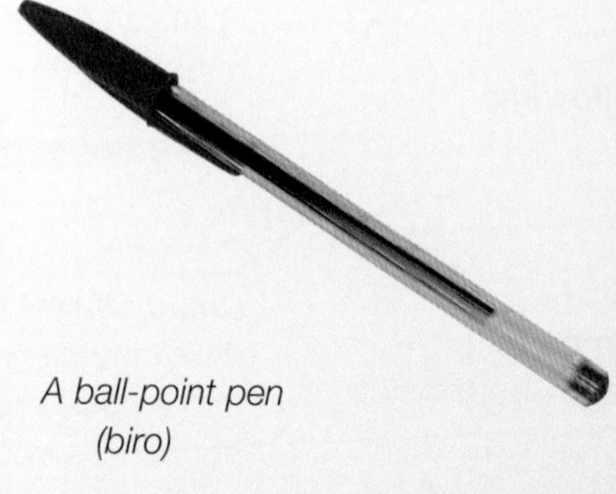

A ball-point pen (biro)

3 Three hundred dollars for a ball-point pen?

A Chicago salesman named Milton Reynolds was on holiday in Argentina and **came across** Biro's pen in a shop. He copied the design, went back to the USA and set up a factory with 300 workers who began making the revolutionary new pens.

The success of the ball-point pen in the USA was incredible.

In October 1945, the new pens went on sale at Gimbels Department Store in New York and the store was astonished when *five thousand* people **turned up** on the first day hoping to buy one. The day before, the company had put an advertisement in the *New York Times* which described the new pen as a 'miraculous fountain pen, guaranteed to write for two years without re-filling!' On that first day of sales, Gimbels **sold out** its entire stock of 10,000 pens – at $12.50 each! At that time, $12.50 was about a week's wages for a factory worker in the USA. It's the equivalent of three hundred dollars at today's prices.

A French manufacturer of pencil cases, Marcel Bich, improved the design of ball-point pens and his design is still in use today. In1952, he **brought out** a new, cheap ball-point pen called the Ball-point Bic.

Today, Biro is still the name used for ball-point pens in most parts of the world. The modern version of Biro's pen is called the Bic Crystal, and fourteen million of them are sold worldwide every day. The manufacturers claim that a Bic crystal will produce more than eight kilometres of writing before running out of ink.

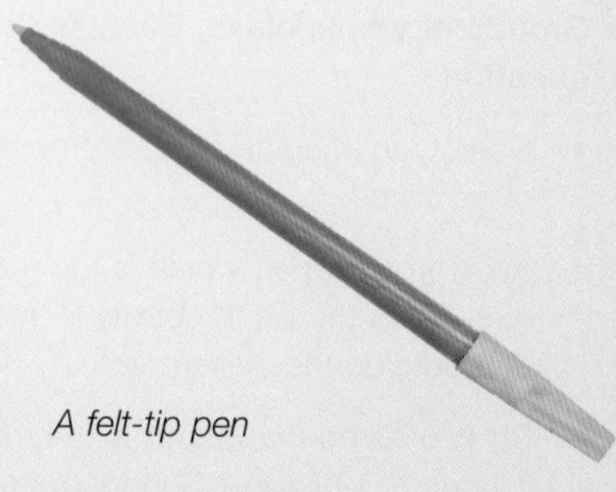

A felt-tip pen

1 **Conduct a quick class survey and answer this question.**

What are people in the class writing with?

- a ball-point pen
- a felt-tip pen
- a fountain pen
- a marker pen
- a pencil
- a crayon

2 **Before you read the text, try to answer the following questions. Don't worry if you don't know the answers – you will find out in the text.**

1 The first pens were called quill pens. Where do quills come from?
2 What did people stop using when fountain pens were invented?
3 Why do we call ball-point pens *biros*?

3 **Now look at the titles of the different parts of the reading text and predict the content. Choose one of these possible explanations.**

1 Quills, leaks and smudges
  a old-fashioned pens and what happened when you used them
  b problems faced by children learning to write
  c what happens when you take a feather from a bird
2 The incredible Mr Biro
  a the story of a man who looked like a ball-point pen
  b the man who invented the ball-point pen
  c the story of the ball-point pen is not true
3 Three hundred dollars for a ball-point pen?
  a the money that some people pay for pens today
  b the value of an antique ball-point pen
  c the equivalent cost today of the first ball-point pens

4 **Skim part 1 of the reading text and find the names of seven birds and then answer these questions.**

1 Do people in your country eat any of these birds?
2 Which of them usually live on a farm?
3 Which of them usually come out at night?
4 Which of them are hunters?
5 Which one is usually black?

5 **Read part 1 more carefully and answer these questions.**

1 Why was it important to use feathers from the left wing of a bird?
2 Why were swan's feathers more expensive?
3 Where did people who used quill pens keep their ink?
4 How long did quill pens last? Did people immediately throw them away?
5 Why was Lewis Waterman so keen to design a better fountain pen?

6 **Skim part 2 of the reading text and find the following information:**

1 the nationality of Ladislas Biro
2 the year he invented the ball-point pen
3 his brother's name and occupation
4 the occupation of Augustine Justo.

7 **Now read part 2 more carefully and decide if the following sentences are true or false. If they are false, explain why.**

1 The Biro brothers studied subjects that were very similar.
2 Ladislas's profession was not an obvious choice, considering what he'd studied.
3 He arranged to meet the president of Argentina on the beach.
4 Justo was reluctant to let them open a factory in Argentina.
5 The pens didn't work very well because you had to hold them in a particular way.

8 **Read part 3 and explain these references.**

1 Line 4: *He copied the design* – the design of what?
2 Line 13: *Five thousand people turned up there* – turned up where?
3 Line 15: *The company put an advertisement in the New York Times* – which company?
4 Line 24: *It's the equivalent of three hundred dollars at today's prices*. What is?

9 Complete these questions and answers.

1 What did Marcel Bich __________? Pencil cases.
2 When __________? 1952.
3 Is Biro __________? Yes, __________.
4 How __________ every day? Fourteen __________.
5 How many? Eight __________.

10 **Look back at the verbs in bold in the text. Complete these sentences using one of the phrasal verbs.**

1 I wanted to buy some chocolate but the shop had __________ of the kind that I like.
2 I first __________ Charles Dickens when I read one of his stories in a book.
3 She was quite upset when no one __________ at her party.
4 I can't write any more. My pen has __________ ink.
5 You won't believe who I __________ in the market today!
6 Reebok have __________ a new kind of trainer – it looks really good!
7 My uncle is going to __________ a travel agency.

Then write your own sentence with the verb that you didn't need to use.

2 GRAMMAR PRACTICE

1 active v passive
2 word order with phrasal and prepositional verbs

1 Rewrite the following sentences beginning as indicated and keeping the same tenses.

1 People were using gold and silver to make jewellery thousands of years ago.
Gold and silver ....

2 Someone gave my great grandfather one of the new ball-point pens in 1945.
My great grandfather ....

3 People have claimed that the Bic pen will write for eight kilometres.
It ....

4 President Justo urged the Biro brothers to set up a factory in Argentina.
The Biro brothers ....

2 Write the questions. Choose verbs from the box.

import	pack	buy	design	maker

(Subject: your blue shirt)

1 ....? Of imported cotton.
2 ....? From Egypt.
3 ....? For my father. It's his birthday.
4 ....? In tissue paper and a cardboard box.
5 ....? By Georgio Armani.

Important – read this!

Look at the passive forms in these sentences.

1 Clothes made of silk *should be dry-cleaned*.
2 I think that bicycle *may have been stolen*.
3 He's unhappy about *being required to wear* a formal shirt.
4 They want *to be invited* to the party.
5 We were *advised to wear* warm clothing.

3 Now complete the following using examples of the passive structures above. Choose verbs from the box.

remove	tell	take	ask	deliver

1 I don't enjoy .... to sing in public – even if it is done politely!
2 It's three weeks since I ordered that cotton jacket. It .... to the wrong address.
3 This car needs .... to the garage today.
4 Shoes .... before entering a mosque.
5 They .... very clearly to arrive on time.

4 Can you explain the difference to Helmut?

I've been reading about Mr Reynolds and his new ball-point pens.
Really? When did he bring out them?
No, Helmut. We say 'When did he bring them out?'
Thanks, Ali. I'll remember that.
Great. Anyway, the answer is in 1945. But he came across the idea in a surprising place.
Really? Where did he come it across, Ali?
Sorry, Helmut. That's 'Where did he come across it?'
What!? But ...
Yes. You'd better check section 16 in the Grammar Reference!

1 **Explain the difference in meaning, if any, between these pairs of words.**

long-sighted – short-sighted
spectacles – glasses
contact lenses – glasses
concave – convex
invent – discover

2 **Read the text below quickly. Match the definitions below with the words in bold.**

1 pieces of curved glass or plastic
2 different, with different types
3 to make a large number of the same object
4 to make something look bigger than it is

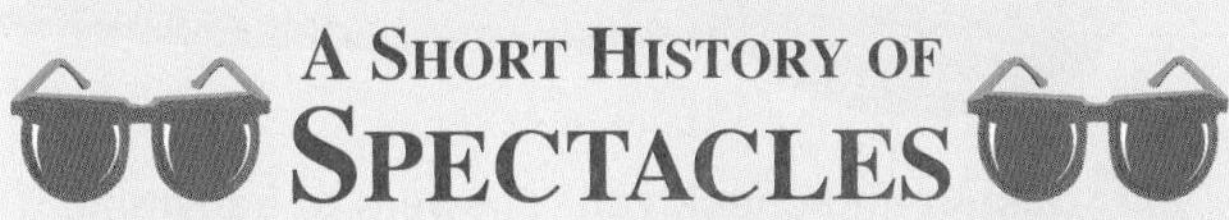

A SHORT HISTORY OF SPECTACLES

It is said that the Roman writer Seneca, who was born about two thousand years ago, read books by looking at them through a glass vase full of water. The water **magnified** the words and he was able to read them. This was a clever idea, but the Romans did not know how to make **lenses**. The 'reading stone', which we call a magnifying glass, was developed about a thousand years ago. Convex in shape, it was placed on reading material to magnify the letters. But the first real spectacles were made between 1268 and 1289 in Italy. In 1306, an Italian described spectacles as 'one of the most useful things on earth'.

One of the most important developments in the history of spectacles was the sixteenth-century invention of concave lenses for short-sighted people. Spectacles became increasingly popular and their use spread from Italy to Germany, Spain and France. However, there was a big problem with spectacles – how to keep them on your nose! It was not until 1730 that spectacles were invented with sidepieces that sat on the ears.

For many centuries glasses were very expensive. In the early eighteenth century in America they could cost as much as US$200, the equivalent of about $10,000 today. Then, in the second half of the nineteenth century, an American company started **mass producing** spectacles and they became cheaper.

In the 1930s, spectacle frames became more **varied** and sunglasses appeared and became popular. Contact lenses became available in America in the 1940s and by 1964 over six million people in the United States were wearing them. But today many people still continue to wear glasses.

3 **Read the following summary of *A Short History of Spectacles*, which only contains essential information. Underline the information in the original which has been omitted in the summary.**

Summary

An early kind of magnifying glass was developed a thousand years ago, but the first real spectacles were made between 1268 and 1289 in Italy. *In the sixteenth century, concave lenses for the short-sighted were invented and the use of spectacles spread from Italy to Germany, Spain and France.* However, sidepieces to keep the spectacles on the nose did not appear until 1730. *Glasses were very expensive until the second half of the nineteenth century when mass production began.* Spectacle frames became more varied in the 1930s and sunglasses also became popular at this time. Contact lenses appeared in the 1940s.

4 **Look at the sentences in italics in the summary. Compare these sentences with the sentences in the original text. How have the sentences been changed? What information has been omitted?**

5 **Connect the phrases in italics in the sentences below. You may have to change the word order or use connecting words. Use the words in brackets to connect the phrases.**

1 In the eighteenth century, *many French men and women preferred to wear glasses in private*. However, *in Spain, glasses were very popular* because people thought they make them look important. (although)
2 It is said that *the Roman writer Seneca*, who was born about two thousand years ago, *read books* by looking at them through *a glass vase of water. The water magnified the words* and he was able to read them. (using, that)
3 *The Ancient Egyptians invented papyrus*, the first substance that resembled paper as we know it. Papyrus was *a woven mat of reeds, pounded together into a hard, thin sheet.*
4 *A French manufacturer* of pencil cases, *Marcel Bich*, improved the design of ball-point pens and his design is still in use today. *In 1952, he brought out a new, cheap ball-point pen called the Ball-point Bic.*
5 *Waterman wanted to improve the early fountain pen designs.* He had a good reason. *He had destroyed a valuable sales contract when ink leaked from his pen.* (because)

6 **Read the text entitled *The Incredible Mr Biro* on page 22. Write a summary of the text, using about 100 words.**

7 **Optional writing task. Write a summary of the text entitled *Quills, leaks and smudges* on page 22. Write about 100 words.**

4 LISTENING AND SPEAKING

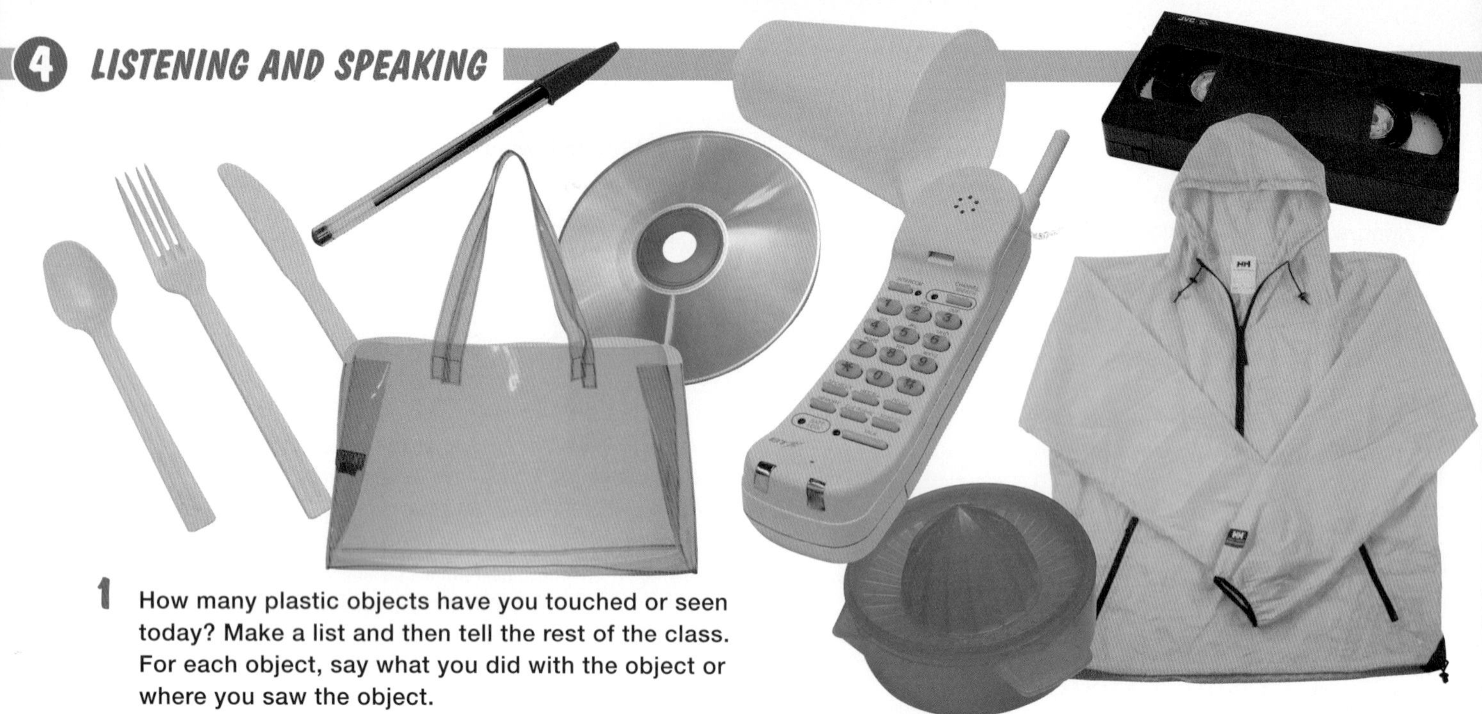

1 **How many plastic objects have you touched or seen today? Make a list and then tell the rest of the class. For each object, say what you did with the object or where you saw the object.**

EXAMPLE: I cut my finger this morning and put a small plastic plaster on the cut.

2 **Before you read the information below, check the meaning of the following words.**

1 *synthetic*: does this mean (a) something made from natural materials or (b) artificial ones?
2 *rigid*: does this mean (a) something that cannot bend or (b) something that bends easily?
3 *derive*: does this mean (a) to make something from something else or (b) to make something new?
4 *biodegrade*: does this mean (a) to become smaller or (b) to disappear into the earth?
5 *produce*: does this mean (a) to make or (b) to sell?

3 **Read the following information about plastic. There are two pieces of information which are not true. Which do you think they are?**

1 Plastic is a synthetic material that is heated so that it becomes soft. Later it becomes rigid or semi-rigid.
2 Plastic has many different uses. For example, it is used in paints and cosmetics and to build car bodies, boats and aircraft.
3 Plastic is an ingredient in Coca Cola.
4 The first form of plastic was introduced in Britain in 1862. It was made from natural materials and was not synthetic.
5 The first completely synthetic plastic was invented in 1907.
6 Today's plastics are mostly derived from wood.
7 Ordinary plastic takes a very long time to biodegrade – in other words, to break down into small parts that do not harm the environment.
8 In 1990, a new kind of plastic was invented that is biodegradable. It costs three to five times as much as ordinary plastic to produce.

4 **Listen and check your answers to activity 3.**

5 **Listen to these phrases and sentences from the listening passage in activity 4. Some of the words are linked together. It is usual to do this when we speak English. If not, we sound too formal. Can you say which words are linked together and why?**

1 What's it made of?
2 Plastic is a wonderful material.
3 No one knows what to do with them.
4 That's a ridiculous idea!
5 It has so many uses.
6 I think we should stop producing it.

Now listen again and repeat the sentences.

6 **Read the following arguments in favour of plastic. Then try and think of some arguments against the use of plastic.**

1 Things made from plastic are often cheaper than things made from natural materials.
2 Twenty-first-century society couldn't continue without plastic. It has very many uses.
3 A form of biodegradable plastic has been invented.
4 This biodegradable plastic will become cheaper in the future.

7 **Listen to this conversation between two young women about plastic. Make notes about the arguments given against the use of plastic. Were they the same arguments as yours?**

8 **Discussion: Work in groups of four. Two students must argue in favour of plastic and two students argue against its use. Tell the rest of the class if any new arguments are used.**

Word watch – Suffixes

A suffix is a letter or group of letters added at the end of a word to make a new word. Suffixes can, for example, turn verbs into adjectives.

Look at these examples:

1 break**able** is an adjective – it is used to describe an object that it is possible to break. You could use it to describe a valuable ornament, for example. What do the following words mean and what kind of thing would you use them to describe?

washable moveable changeable loveable

2 colour**ful** means that something contains a lot of colour. You could use it to describe a painting, for example. What do the following words mean and what kind of thing would you use them to describe?

powerful painful truthful wonderful careful

3 **-ist**, **-er** and **-or** can be added to words to make an occupation (eg art**ist**, teach**er** and act**or**). What suffix can you add to these words to make an occupation?

drive paint type programme invent guitar

Lessons in logic

Five people, Scarlett, Claire, Natalie, Elizabeth and Helen are standing in a circle holding hands. Only one of them faces outwards – all the others face inwards.

Claire holds Scarlett's right hand in her left hand and Helen's right hand in her right hand. Natalie is not beside Scarlett and Elizabeth is not beside Helen.

Who is between Helen and Elizabeth? _______. Who is holding Natalie's right hand? _______.

Which two people are holding each other's left hand? _______ and _______.

Helen leaves and the others close up the circle. Whose hand is Claire now holding with her right hand ? _______. Is it their left or right hand? _______.

Punctuation

1 Can you name these punctuation marks?

.	,	;	:
( )	–	*	‘

!	?	“ ”	-

2 Which one:

1 is used to show surprise, force and sometimes irony? _______
2 can be square or round? _______
3 shows a letter or letters have been omitted? _______
4 is often used to indicate there is a comment at the bottom of the page? _______
5 is used in some people's names? _______

3 Write out the following dialogue with all necessary punctuation and correctly set out. Remember to start a new line for each new speaker.

where is anna asked the teacher we cant get started until everyones here I think I saw her outside the head teachers office said petra really said the teacher whats she doing there I dont know replied petra at that moment anna came in im sorry im late she said ive been waiting outside the head teachers office but she isnt here today thats ok said the teacher now that youre here we can start open your books at page 26 everyone but dont read anything until I tell you to

Did you know? Surprising statistics

20% of Britons would like the national anthem played before films and plays.

The British national anthem is rarely played nowadays (only on special state occasions). Is your national anthem frequently played and when? Would you like it to be played more or less? Do you feel it is right to play the national anthem of the winners at the Olympic Games or should sport be more international? Is it always good to be proud of your country?

What do you think?

4 SWITCH IT OFF!

INTRODUCTION AND VOCABULARY

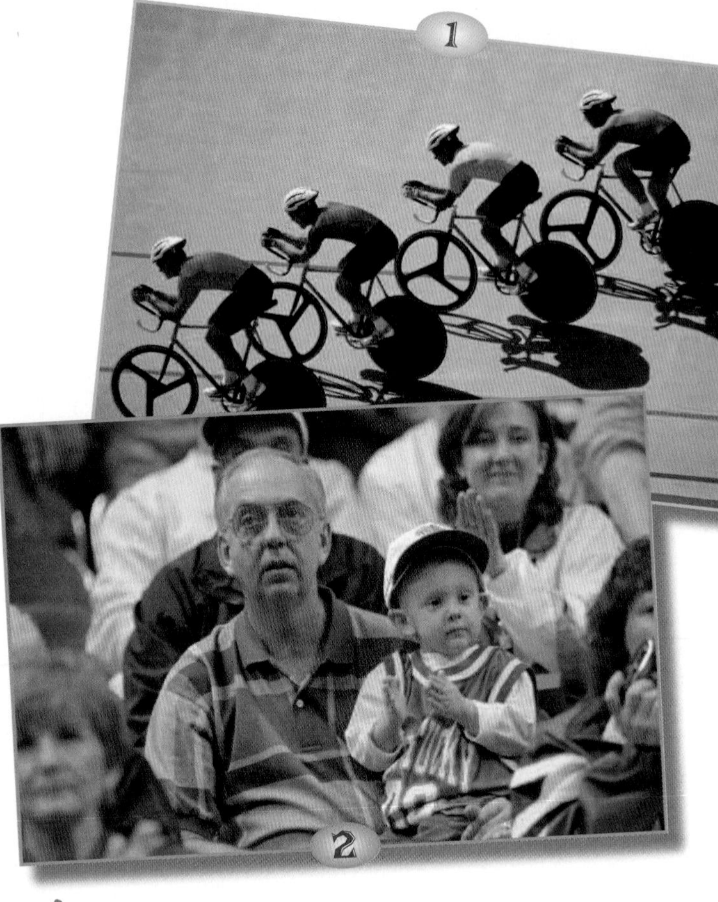

1 **Work in groups. How long do you spend doing the following things every week? Make notes.**

EXAMPLE: In this group, the total time that we sleep is 245 hours.

sleeping studying at school listening to music reading watching TV taking exercise doing homework doing nothing

2 **Compare your answers with other groups. Which group spends most time sleeping/studying etc?**

3 **Look at the photos on this page and answer these questions.**

1 What kind of sport are the people in picture 1 participating in?
2 What kind of sport are the spectators in picture 2 watching?
3 What are the people in picture 3 doing and is it good for you?
4 Which of the activities are 'active' pastimes and which are 'passive' pastimes?

4 **In pairs. Read the conversation between a parent and a child.**

PARENT: What are you doing?
CHILD: *I'm watching a programme on Discovery Channel.*
PARENT: Why do you spend so much time doing that?
CHILD: Because *I learn a lot. I watch Discovery Channel to improve my English.*
PARENT: You spend too much time *watching television*. It isn't good for you.
CHILD: Why not?
PARENT: Because you need to take some exercise.
CHILD: Really?
PARENT: Yes. Go and play football.
CHILD: OK.

5 **Now devise a new conversation. Follow these instructions.**

- Change all the words in italics.
- Choose a new activity from this list:

work on my computer *read a magazine*
listen to a cassette *write a story*

- Make a different suggestion for exercise. Change the underlined section.

EXAMPLE: Go for a ride on your bicycle.

6 **Discuss the following:**

- How much TV do you watch every day?
- What kind of programmes do you watch?
- Is anyone in the class worried about the amount of time they spend watching TV?
- Is there a connection between the amount of TV you watch and how fit you are?

What is the White Dot Campaign?

White Dot is an anti-television campaign group which thinks that television as anti-social and dangerous. The group has published a book which aims to persuade people to give up watching television. The following is an extract.

GET A LIFE – TURN OFF YOUR TV SET

The average time that people spend watching TV is four hours a day – in other words, more than one day a week. People spend a day a week doing nothing but staring at a box in the corner of the room.

Add it up. One day a week equals 52 days a year – nearly two months. In your lifetime, that means more than ten years! Do you really want to waste ten years of your life staring at a box? At the end of your life, if someone offered to give you back those missing ten years, would you accept their offer? Or would you say: 'No thanks, I'm glad I spent that time watching TV'?

If you give up watching TV, you double your free time. All you have to do is turn it off – it's that easy! You'll be amazed at what happens next. You have an extra ten years to do what you want to do.

What do you get from television? Excitement? Friendship? Education? A plastic box can't give you any of these things. So switch it off!

One day, people will look back on television and say 'that was a really dangerous experiment on human guinea pigs'. Your descendants won't have anything to do with it. Instead of saying: 'How could I live without it?' they'll say: 'Wow! We almost didn't live through it!' They'll be shocked at what you did with your time.

To help you decide, use the chart below. Assuming that you live to be 80, it can tell you how much of your future life you'll spend watching television. Cut it out and tape it to your TV remote control.

This chart tells you how many of your remaining years will be spent watching TV:

YOUR AGE	0	10	15	20	30	40	50	60	70
YEARS LEFT	80	70	65	60	50	40	30	20	10
TV YEARS LEFT	13.3	11.7	10.9	10	8.3	6.7	5	3.3	1.7

7 **Read the introduction to the text. In your own words, explain the aims of the White Dot Campaign.**

8 **Read the complete text and answer these questions.**

1. What is the campaign's main reason for suggesting that we stop watching television?
2. What predictions does it make about people's attitudes to TV in the future?
3. Do you think the statistics in the chart are true about you now?
4. Will they be true in the future?

9 **Work in groups of four. Each group should divide into two pairs.**

PAIR 1: Write down arguments in favour of watching four hours of TV every day.

PAIR 2: Write down arguments in favour of watching no TV at all.

Discuss your ideas in your groups and then have a class discussion.

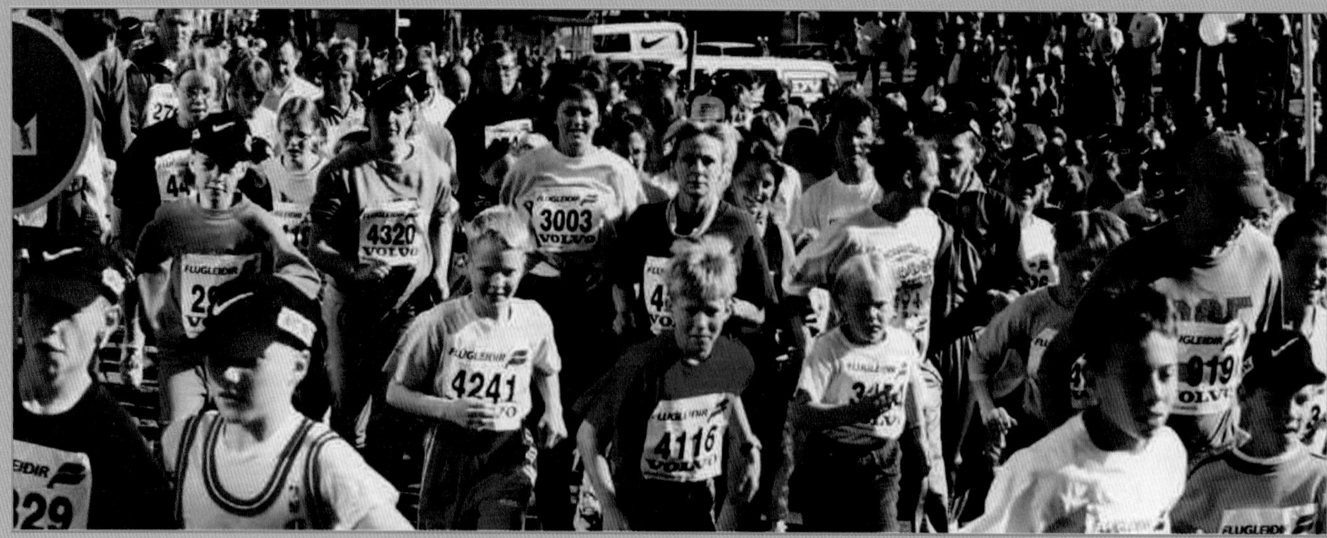

1 Hitting the wall

Marathon is the name of a village in Ancient Greece and also the name of the nearby plain where the Athenians defeated the Persian army two thousand five hundred years ago. A man called Pheidippides ran to Athens with news of the victory. It is said that the distance he ran was 42.2 kilometres, which is now the length of a marathon race. In fact, the distance from Marathon to Athens is about 35 kilometres.

The marathon was one of the events at the first modern Olympic Games in Athens in 1896 and was won by Spyridon Louis, a Greek shepherd, in a time of two hours, 58 minutes and 50 seconds. The 2000 Olympics marathon was won by Gezahgne Abera, a 22-year-old Ethiopian runner, in a time of two hours, ten minutes and 11 seconds. In other words, in the intervening 104 years, humans were able to slice more than three-quarters of an hour off the Olympic-winning time.

The marathon continues to be the supreme test of fitness and stamina. Nowadays, most of the world's major cities, from Buenos Aires in Argentina to Shanghai in China, have an annual marathon race. In Egypt, there is a marathon which starts and finishes at the Great Pyramids. The half-way point is Sakkara, the location of the oldest pyramid, the Step Pyramid. Runners who only want to run a half-marathon stop there, while runners who want to complete the whole marathon run back to the Great Pyramids and end the race at the base of one of the seven wonders of the world.

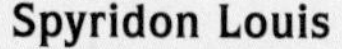
Spyridon Louis

Gezahgne Abera

1 Look at the photograph and discuss these questions.

1 What is the name of the kind of race that the people are taking part in?
2 Is there a race like this where you live?
3 Do you know anyone who has taken part in a race like this?
4 Would you like to take part in a race like this?

2 Look at part 1 of the reading text. What do you think the title might mean? Discuss with other students and then check your answer at the bottom of page 35.

3 Now read part 1 and complete these sentences with the correct answers.

1 Pheidippides
- **a** ran from Athens to Marathon.
- **b** ran 42.2 kilometres.
- **c** took news of a military victory to the capital.

2 The first marathon of the modern era
- **a** was won by an Ethiopian shepherd.
- **b** was completed by the winner in less than three hours.
- **c** took place in the eighteenth century.

3 Nowadays, there are lots of marathon races
- **a** in China and Latin America.
- **b** in many major cities.
- **c** to and from the Egyptian pyramids.

2 The Phantom Japanese runner

The first London marathon took place on Sunday the 29th of March 1981. Three days later was the first of April (April Fool's Day), when people in Britain traditionally play practical jokes on each other. National newspapers often contain photographs and articles that are in fact practical jokes.

On Wednesday the first of April, the *Daily Mail* published a photograph of a Japanese athlete taking part in the London marathon. The article said that the runner, who could not speak English, thought that the race lasted for 26 *days* rather than 26 miles. According to the report, he was last seen on Sunday evening heading north.

In fact, the man in the photograph was Japanese fashion model Riuchi Yamamoto, who was in his London flat when the article appeared.

Hundreds of people telephoned the newspaper saying that they were sure they had seen the Japanese runner at various different locations in the country. The next day, the Japanese Embassy called, wanting to know if they could help with the search. On Friday, the *Mail* took the Japanese 'runner' to the outskirts of St Albans, a small town near London. Yamamoto started running and arrived in the centre of the town at about midday.

He was seen by hundreds of people who, having read that he spoke no English, tried to stop him, shouting 'Finito!' and 'Kaput!' Yamamoto continued running until he reached a petrol station on the other side of St Albans, where a reporter from the newspaper picked him up.

On Saturday, the *Daily Mail* eventually admitted that the story was false.

3 Is marathon running good for you?

Training for the marathon improves your overall fitness and strengthens a lot of muscles, and most marathon runners develop a life-long habit of regular exercise. But is marathon running good for everyone? Here's how the race can affect different parts of your body.

1 Many runners find that their hearing improves after running a marathon. The reasons are unclear but it might be because of improved circulation of the blood.

2 The soles of a runner's training shoes hit the road an average of 30,000 times during a marathon, each stride sending a shock equivalent to three times your body weight through your body. This can be a problem for heavier runners. The most common marathon injuries are cramp and blisters.

3 Some runners are one centimetre shorter at the end of the race, due to the fact that the repetitive pounding on the streets causes muscles to compress.

4 Runners can lose up to five kilos during the race, due to fluid loss. Runners put it all back on when they drink water after the race. It can be dangerous if marathon runners don't drink lots of water at the end.

5 You do at least ten times more breathing during a marathon, which means your respiratory system works considerably harder than normal. For this reason, it is very important to be fit when you take part in the race.

4 Before you read part 2, answer these questions.

1 Why is the first of April a special day in Britain?
2 Is it a special day in your country?
3 What is a practical joke? Can you give an example?
4 Do you like playing practical jokes on other people?
5 Do you like it if people play practical jokes on you?

5 Look at the title of part 2 and predict the content.

6 Now read part 2 and, in your own words, say what happened on the following dates in 1981.

1 29th March
2 1st April
3 2nd April
4 3rd April
5 4th April

7 Part 3 of the reading text is about the effects of marathon running on your body. What does each point refer to? Read the text and choose from this list:

ears eyes feet and legs heart height lungs weight

8 Read part 3 again. Which of the effects of the marathon are good for you, and which could be bad for you?

9 Make notes about what you have learnt about the following. Try to do this from memory, but refer to the text for details, such as dates.

- The history of the marathon
- An April Fool's Day event in 1981
- How running a marathon can affect you

10 Close your books and read your notes to the rest of the class.

1 Infinitives and gerunds
2 Nouns/adjectives + prepositions

1 **Explain the use of the forms in italics.**

CLUE: several explanations depend on the word[s] before the italics.

If you need help, look at section 15 of the Grammar Reference.

1 *Training* for the marathon improves your overall fitness.
2 Your descendants won't have anything *to do* with it.
3 *To help* you decide, check the chart below.
4 Instead of *saying* that, they'll say 'Wow!'
5 They didn't know where *to look* for him.
6 It is very important *to be* fit.
7 His trainer told him *not to run* too fast.
8 Some people enjoy *training*.
9 Some people want *to run* but can't.
10 *To enter* your first marathon takes a lot of courage.

2 **Write a new sentence with the same infinitive or gerund structure for each of the sentences in Exercise 1.**

NOTE: The infinitives and gerunds in exercises 1 and 2 are the simple forms. With *some* structures, other forms are possible.

3 **Look at these examples and say which numbers (1–10) in exercise 1 each corresponds to.**

The perfect:

a *Having prepared* carefully gives you more confidence.
b In spite of *having won* the race, she was unhappy with her time.
c It is very important *to have trained* properly.
d I hope *to have finished* my homework before tomorrow.
e *To have won* this race is like a dream come true.
f Running a marathon is something *to have experienced* at least once.

The passive:

a *Being overtaken* by hundreds of people is a bit depressing!
b *To be admitted* to the race you must show your card.
c After *being beaten* in the race, he was very disappointed.
d It's extraordinary *to be surrounded* by so many people.
e Of course no one wants *to be beaten*.
f Most children don't like *being told* to turn off the TV.
g There's nothing *to be discussed*.

The continuous:

a I never expected *to be standing* here at the start with so many people.
b Just *to be taking part* in this race is wonderful.
c It's difficult for me *to be watching* the race instead of taking part.

4 **Help Helmut with his prepositions after nouns and adjectives.**

What are you studying, Helmut?
Prepositions, Ali. You are already familiar about my interest.
What?
About my interest for prepositions.
Er, yes. Do you find them easy, Helmut?
Well, no. I'm not very good in them, am I? And of course I suffer from a fear to make mistakes.

1 **In pairs. Discuss the following questions.**

1 Do you play computer games? If so, how much time do you spend playing them?
2 What is a games console?
3 Do you have one or would you like one?
4 If you play computer games, which is your favourite game? Say why.
5 Can you think of three good things about computer games?
6 Can you think of three bad things?

2 **Before you read the essay below, read these notes.**

This is a For and Against essay. In other words, it looks at the arguments in favour of something and the arguments against something.

A For and Against essay has four parts:
Introduction
Arguments for
Arguments against
Conclusion

3 **Now read the essay. Does it include the good and bad things that you thought of in activity 1? Are there others that you didn't think of?**

THE ADVANTAGES AND DISADVANTAGES OF COMPUTER GAMES

Computer games first appeared about twenty-five years ago. They have become more and more popular and sophisticated. These days, computer games are extremely realistic. People of all ages play them, but they are especially popular with children and students.

Computer games have great advantages. Firstly, they are a lot of fun and they prevent boredom. If you have a Gameboy, you can play games while you're on a train or sitting in a cafe. **Secondly,** computer games teach you to think fast and have quick reactions. There are many different kinds of computer games and some really test your intelligence.

But there are disadvantages to computer games. They are very addictive and people can spend far too much time playing on them. People can develop physical problems with their thumbs from using them so much. **Also,** it isn't good for children to spend a long time looking at a screen. Some children play games instead of taking exercise. **Furthermore,** computer games are expensive. Some people spend too much money on them.

In conclusion, in my opinion, computer games are a wonderful form of entertainment and can help you to think fast. But we must be careful not to spend too much time playing on our computers. There is more to life than computer games!

4 **Read the essay again and then say if the following statements are true or false.**

1 The first paragraph gives some general facts about the subject.
2 The second paragraph gives the arguments against the subject.
3 The third paragraph gives the arguments in favour of the subject.
4 The fourth paragraph gives the writer's final opinion, with the reasons for this opinion.

5 **Look at the words and phrases in bold in the essay in activity 3.**

1 Find four words used when we make a list of arguments.
2 Find a phrase that is used when we state what we believe.
3 Find a sentence that introduces the disadvantages of computer games.
4 Find a phrase that means *to decide* after looking at all the information.
5 Find a sentence that introduces the advantages of computer games.
6 Find a word that means the same as *also*.

6 **You are going to write an essay with the following title: *The advantages and disadvantages of television.* Work in small groups. Make notes under the headings for each paragraph in activity 2. Look at the reading text on page 29 of this unit for ideas. Then share your ideas with the whole class and write down good ideas from other groups.**

7 **Now write your essay. Try and use some of the phrases below. Write about 150 words.**

Ways of introducing advantages/disadvantages: (Computer games) have great/a number of/several advantages. There are (some big) disadvantages to (computer games).

Ways of listing points: firstly, secondly, thirdly, finally, lastly

Ways of adding points: also, furthermore, in addition, what is more

Ways of concluding: to conclude, to sum up, in conclusion

8 **Optional writing task. Write a summary of reading text 2 on page 31. Turn to page 25 for help with writing a summary. Write about 100 words.**

Are you a couch potato?

1 How much time do you spend watching TV? ☐
a Less than 8 hours a week
b 8-16 hours a week
c More than 16 hours a week

2 Which do you prefer doing? ☐
a Eating in a restaurant
b Eating at the table with your family
c Eating in front of the TV

3 Which of these is your idea of exercise? ☐
a Running five kilometres
b Going for a swim or taking a fast walk
c Turning off the TV and leaving the room

4 If you missed your favourite TV programme, how would you feel? ☐
a OK. TV isn't that interesting anyway
b Unhappy. But hopefully a friend has videoed it
c Terrible. Life would never be the same again

5 What of these things do you enjoy most? ☐
a Being outside in the fresh air
b Seeing friends
c Watching a video

6 Do you know what is on TV this evening? ☐
a I have no idea
b I can tell you about a couple of programmes
c Of course I do

7 If you went on holiday to a place without a television, how would you feel? ☐
a OK. It's good for you not to watch too much television
b I'd miss the TV for one or two days, then I'd be fine
c Awful. I would never do such a thing

8 When you watch TV, which of these do you do? ☐
a Watch for a short time and then go and do something active
b Sit in a sofa or armchair
c Lie on a sofa with a bag of sweets

1 **Work in pairs. The following words and phrases are all connected with television or watching television. Can you explain what they mean?**

couch potato   the box   remote control   soaps

***Couch* is another word for *sofa*. Why do you think we use the expression *couch potato*?**

Read the notes about these words at the bottom of page 35.

2 **Read the quiz at the top of the page and choose the answers that are most true for you.**

3 **Count up the number of a), b) and c) answers you have. Compare your answers with other students in the class.**

4 **Read the explanation below. In your opinion, is the quiz right about you?**

If you have:
mostly (a): You are an active kind of person. Just make sure that you give yourself a rest from time to time.
mostly (b): You are Mr/Miss Average. You watch quite a lot of television but you have other interests too.
mostly (c): You are a real couch potato. Get off the sofa and do something!

5 **You are going to hear a man called Jim being interviewed about his TV viewing habits. The interviewer asks Jim most of the questions in the quiz above. Listen and tick Jim's answers.**

6 **Answer these questions.**

1 There is one question that isn't in the quiz. What is it?
2 What is Jim's reply?
3 Do you think Jim is serious or is he joking?

7 **Look at these words in bold in these questions from the listening passage. Does the intonation go up (↗) or down (↘) on these words?**

1 Which would you rather do, eat in front of the **television** or go out to a **restaurant**?
2 Which do you prefer doing, seeing friends, watching a **video** or being **outdoors**?

8 **Now listen again, check your answers and repeat the sentences.**

Word watch – Root words

Identifying the root word will help in working out the meaning of unfamiliar vocabulary. Underline the root word and then try to find two or three more words with the same root.

Word (underline the root word)	**Examples** (of other words with the same root)
Impersonal	
Onlooker	
Defrosted	
Unreliable	
Heroically	
Disagreement	
Endangered	
Impressively	

Lessons in logic

1 If there are more letters in CORRESPONDENCE than there are in CELEBRATION, put a ring round X, unless there are fewer letters in UNDERLINE than in EXTERIOR, in which case you should put a ring round Y.
X Y

2 If Rosa has twice as many stamps as Edward and Edward has half the number owned by Colin, put a ring round X if Edward has the most stamps, a ring round Y if Colin has more stamps than Rosa or a ring round Z if Rosa and Colin have the same number.
X Y Z

3 If Tom tied with another child in a race and came fifth, beating six others, put a ring round W if there were 11 runners, X if there were 9 runners, Y if there were 12 runners and Z if we do not know how many runners there were in the race.
W X Y Z

4 If the day before yesterday was Thursday, put a ring round the second letter of the day after tomorrow.
O U E A H R

Focus on reading

1 Underline the two words that have to change places for the sentence to make sense.

1 Martin's been trying to days for finish his school project.
2 The teacher made good that all her class got sure results in the end of year tests.
3 The medicine had an unpleasant swallow so she had to taste it quickly.
4 Angela saw through the telescope and looked the new satellite.
5 Although Robert was still very tall, he was not in the basketball team.
6 There were lots of children picking into berries to make wild jam.

2 Select one word from each group in brackets to complete the sentence sensibly.

1 The (cloud/sky/sun) looked lovely as it (blew/brightened/disappeared) at the approach of (wind/dawn/summer).
2 The (leaves/roots/petals) of the (flowers/branch/tree) grew deep in the (earth/vase/autumn).
3 Sophia put (coffee/money/flour) and water in a (bag/bowl/kitchen) to make some (party/bread/meal).
4 The (author/ending/cover) of the (book/poem/story) was (washed/answered/torn).

Did you know? Surprising statistics

Two-thirds of professional footballers and 97% of referees think that the top Premiership players are taking too much out of the game.

Top football players have huge salaries and earn a lot more than doctors, teachers, lawyers and even the Prime Minister. Do you think this is right? Should their pay be limited? Or is it OK because their careers are short and they give lots of pleasure to their fans?

It's time to say what you think.

ANSWERS TO ACTIVITY 1 PAGE 30
Hitting the wall: *At a certain point in marathon races, usually after 20-25 kilometres, many runners feel that they can't go on, and it's a big struggle for them to continue. This experience is called 'hitting the wall'. It occurs when the body runs out of carbohydrates. The body actually has enough fat reserves to complete 35 marathons one after the other!*

ANSWERS TO ACTIVITY 1 PAGE 34
a couch potato *is someone who doesn't take exercise and spends most of their time sitting on a couch (sofa) and watching television*
the box *is a slang word for television*
a remote control *is the machine you use to change channels etc without getting out of your seat*
soaps *(or soap operas) are TV dramas; there is usually an episode at least once a week, and sometimes every day*

5 WHAT DO YOU WANT TO BE?

INTRODUCTION AND VOCABULARY

1 **Look at the people in the illustrations. What are their jobs? Choose from this list.**

architect barrister civil engineer dentist
doctor flight attendant lawyer pilot solicitor
surgeon veterinary surgeon (vet) zoo keeper

2 **Answer these questions about all the occupations in activity 1.**

Which of these people …

1 are involved in the construction of buildings?
2 help people who are sick?
3 work with animals?
4 work for airlines?
5 help people with their legal problems?

3 **Match the numbers with the occupations in activity 1 and complete the sentences. Be careful – some of the answers are singular, some are plural.**

1 (1), (2) and (3) are all involved with medical care. (1) look after your teeth, (2) look after your general health and (3) perform operations.
2 (4) and (5) both work on planes. A (4) flies the plane and a (5) looks after the passengers.
3 Many people are involved in the construction of, for example, bridges. (6) draw the original designs. (7) also work on the designs and are involved in the actual building of the bridge.
4 A (8) is someone who looks after the health of animals. (9) look after animals in captivity.
5 In the British legal system, there are two kinds of (10). The person who gives legal advice is a (11), and the person who represents you in a high court is a (12).

NOTE: If you can't answer question 5, see the note at the bottom page 43.

4 **Complete these three sentences, using one of the professions in activity 1. Add a second sentence of information to your answers, if you like.**

1 I would like to be a ______________ because ______
____.
2 I wouldn't like to be a ______________ because ____
____.
3 I don't think I would be a very good ______________ because ______________________________.

5 **Read what four teenagers wrote about their plans and ambitions 10 years ago. Then answer these questions.**

1 Who wanted a job that would allow them to work in the open air?
2 Who wanted to help sick people?
3 Who wanted to do something similar to one of his parents?
4 Who wanted to take some time off before deciding what to study?
5 Which of them had a clear idea of what they wanted to do?
6 Which of them didn't have a clear idea of what they wanted to do?

1

Name: Helen Carter
Age: 17
Home: near York, England

I live on a farm in the north of England and my ambition is to be a country vet – in other words, a vet who mostly looks after farm animals. Next year, I'm starting my A-level* courses, which take two years. I'm going to do Chemistry, Physics and Mathematics. The following year, I'm going to apply to all the veterinary schools in England. I'm also interested in wild animals. In ten years' time, I hope I'll either be working on a farm in the countryside here in England – or an a safari park in Africa.

***A-level** = Advanced level examinations, which are national examinations taken by UK students at about the age of 18.

2

Name: Lloyd Coleman
Age 17
Home: Memphis, USA

My father is a lawyer and I want to work in the same area. When I leave school, I'm going to study law. I want to specialise in criminal law and become a courtroom lawyer. I like the idea of working in a courtroom and persuading a jury that my client is innocent. Law isn't a subject at my school, but I'm going to apply to law school next year. In ten years' time, I imagine I'll be working as a lawyer and making a lot of money!

3

Name: Hussein Al-Mossawi
Age: 18
Home: Cairo, Egypt

I'm leaving school at the end of this year and I'm going to university here in Cairo to study medicine. Eventually, I would like to be a heart surgeon, like Magdi Yacoub, the famous Egyptian surgeon who works in England. In ten years' time, I hope I'll be working in a hospital – either here in Egypt or in another country.

4

Name: Madeline Patrick
Age: 16
Home: Sydney, Australia

I'm leaving school in two years' time and I haven't a clue what I want to study! I'm going to take a year off and travel round the world. I particularly want to visit Europe and the Middle East. Then I'll come back to Australia and study something – maybe I'll become a dentist, like my mother. I have absolutely no idea what I'll be doing in ten years' time.

6 **Now read what three of the people wrote 10 years later. Which of the four wrote these words?**

I'm very amused now when I think about what I was planning to do when I was a teenager. Things went according to plan - for about a week! When I left school, I was going to spend a year travelling, so I decided that the best way to do this was to become an airline flight attendant. I thought I would do that for about a year. Well, here I am - ten years' later, and I'm still a flight attendant! In fact, I'm a chief flight attendant with our national airline, and I love every minute of it! And do you know what I plan to do next? I'm going to train to be a pilot!

Ten years ago, I had a very clear idea of what I wanted to do, but that was before I got the chance to travel. When I left school, instead of going to university, I decided to go to Europe. When I reached Paris, I completely fell in love with the place and I stayed. I worked as an English teacher for a year, before going home and studying law. But what I really wanted to do was return to the Middle East. So now I'm back in Beirut and teaching law at the university.

I remember what I wrote about my plans and it's amazing how things can change! I was offered the chance to work in the famous Bronx Zoo in New York. When I got there, I fell in love with the city and have lived in New York ever since. I got married seven years ago and I've got two children, Sandy and Alex. In three years' time, when Alex goes to elementary school, I'm going to apply to go to veterinary school again. It's ten years later than I expected, but - better late than never!

7 **Answer these questions about the three people you've just read about.**

1 What were they planning to do when the left school?
2 How did their plans change?
3 What are they doing now?

1 **Look at the photos on the next page. What do you know about these places? Share your ideas with a partner and tell the rest of the group. Then answer these questions.**

1 Which of the three places does the class know most about?
2 Who in the class has the most interesting information?
3 Where did they get this information from?

2 **Read the three reading texts on the next page quickly. They all refer to training for a profession. Which professions do they refer to? Choose from the list on page 36.**

3 **Now read the three texts a little more carefully. What kind of texts are they? Choose from these lists.**

1 The first text is
   a a series of questions from someone who wants to train as a vet
   b a series of questions to someone who wants to train as a vet
   c an explanation of the exams you need to take to be a vet.
2 The second text describes
   a the exams you need to take to be a lawyer
   b the life skills you need if you want to be a lawyer
   c the English you need to be a lawyer.
3 The third text is about a student
   a who studied architecture in Australia
   b who is spending a year studying in Australia
   c who wants to study in Australia.

4 **The first text is from a University of Cambridge website. Look at the words in bold and choose the correct meaning from these choices.**

1 **mandatory** – does this mean (a) you can do it if you like or (b) you must do it?
2 **disadvantage** – does this refer to (a) a problem or (b) a qualification?
3 **currently** – does this mean (a) at the moment or (b) always?
4 **aptitude** – does this refer to (a) what you have learnt or (b) natural ability?
5 **specifically** – does this mean (a) for one particular thing or (b) for many things?

5 **Read the first text more carefully and answer the following questions about specific lines.**

1 *Some colleges insist that you have studied Biology.*
   Is this the same as saying that they prefer you to have studied Biology?
2 *It offers the chance to show that you have the mental attitude to succeed in Cambridge veterinary or medical courses.*
   What aspects of your mental attitude do you think the colleges want to find out about?
3 *You certainly should not give up other valuable forms of extra-curricular activity, eg sports or music, in order to undertake work specifically with animals.*
   Does this mean that you shouldn't try to get experience of working with animals at all?

6 **Read the second text, which is from the website of the University of Louisiana in New Orleans, USA. Which of the following sentences is a good summary of what it says?**

1 If you are planning to study law, the most important thing is your choice of school subjects.
2 If you want to study law, the most important thing is to get good grades.
3 Practising law requires certain life skills, and law schools will be looking for them when they interview students.

7 **Read the second text again and decide if the following are good examples of the qualities they are looking for. If they aren't, think of a better example.**

1 **reasoning skills** – if you can argue in favour or against something, using clear and intelligent arguments
2 **curiosity** – if you like looking in other people's bags to see what they've got
3 **good verbal skills** – if you can speak louder than everyone else in the room
4 **thorough** – if you check that you have answered all the questions completely before you hand in your homework
5 **well-organised** – if all your work is filed neatly in folders

8 **Read the third text, which is taken from a website about studying in Australia, and answer these questions. When there is a second question, you need to give your personal opinion.**

1 What was the reaction of Raul's family when he chose to study in Australia? Why do you think they had this reaction?
2 Why does Raul think that being in a new country makes you 'more open'? Do you think this would be the same for everyone?
3 What does 'there were a lot of people in the same boat' mean? Is there a similar expression in your language?
4 What did Raul think of the facilities?

Sydney, Australia

New Orleans, USA

Cambridge, UK

1

1 *Which subjects should I take at A-level?*
A minimum of 3 A-levels (or equivalent examinations) is necessary. These are normally chosen from Chemistry, Biology, Physics and Maths. Chemistry at A-level is **mandatory**. Some (but not all) colleges insist that you have studied Biology.

2 *What A-level grades do I need?*
In recent years, almost all successful candidates have achieved three As at A-level. If there are special circumstances (eg illness or other serious **disadvantage**) there is a scheme called the Cambridge Special Access Scheme that may be appropriate.

3 *Is there an entrance examination for veterinary candidates applying to Cambridge?*
Yes. Applicants who want to study Medicine or Veterinary Medicine take the Medical and Veterinary Admissions Test in November.

Currently, the two-hour test consists of three sections, A, B and C. Section A is a test of scientific **aptitude**, while Section B tests scientific knowledge. Section C offers the chance to show that you have the mental attitude to succeed in Cambridge veterinary or medical courses.

4 *Will it be a problem if I can't get experience of working with animals?*
The most important reason for doing work experience is to help you find out what the job is like. It is not essential to spend a long time doing this kind of work. You certainly should not give up other valuable forms of extra-curricular activity, eg sports or music, in order to undertake work **specifically** with animals. Indeed, some successful candidates have not had much experience of this kind of work.

2

Law schools are looking for certain qualities in the way you work, rather than the subjects you actually study. The development of reasoning skills is more important. Students who want to study law need to show that they not only have curiosity and good verbal skills, but also that they are thorough and well organised.

However, some school subjects are more useful than others. In order of preference, they are: English language and literature, government, economics, history, mathematics, Latin and philosophy.

Just taking the courses, however, is not enough. You must also do well – grades are important. Consequently, you want to major in a subject in which you are interested and one in which you will have to work hard to do well. Take challenging courses appropriate to your strengths; choose courses in which hard work will be rewarded with good grades.

3

Raul Mendoza, an architecture student, was offered the chance to study for a year in an English-speaking country. To the amazement of his family in Spain, he chose to study in Australia. But Raul hasn't regretted his decision at all.

'My English has gone from strength to strength during the six months that I've been here. It's a terrific place to study – you meet people from all over the world and experience different cultures and different attitudes. Being by yourself in a foreign country makes you more open to other people and their cultures. Plus, you really have to go out and do things – otherwise you don't meet anyone at all.'

'There were a lot of other people in the same boat and it was very easy to meet people and make friends,' he said. 'The university organises events such as barbecues and harbour cruises where you can meet other students from all over the world.'

Raul was very impressed by the facilities. 'The University has the best architecture library I've ever seen. Also, there are a lot of optional subjects – they're called 'elective workshops'. I chose photography, and now I spend a lot of time taking photographs around Sydney. Architecture has been my passion but now I get a lot of pleasure from photography as well. I have a great teacher who has really motivated me.'

Raul hasn't seen much of Australia but plans to travel round the country before going back to Spain to complete his degree. After graduating, he hopes to work for a couple of years then perhaps come back to the University of Sydney to do a Master's course. 'The time has gone so fast,' he says. 'It's quite scary thinking about leaving.' He has this advice for students who are thinking about studying abroad: 'I would definitely recommend studying abroad. It's brilliant!'

2 GRAMMAR PRACTICE

1 Future
2 Future in the past

1 Match the uses of the tense forms in italics with explanations 1-6.

1 Making a promise
2 Expressing a plan
3 Talking about a fixed arrangement
4 Making a prediction
5 Talking about timetables
6 Following a future time conjunction

NOTE: they are all in relation to the future.

ALAN: What *are you doing* in the holidays? ____
VIOLET: *I'm going to study* Italian in Perugia. ____
ALAN: *That'll be exciting*, I imagine. ____
VIOLET: I hope so. I *leave* tomorrow at 8.15. ____
ALAN: Well, send me a postcard when you *get* there! ____
VIOLET: I *will*! ____

2 Underline the more appropriate future tense in each case. Explain your decisions.

Hi Alan!

I've been in Perugia for about three weeks now and the studies are going quite well. Anyway, we'll see/we're seeing tomorrow because we have/we will have a test at 9 o'clock. I'm studying/I'm going to study a lot this evening! As soon as the test will finish/finishes, Sue and I are leaving/leave for a weekend in Rome.

I'm sure we are enjoying ourselves/will enjoy ourselves a lot there! I promise I'll send/I send you another card from there.

Best wishes,
Violet.

3 Complete this paragraph with future tenses from exercise 1, and those forms exemplified in the box.

will/would be talking	will/would have talked
is/was about to talk	am/was going to talk

William was getting very anxious. Jane hadn't come downstairs yet and the bus __________ in a couple of minutes. 'The bus __________ in a couple of minutes, you know. It __________ for us', he called out. He couldn't understand Jane. In another minute or two she __________ hour. 'Do hurry, Jane. That bus __________ arrive. There'll be plenty of time when we __________ at the airport for you to phone Jake', he shouted. 'Here I am, William', answered Jane, 'I __________ phone Peter, too, but you're right, I'll do it at the airport.' William opened the front door and hurried out. Fifty metres away the bus was at the bus-stop and it __________ go!

4 Ali says: Write in the six missing 'futures'.

1 **Read the student profile below. What career would you suggest for Craig? Explain why.**

Craig Roberts, an eighteen-year-old student from the north of England, is in his final year at school. He is taking A-levels in English, French and History and has a place at university in September. Craig is a lively, hard-working student who is good both at academic subjects and sport. His interests include current affairs, reading and films, and he regularly contributes articles to the school magazine, of which he is deputy editor. A member of the school football team, Craig is keen on all kinds of sport. He has a sociable, extrovert personality and enjoys meeting people. Although Craig is unsure about what he wants to do as a career, he knows that it must be something that provides variety and involves meeting people.

2 **In the following conversation, Craig is talking to a career adviser called Mr Shaw. Complete the conversation, using one of the choices below. Use the information about Craig in activity 1 to help you choose the correct answers.**

MR SHAW: Shall we get down to business, then?
CRAIG: **1** ____________________
MR SHAW: You're taking English, French and History. You're not intending to take a year off before going to university, are you?
CRAIG: **2** ____________________
MR SHAW: OK. Do you have any ideas about what you want to do?
CRAIG: **3** ____________________
MR SHAW: How would you describe yourself, Craig?
CRAIG: **4** ____________________
MR SHAW: You've got lots of interests, haven't you?
CRAIG: Yes, I have. **5** ____________________ I'm in the school football team and I'm also deputy editor of the school magazine.
MR SHAW: Actually, I've seen some of your articles, and I must say, I'm impressed. They're not bad at all! Have you thought of a career as a journalist?
CRAIG: **6** ____________________
MR SHAW: I see. Well, you say you love sport. How about being a sports journalist?
CRAIG: **7** ____________________
MR SHAW: Good, well, perhaps we're getting somewhere. Why don't you read this information and then we can talk some more at our next meeting?
CRAIG: **8** ____________________

1 **a** Yes, let's.
b I'm not really interested in business as a career.
2 **a** I haven't made up my mind yet.
b No, I'm not, I want to go straight to university.
3 **a** Something to do with sport, perhaps.
b Not really. But it's got to involve working with people.
4 **a** Me? People tell me I'm pretty extrovert.
b I've got good friends, but like a lot of people, I can be quite shy sometimes.
5 **a** Although if I had to choose one thing it would be sport.
b I'm interested in politics, good novels, movies, meeting people and all sport.
6 **a** Yes I have, but I'm not sure what kind of journalism I'd like to do.
b To be honest, I dislike all kinds of writing.
7 **a** That does sound interesting.
b I think I'd rather take part in sport than write about it.
8 **a** I'll be doing that. Thanks, Mr Shaw.
b I'll do that. Thanks, Mr Shaw.

3 **Find five contractions, four short answers and one interjection in the complete dialogue in activity 2.**

EXAMPLES:
- contractions, eg *isn't* *you're*
- short answers, eg *Yes, I do* *No, I don't*
- interjections, eg *Oh* *I see*

4 **Read the dialogue again. Find:**

1. a phrase meaning *in fact*.
2. a phrase meaning *to make progress*.
3. three ways of making a suggestion.
4. a question that seems to expect the answer *yes*.
5. a question that seems to expect the answer *no*.
6. a phrase meaning *quite good*.
7. a phrase used to emphasize what we are saying.
8. a phrase meaning *to begin the discussion*.

5 **Rewrite these sentences using negative question tags.**

1. Your parents understand how difficult it is.
2. Your sister is going to follow the same career as you.
3. Mr Jones has invited her for an interview.
4. Simon did well in his final exams.
5. You'll be starting a new job soon.
6. There's someone who can help you with this.
7. Somebody will explain how to do it.

6 **Now rewrite the sentences using negative verbs and positive question tags.**

7 **Write a conversation in which a teacher gives you advice about your career.**

- Give information about yourself in answer to the questions.
- Use informal language.
- Try to use at least one question tag.

LISTENING AND SPEAKING

1 **Check the meaning of these words.**

CV (curriculum vitae) qualification to get on with likeable academic fascinated

2 **Which of the following qualities are most important for teachers? Explain why.**

- they can keep discipline
- they explain things clearly
- they like teaching a lot
- they know a lot about their subject
- they love their subject
- they like their students

3 **You will hear two people, Matthew and Sally, being interviewed for their first job as a History teacher in a secondary school. What questions do you think the interviewer will ask? Suggest at least three.**

4 **Listen to the two interviews. Answer these questions.**

1 Were you right about the questions?
2 Who do you think will get the job? Why?

5 **Listen again. In the following extracts, one or two words have changed. Which words have changed? Do the new words change the meaning of the sentence?**

1 I see you've got the right qualifications.
2 I'm a likeable type of person.
3 Do you have many questions you'd like to ask?
4 You're interested in teachers as human beings.
5 I like teenagers, and I like History.
6 I've always wanted to be a teacher, ever since I was a child.

6 **Role play**
Work in groups of three.
STUDENT A: You are the head of a small publishing company that specialises in travel books. You are going to interview someone for a job as a trainee editor. It will be his/her first real job.

- Write down the questions you want to ask.
- Interview the person.

STUDENT B: You are going for an interview for a job as a trainee editor with a small publishing company that specialises in travel. It will be your first real job.

- Think about the questions you are likely to be asked.
- Prepare your answers. Tell the interviewer what travel experience you have had, and what editing experience you have had.

STUDENT C:

- Listen to the interview. Watch for these things:
  - Student B should answer the questions clearly
  - He/she should be positive about himself/herself and enthusiastic about the company
  - He/she should seem friendly and self-confident.
- Afterwards, advise Student B on how he/she can improve his/her interviewing technique.

Examples of advice:
Try and answer the questions more clearly.
Think for a moment before you speak.
You need to smile more.
Sit up straight!

Students A and B role play the interview again. Is student B better this time?

Word Watch – Synonyms

Synonyms are words which have the same meaning – that's the dictionary definition, but of course there is usually some difference between them. Can you find ways in which these synonyms are different from each other? Use a dictionary, if you can.

autumn/fall salt/sodium chloride man/guy slim/skinny stale/rotten

Now find some synonyms. Underline the word in the second column that has the same meaning as the word in the first column.

satisfied	delighted full contented displeased
lazy	unhappy agile idle sleepy
clever	top painstaking bright fast
huge	fierce odd massive affectionate
damage	harm lower control hide
raise	current stage elevate save
free	cheap release available fun
weak	tired feeble poor unpleasant
need	want deed require demand

Lessons in logic

Use your skills in logical thinking and close reading.

Andrew, Robert, Emily and Rose take part in a variety of sports.
Only one person takes part in basketball and that is not Emily or Robert.
Robert is the only person taking part in three sports.
Andrew takes part is swimming and one other sport.
Rose takes part only in swimming and table tennis.
Emily takes part only in badminton.

So, which sport does Robert not take part in? __________

Which person takes part in basketball? ______________

Who takes part in swimming but not table tennis? _______

How many people take part in two sports? ____________

Who takes part in table tennis but not badminton? ______

Alphabetical order

Alphabetical order is a very common way to classify and list items, and you need to know your alphabet well if you want to be able to consult reference works, such as dictionaries and encyclopaedias, efficiently.

1 Put these words into alphabetical order (number them 1-5):

1	flight	flesh	flew	flea	fling
2	spoil	spot	spoof	sport	spoon
3	visible	vice	visitor	visor	vicious
4	attack	attach	ant	attentionaunt	
5	laws	lawless	law	lawyer	lawful

2 A palindrome is a word that reads the same backwards as it does forwards. Underline the palindromes in this list.

revolver chic madam shells tenet rotator secrets civic clinic matter tissue sneezes level solos mum kayak fluff lovely noon sunset

3 Look at this list of words and answer the questions.

decentralise decency decision decimal deceitful

1. Which word contains the letter which is nearest to the beginning of the alphabet?
2. Which word contains the letter which is nearest to the end of the alphabet?
3. Which word has the most consonants in it?
4. Which vowel is used in all the words?

Did you know?

Fewer than 5% of children walk or cycle to school compared with 80% two decades ago.

What do you think?
Is it the same in your country?
What do you think has caused this change?
Do you and your friends consider yourselves to be fit and energetic?

NOTE: ACTIVITY 3 PAGE 36

Lawyers, barristers, solicitors and attorneys

In the UK legal system, a barrister is qualified to represent a client in a high court, whereas a solicitor is merely able to give legal advice. This distinction does not exist in the US. In the US, attorney and lawyer are synonyms – attorney is considered a bit more formal.

6 MAKING MOVIES

INTRODUCTION AND VOCABULARY

Gunfight at the OK Corral

Men In Black

Jungle Book

1 **Look at the film posters on this page and answer these questions.**

1. Have you heard of or seen any of the films?
2. Did you see them on TV, on video or at the cinema?
3. Is the title different in your language?
4. Do you know any English language films where the title is different in your language?

2 **Read the following list of film styles. Describe what happens in films like this and, if you can, give an example of each style.**

EXAMPLE: *In action films, there is a lot of action and not much dialogue. Men in Black is an example of an action film.*

action film   cartoon   comedy   disaster film
gangster film   horror film   musical   silent film
science fiction film   western

NOTE: You can say
Jungle Book is a cartoon film. OR Jungle Book is a cartoon.
Men in Black is an action film. NOT Men in Black is an action.

3 **Look at the cartoons and explain the difference between the two sentences.** ***He's gone to the cinema*** **and** ***He's been to the cinema.***

1 Where's Tom?
He's gone to the cinema.
2 Where's Tom been?
He's been to the cinema.

4 **Work in pairs. Complete the following dialogue and act it out the for the rest of the class.**

DETECTIVE 1: I've been waiting for you for hours! Where have ... ?
DETECTIVE 2: I ... to the police station.
DETECTIVE 1: Why ... there?
DETECTIVE 2: I ... there to see Sergeant O'Leary.
DETECTIVE 1: And did you see him?
DETECTIVE 2: No. He wasn't there. He's ... to Los Angeles.
DETECTIVE 1: Why ... Los Angeles???
DETECTIVE 2: I don't know.
DETECTIVE 1: Did you see Detective Starkey?
DETECTIVE 2: No.
DETECTIVE 1: Why not?
DETECTIVE 2: Because he ..., too.

5 **Read the following list of words about movies. Which ones refer to (a) people (b) places or (c) other things?**

actor/actress   cameraman   director   location
plot   producer   script-writer   set   studio

6 **Complete the information about films and film people, using six words based on words in activity 5. Be careful – you may have to change the words, eg from noun to verb.**

On the Waterfront (1954)

Winner of seven Academy Awards, this powerful story focuses on the hopes and despair of New York dock workers. Marlon Brando, who was already known as one of the most talented ... of his generation, played Terry Malloy. The film was ... by Elia Kazan and the ... was written by Budd Schulberg, with award-winning ... Boris Kaufman taking the pictures. Kazan hated making films in ..., and *On The Waterfront* was filmed it almost entirely on ... at the docks in Hoboken, New Jersey.

Brad Pitt
Was he in a rock band?

Nicole Kidman
Did she want to be a vet?

Leonardo DiCaprio
Did he have to wear a chicken costume?

Russell Crowe
Was he a child actor?

Julia Roberts
Did she want to be a ballet dancer?

Five movie stars – but who are they?

1 Brad or Leonardo?

Born in Los Angeles in 1974, he appeared in milk commercials on TV while he was still a child. As he grew older, he had lots of bit-parts in movies and was nominated for Best Supporting Actor at the age of 19 for his performance in a film called *What's Eating Gilbert Grape?* He became a huge star in the record-breaking movie *Titanic*. *Titanic* won a lot of Oscars, although he didn't get one. Since making *Titanic*, he has been offered parts in many big movies, many of which he has turned down. In 2002, he appeared in the Steven Spielberg film *Catch Me If You Can*.

2 Nicole or Julia?

Born in Honolulu in June 1967 and brought up in Australia, she wanted to be a ballet dancer but turned to acting and has never looked back. She won an Oscar in 2003 for her portrayal of Victorian British novelist Virginia Woolf in *The Hours*.

3 Russell or Brad?

He was born in 1963 in Oklahoma. His father owned a truck company, his mother was a school counsellor and he was a choirboy at High School. His first job in Hollywood was standing in the street, dressed as a chicken, offering free cigarettes to passers-by. His breakthrough was when he got a part in the 1980s TV series *Dallas*. He got his first Oscar nomination for his performance in *Twelve Monkeys* in 1996. His most famous films are *Fight Club* and *Ocean's Eleven*.

4 Julia or Nicole?

Born in Georgia in October 1967, she wanted to be a vet until she graduated from high school. She appeared in her first film in 1986, was nominated for an Oscar for her performance in *Steel Magnolias* (1989), and finally won one for *Erin Brockovich* (2000).

5 Leonardo or Russell?

He was born in 1964 in Wellington, New Zealand and spent some of his early years in Australia. When he went back to New Zealand, he formed a rock band called Roman Antix with some friends, but they were terrible and never released any albums. His most famous and Oscar-winning role has been the Roman general Maximus in *Gladiator*.

■ The answers are at the bottom of page 51.

7 **Before you read the mini-biographies, check the meaning of these words and phrases.**

- An actor has a *role* or a *part* in a film; what do you think a *bit-part* is?
- When an actor becomes famous through a particular role, do we call it a *breakthrough* or a *breakdown*?
- What do you think it means if an actor *turns down* a part?
- If someone has started a career and has never *looked back*, does that mean he/she is successful or unsuccessful?
- An Oscar is an award given to Best Actor, Best Film etc. What's the difference between *winning* an Oscar and being *nominated* for an Oscar?
- What does it mean if a film breaks *box office* records?

8 **Read the mini-biographies of the five actors and actresses and match them with the photographs. Then answer the questions under the photos.**

EXAMPLE: Was Brad Pitt in a rock band?
No ... was in a rock band.

9 **Read the information again and answer these questions.**

1 Which of the actors/actresses have won Oscars?
2 Which of them have been nominated for Oscars?
3 Which of them have appeared in TV commercials?
4 Which of them are not American?
5 Who's the oldest actor or actress in the group?

10 **Look at the names of films and TV programmes in the text (in italics) and answer these questions.**

1 Which of the titles are or contain people's names?
2 Which one is a command?
3 Which one is the name of a boat?
4 Which one is the name of an American city?
5 Which one is a question and what do you think the question means?

11 **Now discuss the following points.**

1 What do you know about the film industry in your country?
2 Research how your country's film industry started.

Steven Spielberg – movie magician

Steven Spielberg, who was born in Cincinnati Ohio in 1946, has written, acted in, directed and/or produced some of the most successful movies of all time. Spielberg has been fascinated by the movie industry since he was a small child. When he was nine years old, he charged admission to his home movies – 'action films' which involved train crashes with his train set. His sister sold popcorn to the audience. At the age of 13, Spielberg won a prize for a 40-minute film he made called *Escape to Nowhere*. In 1963, when he was 16, his film *Firelight* was shown in a local cinema and made a $100 profit. *Firelight* inspired his later film *Close Encounters of the Third Kind*.

Astonishingly, this naturally talented filmmaker was unable to get a place at film school! Instead, he went to California State University to study English. When he left, he was determined to make it in the movies. His life changed on the day he decided to jump off a tour bus at Universal Studios in Hollywood and wander around the studio. The story is that he found an abandoned store room and turned it into an office. He then dressed smartly and went to work in his new 'office' every day. The security guards saw him so often that they presumed he was a genuine employee of the studio and allowed him to enter.

Eventually, Universal gave Spielberg $15,000 to make his first film, *Amblin*, which was 24 minutes long and won several film festival awards. As a result, the studio gave him a seven-year contract to make films for TV. They soon realised that Spielberg was a rare talent and in 1974 they asked him to direct his first cinema film, *The Sugarland Express*. His second film, *Jaws* (1975), made Spielberg an international superstar. Two years later, he made the science-fiction classic *Close Encounters of the Third Kind*.

Spielberg then made some less successful movies but in 1981, he struck gold again with *Raiders of the Lost Ark*, starring Harrison Ford. One year later, Spielberg's next film *ET The Extra Terrestrial* became the biggest movie of all time at the US box office. In 1993, he made another record-breaking movie, *Jurassic Park*, which earned a hundred million dollars in just nine days after its release, beating *ET*'s box office record.

Film critic Roger Ebert said in 2002: 'If Spielberg never directs another film, his place in movie history is secure. No other director has been more successful at the box office and few directors have directed so many great films.'

1 **Before you read the text about Steven Spielberg, complete the KWL chart below. Working in groups, complete the first part by saying what you know (or think you know) about Steven Spielberg and his films.**

What we Know	What we Want to know	What we Learned

2 **Now complete the second part by listing what you want to know.**

3 **Skim the text about Steven Spielberg and answer these questions.**

1. Why are the following years mentioned in the text?
   1946 1963 1982 1993
2. Why are the following sums of money mentioned in the text?
   $100 $15,000 $100 million

4 **Look at the following lines in context and choose the correct meaning.**

1. **Line 12:** He charged admission to his home movies. Does this mean **a** he asked people for money to see his films or **b** he forced his friends to watch the films?
2. **Line 22:** *Firelight* inspired his later film *Close Encounters of the Third Kind*.
   Does this mean that *Firelight* **a** was better than the other film or **b** gave him the idea for the other film?

3 **Line 24:** This naturally talented filmmaker was unable to get a place at film school.
Does this mean that **a** he didn't want to go to film school or **b** the film school didn't want him to attend?

4 **Line 34:** He found an abandoned store room and turned it into an office.
Does this mean **a** he stopped working in a store room and moved to an office or **b** he transformed a store room into an office?

5 **Line 39:** They presumed he was a genuine employee of the studio.
Does this mean that they **a** thought he worked for the studio or **b** didn't think that he worked for the studio?

6 **Line 58:** He struck gold again with *Raiders of the Lost Ark*.
Does this mean the film was **a** a success or **b** a failure?

7 **Line 61:** *ET* ... became the biggest movie of all time at the US box office.
Does this mean that **a** it cost more than any other US film to make or **b** that more people paid to see it?

8 **Line 70:** If Spielberg never directs another film, his place in movie history is secure.
Does this mean that Spielberg will be remembered as a great director **a** only if he never makes another film or **b** even if he never makes another film?

5 Now read the complete text. Which words, phrases or sentences in the text tell you the following?

1 Spielberg had more than just a small interest in films.
2 The story about Spielberg using a store room as an office may or may not be true.
3 Universal Studios had a high opinion of Spielberg.
4 *Raiders of the Lost Ark* was more successful than the films Spielberg made before it.
5 Spielberg has directed a lot of very good movies.

6 Read the first line of the plots of three of Spielberg's films. Then complete the story line with three or four more sentences from the list in the box.

a *Jaws*
The people of the small Long Island town of Amity have become the victims of a man-eating shark ...

b *Jurassic Park*
Jurassic Park is an animal reserve on a small island off the coast of Costa Rica ...

c *Minority Report*
Set in the year 2054, this is the story of a police department which arrests criminals before they commit their crimes ...

1 It is possible to do this because of the extraordinary powers of three young people who help the police by predicting the future.
2 Town officials hesitate to warn people about the shark because they don't want visitors to stay away.
3 The director of the reserve is a scientist called John Hammond, who has managed to clone different kinds of dinosaurs.
4 Then a swimmer is attacked in broad daylight and killed.
5 The company which owns the reserve become concerned that strange things are happening there, and sends experts to find out what is going on.
6 However, one of the officers who works in the department is accused of a future crime.
7 Three people – a police chief, a young marine biologist and a shark expert – decide to try to find the shark.
8 The experts are astonished by what they find, and astonishment soon turns to horror ...
9 He only has a little time to try to stop the crime taking place ...
10 They set out in a small boat, knowing that the shark may get them first ...

7 Now complete the last part of the KWL chart in activity 1.

8 Class survey.
Read the following survey and tick ✔ the answers that are true for you.

1 I like seeing films at the cinema. ☐
2 I prefer watching films on video, DVD or TV. ☐
3 I'm interested in who the director of a film is. ☐
4 I'm not interested in who the director of a film is. ☐
5 I don't care who is acting in the film. ☐
6 My favourite film actor/actress is ...
7 My favourite kind of films are ... (choose a style)
8 My favourite film of all time is ...

9 Discussion 1
Work in groups. Compare your survey results with other students in your group. Then share your results with the rest of the class.

10 Discussion 2
Make a note of your favourite three films. Find someone else (or more than one person) in the class who likes one of the same films. Discuss why you like the film and tell the rest of the class.

2 GRAMMAR PRACTICE

1 Perfect tenses
2 *been* and *gone*

1 Explain the perfect tense uses in the dialogue. Refer to the Grammar Reference, section 4.

MUM: Are you going out, Tom?
TOM: Yes. I'm going to see the new Spielberg film.
MUM: That's the second time you'll have been to the cinema this weekend. Have you written your essay?
TOM: Yes. I've just finished it. I've been working for hours and I need a break.
MUM: Why don't you stay in and watch this film on TV with me, then?
TOM: I've seen it. It's about snakes and you know I've never liked snakes.
MUM: *The Sound of Music* is on, too. Have you seen that?
TOM: Only about twenty times. And you and Dad had seen it about ten times before I was born!

2 Complete these sentences with perfect tenses. Use the verbs in brackets and include an adverb from the box for emphasis.

ever (never) already yet still just

1 Julia Roberts .... an Oscar before *Erin Brockovich* but she .... for one for her role in *Steel Magnolias*. *(win, nominate)*
2 Brad Pitt .... a popular TV or film actor for almost 20 years now but he .... an Oscar. *(be, win)*
3 When Leonardo DiCaprio starred in *Titanic* in 1997, he .... in front of the cameras for a good many years. He .... to make big movies since then, but some people predict that by the time he's 40 he .... from our cinema screens. *(work, continue, disappear)*
4 Kate Winslet .... in many movies since *Titanic*. Who knows how many film roles .... by 2010, when she .... her 35th birthday. *(star, take, celebrate)*

3 Choose the better perfect forms and explain your choices. Answer the questions.

1 How long has Steven Spielberg *made/been making* major films for the cinema?
2 Which films have most people *watched/been watching* lately in your country?
3 Are you reading a book (novel or other kind) at the moment? How many pages *have you read/been reading*? *Have you read/been reading* it for more than a week?

4 Explain Helmut's confusion.

Tolkein's novel is a screen triumph

by Hank Groves

The Lord of the Rings is an epic fantasy novel by JRR Tolkein which takes place in an imaginary place called Middle Earth. The story is in three parts and *The Lord of the Rings: The Fellowship of the Rings* is the film of the first part. In it, we meet imaginary creatures called hobbits, who are like humans but shorter, with furry feet. A young hobbit called Frodo has been given a dangerous ring. The wizard Gandalf reveals that an evil wizard wants to use it to control Middle Earth. It is decided that the ring must be taken into Sauron's kingdom and destroyed. Nine creatures, each from a different race, agree to perform this almost impossible mission. The film tells the story of the dangers that the nine meet as they travel.

The film was directed by Peter Jackson and was shot in New Zealand, and the scenery is wild and beautiful. The computer-generated sequences are extraordinarily realistic and, although the characters never really develop, this doesn't affect the drama and the action at all. Ian McKellen is superb as Gandalf the wizard and Elijah Wood is just right as the young hobbit who is the hero of the story. The film is fast moving and full of suspense, and has some absolutely terrifying battle scenes. It's a brilliant film. Don't miss it!

1 **The adjectives below can be used to talk about a film. Put them into two groups, positive and negative.**

gripping entertaining disappointing terrible slow frightening sentimental moving brilliant fascinating terrifying superb

2 **Look quickly at the following review of *The Lord of the Rings: The Fellowship of the Ring*. Then answer these questions.**

1 What does the title tell you about the reviewer's opinion of the film?
2 Which paragraph describes the plot?
3 What tense does the reviewer use to describe the plot?
4 Which paragraph gives the reviewer's opinion of the film?
5 Which adjectives in the text tell you what the reviewer thinks about the film?

3 **What do we learn about the following people and characters in the film?**

Gandalf Ian McKellen Elijah Wood

4 **Read the lists of expressions you can use to review a film. Give each list one of these category headings:**

plot final opinion photography acting and direction pace and interest

1
It takes place in …
It tells the story of …
It's about …

2
(Name of actor) stars as (name of character).
It's directed/written by …
(Name of actor) is (superb) as (name of character).
(Name of actor) plays (name of character), who (tries to …).
The characters are not very believable.

3
The photography is superb.
The film looks beautiful/good.
It's visually stunning.

4
It's a fast-moving film.
The film moves (too) slowly/fast.
The film is boring/predictable/full of suspense.

5
This is a film you should not miss.
I can thoroughly recommend this film.
I found the film very entertaining/rather boring.
The film was quite/very enjoyable.

5 **Write a review of a film you have seen. Include:**

- a paragraph describing the plot
- a paragraph giving your opinion.

Try to use the words and expressions you have learnt in this lesson. Write 150 words.

6 **Optional writing task. Write a summary of the text entitled *Steven Spielberg – movie magician* on page 46 of this unit. Write about 120 words. Turn to page 25 for help with writing a summary.**

1 **Discuss the following questions:**

- Is there anyone in the class who would like to work in films?
- What kind of thing would you like to do (direct? write? act? operate a camera?)
- Which of the following are the most interesting things about working in film?
  - It's a glamorous and exciting life.
  - Working in the movies makes you famous.
  - You can work with interesting and talented people.
  - Movie people make a lot of money.
  - There are opportunities to travel.

2 **You're going to hear a young British filmmaker called Paul Tanner talk about his career in films. Below are the stages that he thinks are necessary to become a successful film director. Put them in the order that you think is most probable.**

A make a low-budget, full-length film with professional actors and film crew
B make a short film using professional actors and film crew
C make short films using a video camera with friends
D make a big, Hollywood film
E make music videos and advertisements

3 **Now listen to an interview with Paul. Check your answers to activity 2.**

4 **Listen again. Answer these questions.**

1 How old is Paul?
2 What reasons does he give for wanting to be a film director?
3 When did he first use a video camera?
4 How many prizes did his short film win?
5 How long did it take Paul to write a full-length film script?
6 How long have they been filming this script?

5 **Listen to the second part of the interview with Paul. Below are the questions the interviewer asks Paul. Listen and give Paul's answers to the questions.**

1 What advice would you give young filmmakers?
2 Why is it so hard?
3 Why do you think you've been successful so far?

6 **Listen to the following phrases from the listening passages. You will hear each phrase twice. The second time you hear a phrase, it will have a different intonation. Then answer the questions below.**

A I'm sure you will!
B It's been a lot of hard work!
C It's really difficult, you know.
D It's all I think about!
E Really?
F Really!

1 Which is the main word stressed in each of sentences A–D?
2 Compare the two sentences. In the second sentence, does the speaker's voice rise or fall more or less?
3 How is the mood different in each sentence? Choose from these words:

enthusiastic matter-of-fact emphatic interested neutral

7 **Listen and repeat the phrases.**

8 **Role-play: work in threes.**

STUDENT A: You want to become a film director. Ask Student B and Student C for advice about how to start your career.
STUDENT B: You are a young film director and are very enthusiastic about film. Tell Student A all the good things about working in films.
STUDENT C: You've been working in films all your life but you are a very pessimistic person. Tell Student A all the bad things about working in films.

Try to use some of the following language:
What do I have to do to get started?
How long have you wanted to do this?
If I were you, I'd borrow a video camera.
Take my advice, try something else!

9 **Work in small groups. Contrast what you have learnt about the British film industry with the film industry in your country. Below are some questions to help you:**

- What is the state of the film industry in your country? For example, is it successful or does it have financial problems?
- Is there such a thing as a 'typical' film made by your country's film industry? Do you enjoy these films?
- Is your country's film industry easy or difficult to get into? What are the best ways to get into it?

Word watch – Antonyms

Antonyms are words that are opposite in meaning. Some of the most commonly used are big/small, first/last, few/many, bad/good, black/white and they may often occur close together in the same sentence. Can you think of an example?

1 **Underline the two words – one from each group – that are most opposite in meaning.**

fear thought sadness	pain joy memory
deep dangerous anxious	easy excited shallow
shiver improve hope	deteriorate cry warn
enlarge divide elevate	reveal damage multiply
guilty wrong criminal	judge innocent punishment
active energy health	tired passive exercise
crazy lost wild	ordinary tame fierce
fake bargain cheat	genuine copy special
seldom ancient tiny	age colossal odd
discontented lazy fit	clever satisfied excessive

2 **Make antonyms for these words by adding a prefix:**

_______obedient _______correct _______probable
_______understand _______necessary

3 **Make antonyms for these words by changing the suffix:**

careless_______ starry_______ sensible_______

Lessons in logic

Use your skills in logical thinking and close reading.

Five friends – Pauline, Emily, Jessica, Carol and Nicola – went shopping for clothes, books and computer games. Only Emily and Carol didn't buy clothes. Emily was the only person who bought only one item and it was a book. Only Pauline and Nicola did not have buy books. Four of them bought computer games.

So, who bought only books and computer games?

____

Who bought clothes, books and computer games?

____

Which two friends bought the same items?

____

Altogether how many items did they buy?

____

Revitalise your vocabulary

1 **Look at the four words on each line and find the missing letter to end the first word and start the next one. Note that it is the same letter for both pairs of words.**

PAT	( )	EAL	EAC	( )	EAR
MAI	( )	ESS	DIA	( )	END
WA	( )	ED	CA	( )	OAD
WAL	( )	NOW	BAC	( )	NOT
LES	( )	EW	WA	( )	POT
ZO	( )	NE	SOL	( )	UR
GAN	( )	UESS	WI	( )	OOD
AN	( )	ELL	FL	( )	OU
LIK	( )	VEN	TIL	( )	GG
OW	( )	EW	JOI	( )	EWS

2 **Add one letter to the following words to make a new word that has the meaning given.**

HOST	a spirit or phantom	__________
SIT	an outfit of clothes	__________
PLAN	simple	__________
RUSH	used for sweeping	__________
STEAM	a small river	__________
REIGN	to give up, leave	__________
EACH	fruit	__________
RAVE	courageous	__________
EAST	an animal	__________
RELY	answer	__________
HEEL	on cars and bikes	__________
LAME	fault	__________

3 **Make words from the letters of the word CONGRATULATIONS that mean the following:**

EXAMPLE: on your own *solo*

a kind of fish _________
a kind of heavy metal _________
also _________
a locomotive _________

Now try and find at least five more words yourself:

____
____
____

ANSWERS TO ACTIVITY 9 PAGE 45

1 Leonardo DiCaprio *2 Nicole Kidman* *3 Brad Pitt*
4 Julia Roberts *5 Russell Crowe*

7 ACROSS CULTURES

INTRODUCTION AND VOCABULARY

Prime Minister Megawiti Soekarnoputri

Prime Minister Koizumi

1 **Look at the following expressions. When do English speakers use them? Which of them are usually spoken and which are usually written?**

1. Many happy returns of the day!
2. Congratulations!
3. Well done!
4. Don't mention it.
5. Very pleased to meet you.
6. Looking forward to seeing you.
7. Please accept my sincere apologies.
8. I'm so sorry to hear that.

2 **Work in pairs. Devise a mini-conversation, which uses at least one of the expressions in activity 1.**

3 **Look at the photos on this page and try to answer these questions.**

1. What do you think the people in the first picture are doing?
2. What do the two people in the second and third pictures do?
3. What cultural problems do you think they face when they meet?

4 **Read this email from an English teenager to her penfriend in another country. Work out how it relates to the young people in the photograph on this page.**

Hi ...

Well, the waiting is over! The results finally arrived yesterday. My friends and I all went to school to find out the news. I got straight As! It means that I'll get the place that I wanted at university. It felt so good when I read them. Most of my friends did pretty well, too, but I'm the only one with an A in every subject! We're going to have a party on Saturday. I wish you could come!

Love,
Janet

5 **Now answer these questions about your society's cultural habits.**

1. Look at the first picture again and answer these questions:
   - What do you do to celebrate leaving school or passing examinations?
2. Look the second and third pictures again and answer these questions.
   - What happens when your country's head of state meets the head of state of another country?
   - Do the visitors receive anything when they arrive? Flowers, for example?
   - Where are they taken to? The presidential palace, for example?
   - Which other places are they shown? National monuments, for example?

6 **Imagine that someone has sent you the following email or letter containing a number of questions about cultural differences between their country and your country. Read the text and make notes of possible answers to the questions. The questions are underlined.**

I will arrive in your country on 14th June. A friend of my parents is meeting me at the airport. His wife and his daughter will be there to meet me, too. I've never met them. <u>Should I shake hands with them?</u>

I'm staying in a hotel, but I'm going to their house for dinner. <u>Should I take some flowers or another kind of gift?</u> If they tell me to be there at 8pm, <u>should I arrive a little early or exactly on time?</u> <u>What should I wear when I visit them?</u> <u>Should I wear a suit and tie, or can I dress more casually?</u>

Also, I think it's their daughter's birthday the day after I arrive. She'll be 15. <u>Would it be appropriate for me to buy her a present?</u> <u>What would you buy for a 15-year-old girl?</u>

7 **Write a short email answering the questions.**

8 **Read the information and then answer the questions about birthdays in your country.**

There are some birthday traditions that are common in many parts of the world – for example, birthday cakes, birthday parties, birthday presents and birthday cards.

The tradition of birthday cakes began with the Ancient Greeks, who made circular cakes and took them to the temple of their goddess of the moon, Artemis. The cakes were circular to represent the moon. The Greeks are said to have placed candles on the birthday cakes to make them look as if they were glowing like the moon. In medieval Britain, birthday parties were held because people thought that evil spirits visited them on their birthdays. They stayed close to their family and friends for protection. It was the late nineteenth century when parties became social gatherings where friends and family would bring presents or flowers. The tradition of sending birthday cards started in England about 100 years ago. Originally, cards were sent as an apology when someone couldn't visit in person.

On your birthday ...

1. Do people in your country give and receive birthday presents?
2. If so, what kind of presents are typical for people of your age?
3. Do you send birthday cards?
4. If so, what messages do you write on them?
5. Do you have a party?
6. If so, what happens?
7. Do you have a birthday cake?
8. If so, what's it made of?
9. Do you put candles on the birthday cake?
10. Are there any other special traditions on your birthday?

9 **Now look at the illustrations. They all have something to do with birthday celebrations. Describe what seems to be happening.**

EXAMPLE: *It looks as if the girl is putting something on her friend's nose.*

10 **Now read *Happy birthday?* and answer this question. Where in the world do the following things happen on birthdays?**

1. A flag is flown outside your house.
2. People pull your ears.
3. They put butter on your nose.
4. The person whose birthday it is wears clothes of a particular colour.
5. The person whose birthday it is gives chocolates to everyone in their class.
6. They turn you upside down and bump you on the floor.
7. The person whose birthday it is (and friends) wear blindfolds and hit a papier mâché animal with a stick.
8. The person whose birthday it is has to dance in front of the rest of the class.

Happy birthday?

In some countries in Latin America, particularly in Argentina and Brazil, it's a tradition to pull people's ears on their birthday. They pull your earlobe once for each year of your life. In Ecuador, there is a special celebration for girls when they reach the age of fifteen. There is a big party and the girl wears a pink dress. The father dances the waltz with her and fourteen other girls and fourteen boys dance as well. In India, girls also wear brightly-coloured dresses and give chocolates to all the students in their class.

In Ireland, there is a tradition called Birthday Bumps. On your birthday, friends lift you upside down and bump you on the floor for good luck. The number of bumps is your age, plus one for extra good luck.

You should avoid going to Canada on your birthday, where they grease your nose with butter or margarine! Canadians believe that a greasy nose means you are too slippery for bad luck to catch you.

In Denmark, a flag is flown outside a house to indicate that someone who lives there is having a birthday. In Norway, you have to stand in front of your class and choose a friend to dance with you. While you dance, the rest of the class sings a birthday song.

Finally, in Mexico, there is the tradition of the piñata. A piñata is a papier mâché animal which is filled with sweets and other small presents and hung from the ceiling. The birthday child and friends are blindfolded and they all hit the piñata with sticks until it breaks open. When the presents rain down on the floor, everyone scrambles to collect them.

11 **Discuss the following questions about the traditions.**

- Which traditions seem strange to you?
- Which seem interesting?
- Which traditions would you like to have on your birthday?

1 READING

Mount Snowdon

1 **On the next page there are two texts about cultural differences. They are written in the first person (*I*). Read the first sentence of each text and find out something about the people who wrote them. Do you think it is possible that they were both written by the same person?**

2 **Scan the passages quickly and decide what they are about. Choose from this list.**

1 The first text is about
  a a holiday in North Wales.
  b bad weather in Britain.
  c a summer school for English language students.
2 The second text is about
  a the richness of an African language.
  b the colours of nature.
  c a misunderstanding about the colour green.

3 **Choose a title for the texts from this list.**

1 The first text
  a Having fun in the Welsh mountains
  b A disastrous excursion
  c International attitudes to rain
2 The second text
  a Misunderstandings about the colour green
  b An argument about colours
  c How many greens can you see?

4 **Skim Text 1 and find words beginning with the letter *e* which mean the following:**

1 activities which are designed to amuse people
2 a short journey you take for pleasure
3 to get away from somewhere
4 at the end of a period of time
5 when you feel ashamed or worried about what other people think
6 very angry

5 **Now read Text 1 more carefully and answer these questions. Quote words or phrases from the text to support your answers.**

1 Did the students go on excursions every day?
2 How many Finns asked for the trip to Snowdon to be cancelled?
3 What were the main Italian objections to cancelling the trip?
4 Did the Italians and Finns discuss the problem sensibly?
5 Was there a little rain during the night?
6 Had the Finns changed their minds about the excursion?
7 Did it continue to rain during the day?
8 What condition were the students in when they returned from the excursion?

6 **Read Text 2 quickly and answer these questions.**

1 In which country is the conversation taking place?
2 Which people are having the conversation?
3 Is the conversation taking place indoors or outdoors?

7 **Now read the text more carefully. Answer the following about some of the words and phrases in it.**

1 Explain what *a former Zulu chief* is.
2 Use other words to mean the same *as discussed this at length*.
3 *the language adapted itself to the requirements of its speakers* – does this mean that the language changed or stayed the same?
4 *sensing my inadequacy* – does this mean that the narrator was able to express himself well or badly?
5 What image does the expression *leaves vibrating in the wind* give you?
6 *without raising a sweat* – does this mean it was easy or difficult?

8 **The plural of *leaf* is *leaves*. What are the plurals of these words? Be careful – there's an odd one out!**

loaf calf knife life scarf chief
thief wife wolf shelf

Note: there was an irregular plural activity on page 19. Can you remember any of the words you read there?

9 **Discuss these points.**

- What do the texts tell you about cultural differences?
- What would you have done to make the nationalities in Text 1 communicate better?
- Does Text 2 remind you of anything in your own language?

1

I was once in charge of an English language summer course in North Wales for students from three countries – Italy, Japan and Finland. There was intensive instruction during the day, entertainment in the evenings and occasional excursions to places of scenic or historic interest.

We had scheduled a trip up Mount Snowdon on a particular Wednesday, but on the Tuesday evening, it rained heavily. Around ten o'clock that night, a dozen or so Finns approached me and suggested that we cancel the excursion, as it would be no fun climbing the muddy slopes of Snowdon in heavy rain. I agreed and announced the cancellation. I was immediately surrounded by protesting Italians, enraged at the decision. Why cancel the trip? They were looking forward to it (an escape from English classes), they had paid for it in their all-inclusive fee, a little rain wouldn't hurt anyone and what was the matter with the Finns anyway – weren't they supposed to be tough people?

A little embarrassed, I consulted the Japanese students. They were very, very nice. If the Italians wanted to go, they would go, too. If, on the other hand, we cancelled the trip, they would be quite happy to stay in and take more lessons. The Italians jeered at the Finns, the Finns mumbled and scowled. Eventually, they agreed to go.

It rained torrentially all night and during breakfast the following morning. The bus was scheduled to leave at half past eight, and at twenty-five past I took my umbrella and ran through the downpour to the vehicle. Inside, there were eighteen scowling Finns, twelve smiling Japanese and no Italians.

We left on time and had a terrible day. The rain never let up, we had lunch in clouds at the summit and returned covered in mud at five o'clock. The Italians were drinking tea and eating chocolate biscuits when we arrived. They had sensibly stayed in bed. When the Finns asked them why, they said: 'Because it was raining!'

2

I once met a former Zulu chief, who was one of my students at Oxford University. He told me that the Zulu language had thirty-nine words for 'green'; English only has one. In English, if you wish to modify the shade, you have to add another word (eg bottle green, leaf green). I was interested in how the Zulus could have thirty-nine one-word concepts for green, and discussed this at length with him.

He began by explaining why Zulus need so many words for green. In the days before cars and national highways, the Zulu people would often make long journeys across their savannah grasslands. There were no signposts or maps. Lengthy journeys were described by those who had travelled the route before. The language adapted itself to the requirements of its speakers. The Zulu language, like many African languages, has many beautiful descriptive words for natural objects.

'Give me some examples of different green words,' I said.

My friend picked up a leaf. 'What colour is this?' he asked.

'Green,' I replied.

The sun was shining. He waited until the sun disappeared behind a cloud. 'What colour is the leaf now?' he asked.

'Green,' I replied, already sensing my inadequacy.

'It isn't the same green, is it?'

'No, it isn't.'

'We have a different word in Zulu.' He dipped the leaf in water and held it out again. 'Has the colour changed?'

'Yes.'

'In Zulu, we have a word for 'green shining wet'.'

The sun came out again and he had another word (leaf-green, wet-but-with-sunshine-on-it!).

My friend walked until he was twenty metres away and showed me the leaf. 'Has the colour changed again?'

'Yes!'

'We have another word,' he said with a smile.

He went on to indicate how different Zulu greens described tree leaves, bush leaves, leaves vibrating in the wind, river greens, pool greens, tree trunk greens, crocodile greens … he reached thirty-nine without raising a sweat.

2 GRAMMAR PRACTICE

1 Dynamic and stative verbs
2 Adjectives with copular verbs (*be*, *seem*, etc)

1 Complete dialogue (a) and text (b) by adapting the words in brackets.

a DAVE: What (*they-do*) to Tom?
ANNE: I (*suppose*) it's his birthday and they (*put*) butter on his nose.
DAVE: I (*not-understand*). Why?
ANNE: Because they (*believe*) a greasy nose (*mean*) bad luck can't catch you!

b The Mexican boy in the picture (*try*) to hit a papier mâché animal with a stick. He (*seem*) to be very excited and that is probably because he (*know*) it (*have*) a lot of sweets and other nice things inside. The boy's friends (*cheer*) him, but they (*want*) an opportunity to hit the piñata, too, and they (*wait*) impatiently for their turn.

2 Compare and explain the tenses of the verbs in each of these sentences

1 He was shouting but they didn't hear him.
2 I know you've been listening but have you understood everything?
3 I was weighing myself when you called and was surprised how much I weighed.
4 I think you seem to be right but I'm still thinking about it!
5 He appeared to be very tired when he was appearing on the stage in *Hamlet*.

Important – read this!

Although stative verbs (Grammar Reference, section 5) are not used in continuous tenses, they can be used like dynamic verbs in the gerund (section 15):

Knowing the truth is not always easy.
Seeing is believing.

and in participle clauses (section 14), which here give the idea of explanation:

Not wanting to get a greasy nose, I didn't tell my Canadian friends about my birthday.
Thinking that evil spirits were dangerous on birthdays, friends would join someone on their birthday to protect them.

3 Rewrite these sentences beginning with gerund or participle (*-ing*) forms of the stative verbs in italics and making other necessary changes.

1 It is very surprising *to have* so many words for 'green' in a language.
2 I *doubted* my knowledge of Japanese rules about food and drink, so I checked with my friend.
3 I *imagined* the Italians would come and I was surprised when they didn't.
4 *To like* English can be difficult sometimes.
5 Because I *belong* to the same football club as John, I know him quite well.

4 Helmut is having a bad day with his English. Rewrite everything he says in correct English. And why does Ali say 'No, it doesn't'?

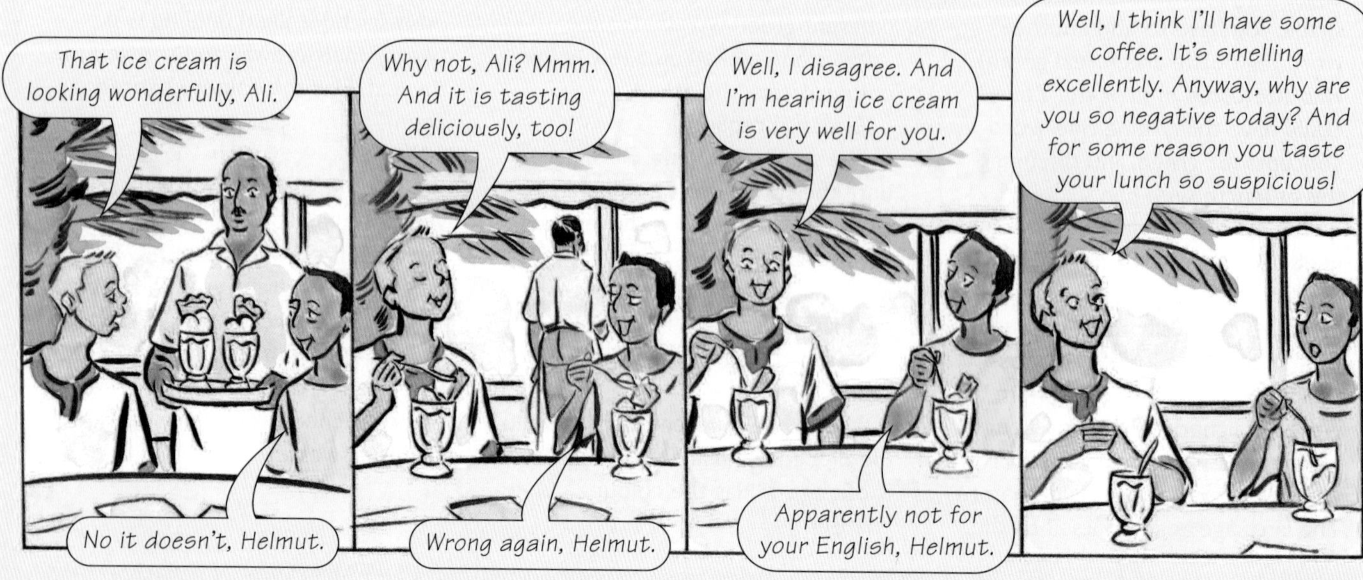

1 **Discuss the following questions.**

1 In your opinion, what are the main needs that human beings have?

EXAMPLE: Everyone needs nourishment.

2 What are the main emotions that human beings feel?

EXAMPLE: All human beings feel fear from time to time.

2 **The essay below is an *opinion* essay. In an opinion essay, the writer gives his or her opinion in both the first and last paragraphs. Read the essay and answer these questions.**

1 What is the writer's basic opinion about the subject?
2 What are the two main reasons for the writer's opinion?
3 What examples does the writer give of different cultures?
4 How is the last paragraph different from the first paragraph?
5 Do you agree with the writer's arguments?

Cultures may be different, but people are the same everywhere in the world

Everyone agrees that there are enormous differences between cultures. At first sight, it may seem that you cannot compare the lives of Inuit people living in the Arctic Circle with the life of a busy business person in Rome. However, in my view, people all over the world are essentially the same.

We are all born with the same basic needs, such as the need for nourishment and shelter. These needs are provided for in different ways by different cultures. For example, one culture may eat rice whereas another may eat wheat, but they are all providing the same thing – food. Another need we all have is the need for love and security. Children who do not receive enough of these things become unhappy and insecure. It is true that different cultures look after their children in different ways. For example, South American Indians carry their babies on their backs while Western mothers put their babies in cots and prams. Nonetheless, this does not change the fact that each culture has ways of giving children what they need: love and security.

Furthermore, all humans have the same emotions of love, fear and anger. These emotions may be expressed differently in different cultures, but the emotion is the same. To give an example, a genuine smile is the same in any part of the world. Similarly, an emotion such as fear is instantly recognisable on someone's face.

To conclude, it is certainly true that cultures are very different. Nevertheless, in my opinion, people everywhere have the same feelings of love, fear and anger. We share the same needs for nourishment, shelter, love and security. Someone once said: 'We are all brothers under the skin.' I think it's true.

3 **Read the essay again. Find:**

1 three phrases used to introduce examples
2 a word that means *but*
3 two words that mean *although this is true*
4 two words used to compare two different situations, people or things

4 **Complete the sentences below using one of the following words or phrases.**

such as | however | to give an example | while | nevertheless | for example | whereas | nonetheless

1 Zulus have many words to describe different shades of green _______,they have a word that means *green-shining-wet* and another that means *river green*.
2 We all need to feel part of a group. _______, we also need the freedom to be ourselves.
3 A tradition _______ the Muslim feast of Ramadan makes us feel that we are part of a group.
4 It was raining heavily. _______, the Italians wanted to go on the trip.
5 Some countries have their main meal at midday _______ others have their main meal in the evening.
6 I do not agree with everything you say. _______, I find it very interesting.
7 Many cultures have similar traditions. _______, many cultures celebrate birthdays with cakes and gifts.
8 The Zulu language has many words to describe different shades of green, _______ English only has a few.

5 **You are going to write an opinion essay with the following title: *Every society needs its own traditions*. Before you start, work in groups and discuss the statement. Here are some questions to help you:**

- How do traditions make people feel?
- What is your favourite tradition? What do you like about it?

6 **Now write the essay. Follow these instructions.**

- Decide on your opinion.
- Write your opinion down using one or two sentences.
- Plan your essay.
- Write your essay. Try to use some of the words and phrases practised in activity 4. Write 150 words.
- Give your essay to another student to check for mistakes.

7 **Optional writing task. Read Text 1 on page 55 of this unit. Imagine that you are a student on the English language summer course in North Wales. Write an informal letter to an English friend telling him or her about the excursion to the mountains. Write about 150 words. Turn to page 9 for help in writing a letter.**

4 LISTENING AND SPEAKING

1 **Discuss the following questions about traditions and customs in your country.**

1 Describe a typical gesture that people in your country make. What does it mean?
2 How do you greet a friend of your parents when you meet them for the first time? What do you say or do?
3 Does the colour white signify anything in your country?
4 If a family visits another family with whom they are friendly, is it customary to bring a gift? If so, what kind of gift should you bring?
5 When people in your country talk together, how close do they stand to each other?
6 Do people make eye contact when they are talking to people they don't know well?
7 Are people direct or indirect when they talk to one another? In other words, do they tend to say what they think, or do they avoid doing this?

2 **Discuss this question: *Do people in your country make generalisations about the Japanese, the Turks and the Italians? If so, what kind of things do you say about them?***

EXAMPLE: People say that the Italians talk a lot.
The Japanese are said to be extremely polite.
Turks are supposed to have wonderful food.

3 **Read and complete the following descriptions of different customs in Japan, Turkey and Italy. Don't worry if you aren't completely sure of the answer. Complete the gaps with one of these words:**

the Japanese   Japan   Turkey   Turks
Turkish   Italy   Italians   Italian

1 _______ tend to avoid making direct eye contact.
2 _______ try to keep a smile, even when they are upset.
3 _______ may greet a close friend with a two-handed handshake.
4 In _______, you may see a man quickly stroke his fingertips under his chin and thrust them forward. This can be a sign of defiance or contempt.
5 _______ are extremely hospitable. When you go out with _______ friends, you will have to fight very hard to pay for the meal, even if you have invited them.
6 The traditional greeting in _______ is a bow.
7 In _______, it is rude to cross your arms while facing someone.
8 _______ talk with their hands, and make very expressive gestures.
9 When invited to someone's home in _______, you should not give gifts of brooches, handkerchiefs or knives.

A Japanese woman wearing a kimono — A Turkish man in traditional costume — An Italian woman wearing traditional dress

10 In _______ restaurants, a toothpick is usually offered at the end of the meal.
11 _______ do not like to be very direct in conversation.
12 In _______, handshakes may include grasping the arm with the other hand.

4 **Now listen and check your answers.**

5 **Listen again. Answer these questions:**

1 In Italy, when you meet someone for the first time, what shouldn't you do?
2 What other greeting do Turks use for close friends of the same sex?
3 What is becoming more and more common in Japan?
4 When speaking to a Turk, what should you avoid doing with your hands?
5 Why shouldn't one give brooches, handkerchiefs or knives as gifts in Italy?
6 What example is given of Japanese indirectness?
7 What should you do when entering someone's home in Japan?

6 **Work in small groups. Choose a country that interests you and that you know something about. Write a short sketch showing some of the cultural differences between this country and your own country.**

- Think of three or four points of difference.
- Think of dramatic and amusing ways of illustrating these differences.
- Write the sketch.

Perform your sketch for the class. The class can then vote for the best sketch.

Word watch – Formation

1 **Make two nouns from the following verbs. For example, (1) a person and (2) an abstract quality.**

EXAMPLE: create – (1) creator (2) creation

manage		
believe		
reside		
invade		
possess		
cycle		
admire		
use		
sing		
advise		

2 **Make adjectives from the words in the first box and adverbs from the words in the second box.**

Root word	Adjective	Noun
health	healthy	lifestyle
mud	muddy	footprints
triangle		
fame		
ice		
explain		

Root word	Verb	Adverb
patience	wait	patiently
persuade	argue	persuasively
tight		
hero		
decide		
deep		

3 **Now read the following nouns and verbs. Match the words in the first box in activity 2 with a noun from the list below. Match the words in the second box with a verb from the list. The first two examples in each list have been done for you.**

shape leaflet fight water ~~wait~~ ~~footprint~~
act ~~argue~~ actor ~~lifestyle~~ hold breathe

Lessons in logic

Use your skills in logical thinking and close reading.

Richard, Michael, Arthur and Peter are playing a tennis match. Each player plays a single game against each of the other three. Richard loses to Michael and Peter. Peter loses to Michael but beats Arthur who beats Richard but loses to Michael.

Who wins the tennis match? __________
How many games does Richard win? __________
How many games does Peter win? __________
How many games does Arthur win? __________
How many games does Michael lose? __________

Vocabulary – words and meanings

Words can often have several different meanings. Underline the word in brackets that can go equally well with both pairs of words outside the brackets.

EXAMPLE: position/job mail/send (office work <u>post</u> stamp)

1. starve/not eat rapid/quick (express gulp hurry fast)
2. take care/look after brain/thoughts (watch soul mind head)
3. run forward/attack cost/payment (charge price rush fear)
4. hour/second tiny/small (little short minute pass)
5. engine/railway teach/educate (form train transport station)
6. sort/type good-hearted/nice (class lovely friend kind)
7. gift/treat here/now (attend prize present free)
8. expensive/costly precious/valued (special dear pricey left)
9. shut/fasten nearby/at hand (there wrap finish close)
10. salt/spices autumn/period (spring season pepper warm)

8 LIVING ON THE EDGE

INTRODUCTION AND VOCABULARY

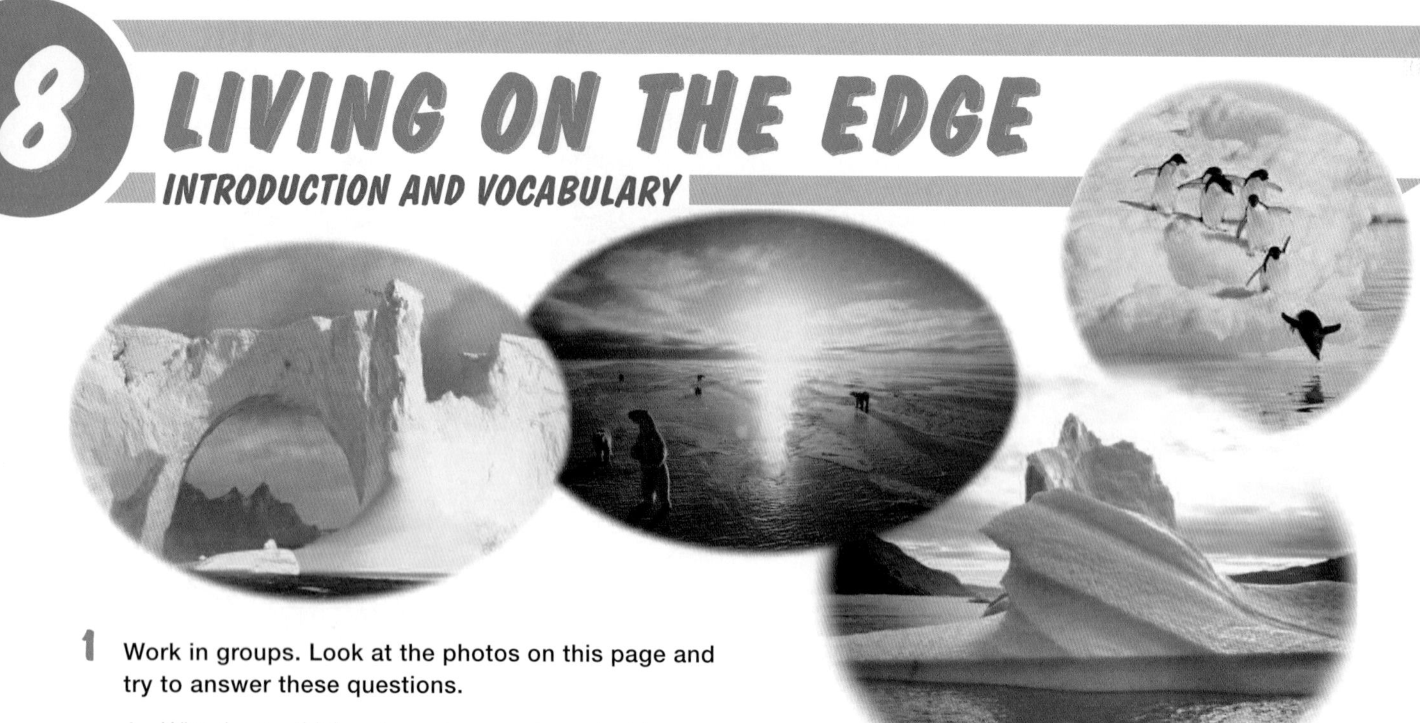

1 **Work in groups. Look at the photos on this page and try to answer these questions.**

1 Why do you think polar regions are important?
2 Is there any way that changes to the polar regions could affect you?
3 Why do you think scientists and explorers spend so much time in polar regions?
4 Can people, animals or plants survive there?
5 Is the Arctic polar region bigger or smaller than the Antarctic?
6 What do you imagine is a normal temperature in polar regions?

2 **Share your information with other groups. Make notes of any new information you hear from other students.**

3 **Write a paragraph about the new information you have heard. Indicate your reaction to the new information, eg surprised, impressed, uncertain, amused.**

EXAMPLE: Peter said that there are insects that can survive in polar regions for months without eating or drinking. It may be true, but I'm not sure if I believe it! Sarah said that polar bears weigh 700 kilos, which is amazing! They must be absolutely enormous!

4 **Look at the last two words in the example in activity 3 again and try to answer these questions.**

1 Enormous is an 'extreme' adjective. Which of the following 'normal' adjectives means more or less the same thing? *tall long fat big wide*
2 You can use *absolutely* with extreme adjectives, for example *absolutely enormous*. Can you use absolutely with normal adjectives, such as *tall* or *long*?
3 What modifying words could you use with 'normal' adjectives?

5 **The adjectives on the left below are 'extreme'. Match them with the 'normal' words on the right.**

EXAMPLE: boiling – hot

boiling	brilliant	hot	cold
deafening	delighted	hungry	loud
devastated	exhausted	angry	tired
freezing	furious	pleased	stupid
ridiculous	starving	good	sad

6 **Work in pairs. For each of the sentences 1–8 make mini-conversations using *absolutely* and one of the adjectives from activity 5. Add more lines to the conversation, if you can.**

EXAMPLE: Were you sad when your team lost in the Cup Final?
Sad?!? I was absolutely devastated!
Oh come on! It isn't that important!
You think so? Obviously you aren't a football fan.

1 Was the rock concert loud?
2 Were you cold after you swam in the lake?
3 Was your friend angry when you broke her watch?
4 Was it hot when you visited the Pyramids?
5 Were you pleased when you passed the examination?
6 Were your friends hungry after they climbed the mountain?
7 Were you tired after you ran the marathon?
8 Did you feel stupid when you had to wear the cow costume in the school play?

7 **Below is a diary kept by a visitor to the Arctic polar region. Before you read the complete text, find the following adjectives in the text and explain what they are describing.**

amazed angry bitter curious disappointed exhausted inviting remote scary smart smooth stiff welcome wild

8 **Now read the diary and answer these questions.**

1. Do you think the author is an explorer or a tourist?
2. Did she travel alone, with a companion or with a group?
3. What were her first impressions when she saw the polar region from the plane?
4. Did she get a different impression when she landed?
5. How much sunlight did the region have at the time of year she visited?
6. What was the plan for the second day of the visit?
7. In what way was she different from her companions?
8. Did she enjoy the experience?

9 **Imagine the writer stayed at the hotel for a week. Write a diary page for the last day of her visit.**

10 **Now imagine that you are a tourist visiting a hot desert region. Write a similar diary of a visit to a hotel or activity area in the middle of the desert.**

Day 1

Our plane landed in a curious kind of twilight, absolutely beautiful, but also a little scary. I had expected it to be windy, but the landing was very smooth. I had a window seat and looked around for signs of life as we descended, but I couldn't see anything. The place seemed to be so far from civilization. How do people survive there? And what do they do to make a living?

In fact, it wasn't very remote at all! The airport was small, but it was modern and had the usual airport paraphernalia - taxis, buses, car rental etc. There was a very smart bus waiting for us - easily big enough for all twenty-five of us.

As soon as we left the airport, it began to feel wild again. It had turned dark, and there was a stiff breeze. It must have been about two o'clock in the afternoon when we arrived at the hotel, but you wouldn't have known. It was like the middle of the night.

When we got off the bus, the cold hit us - it went through you like a knife! We all hurried into the hotel reception area, which was warm and inviting.

Day 2

The plan for today was to travel across the ice to the edge of the Arctic Sea to see some wildlife. Surprise, surprise, it was dark when we got up and still dark when we came out of the hotel and got into the bus. I was a bit disappointed that we started the journey by bus - I had hoped to be able to go on a sled, or something like that. Well, my wish came true eventually!

We arrived at a kind of lodge and we all went in for a very welcome cup of coffee. We were then offered the chance to continue the journey by bus, or to travel on sleds pulled by teams of huskies. I was amazed to find that I was the only one who wanted to travel on the sleds! I had to put on some different clothes, including a special pair of goggles, which were designed to protect me from the glare of the sun but also to stop my eyeballs from freezing in the bitter wind.

Why did the others book a holiday like this if they didn't want to try travelling on a sled? It was absolutely fantastic and not difficult at all. I had a guide who showed me how to control the sled, and what to shout when I wanted the dogs to stop. After about twenty minutes, we reached the edge of the ice floe and saw some polar bears. They didn't seem to take any notice of us at all, but suddenly one of them got very angry. He must have thought that my camera was some kind of gun.

I was absolutely exhausted when we got back but the huskies must have been even more exhausted than me!

1 READING

1 **Work in pairs. Read *Fascinating facts* and follow these instructions. Student A: Close your book and answer Student B's questions. Student B: Ask student A questions about the information you read. Give your partner clues if he/she has difficulty answering a question.**

EXAMPE: What's the average annual temperature at the North Pole?

Fascinating facts

Arctic v Antarctic

– which is more hostile?

Read and decide!

- *The average annual temperature at the North Pole is minus 17 degrees Celsius; the average at the South Pole is minus 50 degrees Celsius.*
- *The South Pole is three thousand metres above sea level; the North Pole is one metre above sea level.*
- *Many animals, including reindeer, foxes, bears and wolves, can survive in the Arctic region. There are no such animals in Antarctica.*
- *There are 450 species of flowering plants at latitude 70 degrees north; there are two species of plant at latitude 70 degrees south.*

2 **Before you read *The coldest place on earth*, check the meaning of the following words and phrases.**

Line 5: tundra
Line 45: moisture
Line 53: gust
Line 57: indigenous population
Line 66: inaccessibility
Line 78: conduct research

3 **Scan the reading text. Which of the following topics are referred to?**

- the lack of rainfall in Antarctica
- wind, rain and snow
- human inhabitation of the region
- similarities to living on Mars
- what Russian scientists actually do there
- the thickness of the ice

4 **Scan the text again and find out what the following numbers refer to.**

Para 1: 270 million
Para 2: 75 metres
Para 3: 327 kph
Para 4: -89°C
Para 5: 6 months
Para 6: 24 hours

5 **Work in small groups. Make a note of three other numbers from the text. Then, with books closed, test each other on what they refer to.**

EXAMPLE: What does two million refer to?
The number of years since it rained in some parts of Antarctica.

6 **Now read the complete text. Find phrases that mean more or less the same as the following:**

1. Water goes into the region for a short time each year.
2. There are winds that make all water disappear.
3. No country has jurisdiction over Antarctica.
4. People have never lived in Antarctica.
5. It is not easy to get there.
6. It isn't easy to find something to eat or build somewhere to live.
7. Living conditions get worse during the winter.
8. People practise there for a possible future visit to another planet.

7 **Class discussion. Give your opinion about the following. Give reasons for your opinions.**

1. Do you think it is a good or bad idea for scientists to work in Antarctica?
2. Do you think space research is a good or a bad thing?
3. Do you think Antarctic tourism is a good or a bad thing?
4. Do you know what could cause the polar ice caps to melt?
5. Have you any idea what we can do to stop this happening?

8 **Class survey. Find out how many people would like to visit the North Pole or the South Pole. When you vote, give reasons for your decision.**

Tick one of the following boxes.

I would like to visit the North Pole. ☐
I would like to visit the South Pole. ☐
I can think of nothing worse than visiting the North or South Poles. ☐

The coldest place on earth

Two hundred and seventy million years ago, the southernmost tip of planet Earth was probably covered with tundra, marshes and forests. Not any more! Nowadays, Antarctica is the coldest and driest place on earth. It is the fifth biggest continent on the planet, comprising ten per cent of the earth's land area, a total of fourteen million square kilometres (km^2) – and that's in the summer! In winter, another two and a half million km^2 of sea ice increases the continent to an incredible nineteen million km^2.

Antarctica contains seventy per cent of the earth's fresh water and the East Antarctic Ice Sheet is the biggest piece of ice in the world – some parts are more than five kilometres thick – that's higher than the Swiss Alps! The ice in Antarctica accounts for 90 per cent of all the ice in the world. If this ice cap melted, the sea level would rise an average of seventy-five metres across the entire planet and would flood almost all the cities which are situated on coasts or rivers, including New York, London, Shanghai and Cairo.

Even with all this water and ice, Antarctica is the world's driest continent. How can this be true? Part of the interior region of the Antarctic is known as the Dry Valleys. These valleys have not seen rainfall for more than two million years! With the exception of one valley, whose lakes are briefly filled with water by inland-flowing rivers during the summer, the Dry Valleys contain no moisture (water, ice or snow) at all. This is because all the moisture is evaporated by high winds, called katabatic winds, which can blow with hurricane force, because – another superlative – Antarctica is the windiest place on earth, with gusts of up to 327 kilometres per hour (kph) having been recorded.

Antarctica, which is owned by no one, is the only continent that has never had an indigenous population of humans because it has always been such an extreme environment. The lowest temperature ever recorded on earth, minus eighty-nine degrees Celsius, was recorded in 1983 at Vostok, the Russian Antarctic base. Not only the cold, but also the inaccessibility of the place and the lack of reliable food and means for constructing shelter, have kept humans away for thousands of years.

But new technology has made it possible for people to reach these icy shores to explore and study the Antarctic in more detail than ever before. Antarctica is now the world's finest laboratory, and there are scientists who live there for part of the year to conduct their research, although hardly anyone stays there for more than six months. The sun rises and sets only ONCE A YEAR in the Antarctic, which means there are six months of daylight, followed by six months of darkness. During the winter, there is no sun and the Antarctic becomes an even more hostile place to be – bone-chillingly cold and with no daylight.

Can you imagine living in darkness twenty-four hours a day? That would almost be like living in space. In fact – it IS like living in space. The freezing temperatures and the absence of water, plant life and animal life are similar to conditions on Mars. Consequently, the Dry Valleys are used as training grounds for astronauts who may one day travel to our neighbouring planets. Antarctica is not only fascinating itself, but also serves as an excellent laboratory for studying the effects of space travel and for developing new technologies.

1 Modal auxiliaries
2 Adverb types and position

1 Modal verbs are different in several ways from 'ordinary' verbs. Say what difference each sentence shows between the two types of verb (see Grammar Reference, section 6).

1 The temperature at the South Pole *averages* minus 50 degrees Celsius, but it *can* fall as low as minus 80 degrees.
2 The Dry Valleys don't *have* much rain and trees *won't* grow there.
3 Do all polar regions *show* the same characteristics or *should* we think of them as representing a whole range of landscapes?
4 Most European people don't want to *visit* the South Pole and think they wouldn't enjoy *visiting* it, but they might *like* it if they went.
5 Human beings have *lived* in almost all parts of the world but, until recently, they had never *been able* to live in Antarctica.
6 Do you *know* the name of the Russian base in Antarctica? Yes, I *do*.
7 *Can* you see the sunrise more than once a year in the Arctic? No, you *can't*.

2 Complete these sentences with suitable perfect modals of verbs in the box.

start	take	feel	be	find	return

EXAMPLE: When pilots rescued the explorer from the North Pole in May 2003, the ice was melting and dangerous. They said he should have started his expedition earlier in the year.

1 The people at Vostok Antarctic base .... very cold when the temperature was minus 98 degrees.
2 Scientists are not sure but they think there .... flowing water on Mars in the past.
3 If we had had the time and money when we were in New Zealand, we certainly .... the Hercules plane to Antarctica.
4 Perhaps we were lucky because I get nervous on planes and there was a small problem that day. Later the pilot said he .... to New Zealand because they had passed the point of no return.
5 They .... that penguin in the Arctic – penguins don't live there.

3 Rewrite these sentences including the adverbs and adverbial phrases in brackets in their normal (unstressed) positions.

1 The weather has been freezing during our visits. (*absolutely, always, unfortunately*)
2 My friend Doctor Jones spoke. (*yesterday, at the museum, brilliantly, quite*)
3 Most scientists had heard of the Dry Valleys. (*actually, never, until recently*)

4 Rewrite Helmut's first two sentences with the correct modals. What does 'You might have told me' mean here? How should Helmut have responded?

An Inuit standing outside an igloo, with his snowmobile

An Inuit about to shoot a caribou

My uncle, a Canadian government official, had invited me on a week's trip to the Northwest Territories in the north of Canada, where the Inuit people live. We flew in a small plane to the small low-lying island of Igloolik, situated about 300 miles north of the Arctic Circle. I stepped out into a dazzling snow-white world, and we drove across the snow in a snowmobile to Igloolik town, which is a community of about 1200 people. Igloolik has rows of bungalows, their roofs covered with snow.

We spent two days in Ingloolik before setting off in snowmobiles north-east towards an Inuit camp called Iglurjuat. The ice was shiny and slippery and the snowmobile slid from side to side. The sun shone in a clear bright blue sky, and sometimes it was hard to know where the sky ended and the snow began. It was strangely beautiful in a rather terrifying way. After ten absolutely exhausting hours, we arrived at Iglurjuat, where there was just one large wooden hut, completely covered with snow. Several steps, cut in the snow, led to the door. Inside, the light in the hut was dim, with a single window located above the door. The hut, a single room heated by an oil stove, was about eight metres square. A family of fourteen lived in the hut, five adults and nine children.

We stayed with the family for three days before returning to Igloolik. The men of the family took me hunting for seal and caribou, a truly exciting experience. I returned to Igloolik having experienced a life-style very different from my own. I shall never forget it.

1 **How much do you know about the Inuit people? Which one of the following statements is false?**

1 Inuits are also known as Eskimos.
2 Inuits live inside the Arctic Circle.
3 They hunt seal and caribou.
4 There are Inuits in the Antarctic.
5 The Inuit culture is about 4,000 years old.

2 **In the descriptive essay on this page, Canadian student Daniel Martin describes a short trip to the Arctic Circle to visit an Inuit settlement. Read the essay and answer these questions:**

1 Which paragraph sets the scene?
2 Which paragraph contains the most description?
3 Which sentences talk about the writer's feelings and reactions?
4 Do you think the final paragraph is necessary? Explain why/why not.

3 **The essay above describes places. When describing places we often use the following kinds of language. Find examples of each type of language item in the essay:**

adjectives
present participles as adjectives (eg boiling)
past participles (eg The Inuits, also known as Eskimos, live inside the Arctic Circle.)
adverbs preceding adjectives (eg extremely interesting)
there is/was
relative pronouns (eg which, where)
preposition *with*
the verb *to have*
apposition – a noun followed by another noun (eg I talked to Ituko, an Inuit from a nearby camp.)

4 **Complete the gaps in these sentences with one of the following words:**

rushing written where hunter with bare surrounded totally

1 We came to a little village, _______ by mountains.
2 The _______ waters made a gurgling sound.
3 He came to a part of the desert _______ nomads had camped for several months.
4 The landscape was _______ enchanting.
5 We met Augustine, a _______ who lived nearby.
6 The _______, lonely sands stretched endlessly towards the horizon.
7 We saw a sign _______ in five different languages.
8 The houses were white, _______ rounded roofs.

5 **Write a descriptive essay about a trip that you have made to an interesting place. Write 150 words. Try and use some of the language items in activity 3.**

PARAGRAPH **1:** Set the scene: say where you went and why. Describe your arrival.
PARAGRAPH(S) **2/3:** Describe the place in detail. Say what you did and how you felt.
FINAL PARAGRAPH: Say how the trip ended and how you felt.

6 **Optional writing task. Imagine that you visit the Inuit camp of Iglurjuat described in the essay above. Write down the conversation that you might have with one of the Inuits. Write about six exchanges.** **Turn to page 41 for help with writing a dialogue.**

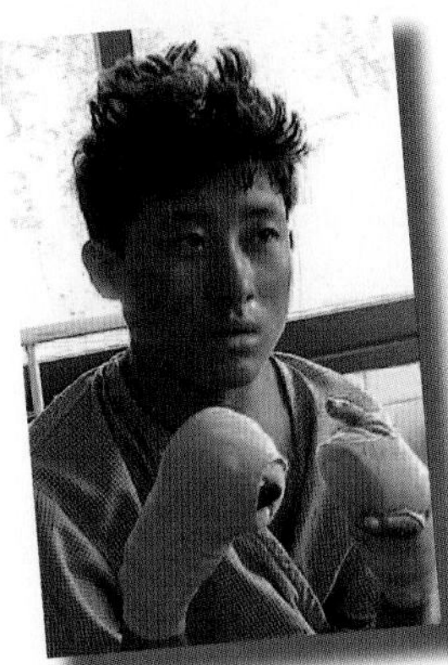

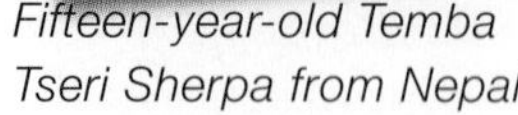

Mount Everest

Fifteen-year-old Temba Tseri Sherpa from Nepal

1 **Look at the two photos above. Answer these questions.**

1 What do you know about Mount Everest?
2 What could the connection be between the two pictures?

2 **The following vocabulary items are all in the listening passage in activity 3.**

amputate frostbite summit expedition
break the record attempt (verb and noun)
determined give up

Find a word or phrase from the box which means:

1 to stop trying to do something
2 to cut off a leg, arm or finger
3 the top of a mountain
4 when your fingers or toes become frozen and badly damaged
5 to do better than someone else at, for example, climbing the highest mountain or running the longest distance
6 to try
7 a long and carefully organised journey, especially to a dangerous place
8 wanting to do something very much

3 **A fifteen-year-old Nepalese boy called Temba Tseri Sherpa almost succeeded in climbing Everest. He was forced to give up because of frostbite. Listen to the information about Temba and other attempts by Nepalese teenagers to climb Everest. Answer these questions. The answers are all numbers or dates.**

1 When did Temba Tseri Sherpa attempt to climb Everest?
2 How far away was he from the summit when he gave up?
3 How many fingers did doctors have to amputate because of frostbite?
4 How many children are there in Temba's family?
5 How old was Shambhu Tamang when he reached the summit?
6 When did Arbin Timilsina attempt to climb Everest?
7 How many people have climbed Everest since 1953?

4 **These statements about Mount Everest are incorrect. The correct information is in the listening passage in activity 3. Correct the sentences, listening to the passage again if necessary. Which words do you need to stress in the corrected sentences?**

1 Everest is almost 8,000 metres high.
2 More than 160 people have died trying to climb the world's highest mountain.
3 Everest was first climbed in 1956.
4 Everest is the second highest mountain in the world.
5 Everest is on the border between China and India.

5 **Listen to the corrected sentences. Did you get the stress right? Repeat the sentences with the correct stress.**

6 **Read the following questions for discussion.**

1 In your opinion, what made Temba Tseri Sherpa attempt to climb Mount Everest?
2 What makes people attempt to do brave but dangerous things, for example, crossing the Atlantic Ocean in a small sailing boat?
3 Should young people be allowed to do dangerous things, as in the example of Temba Tseri Sherpa?

7 **Now listen to two students, a boy called Simon and a girl called Olivia, give their opinion on the questions above. Answer the following questions.**

Who thinks the following?
1 Temba attempted to climb Everest because some of his brothers had done so.
2 Temba attempted to climb Everest because he wanted to be famous.
3 People do brave but dangerous things because they want to be special.
4 People do brave but dangerous things because they want to achieve something and feel really alive.
5 Young people should be allowed to do dangerous things, provided they have the right equipment and support.
6 Temba was much too young to climb Everest and took a big risk.

8 **Work in groups of four. Discuss the questions in activity 7.**

Word watch – Comparatives and superlatives

1 **Complete the chart with the comparative or superlative forms or the adjectives.**

Adjective	Comparative	Adjective	Superlative
fat	________	exact	________
bad	________	good	________
far	________	lovely	________
much	________	little	________
quiet	________	careful	________
catastropic	________	many	________
narrow	________	unhappy	________

2 **A popular way of making comparisons is by using similes, linked by *like* or *as*. Use the words in the box to complete the comparisons. Choose from the words given and then try and use the remaining three in similes of your own.**

picture fiddle sheet pie dust feather
church mouse new pin cucumber gold

as fit as a ________
as easy as ________
as cool as a ________
as good as ________
as poor as a ________
as clean as a ________
as pretty as a ________

3 **Underline the correct construction in these sentences.**

1 Your brother looks *as / the same / like* your uncle.
2 She takes the same bus *like / as / than* I do every day.
3 That's *the more / the most / much more* amazing trick I've ever seen.
4 His accent is *worst than / the worst than / worse than* mine.
5 It's the most expensive television *in / of / from* the shop.
6 We've been waiting longer *that / than / as* you have.
7 *The most / More / The more* you work, the better your results will be.
8 Can you please come *more early / earlier / earliest*?
9 I think Anna's *the nicest of / nicer than / as nice as* all.
10 My sister is *very / much / many* older than me.

Lessons in logic

Howard Ford was born in 1967. His daughter was born 27 years later and his son was born 2 years before his daughter.
When was his son born? ________

When Mr Ford is 50, how old will his daughter be? ________

Mr Ford's watch is 12 minutes fast and the train he is catching is due at 10.38 but is 6 minutes late. When the train arrives, what time does his watch show? ________
The train journey takes 45 minutes. What time does he arrive? ________
What time does his watch show when he arrives? ______

Vocabulary – Words and meanings

Words can be put together in many ways to form compounds with distinct new meanings. What word can you place in front of each of the following?

EXAMPLES: landlord landmark landslide landscape

1	____ball	____step	____print	____note
2	____writing	____bag	____made	____out
3	____graduate	____ground	____stand	____foot
4	____shelf	____shop	____mark	____case
5	____mark	____box	____card	____office
6	____side	____food	____shore	____sick
7	____coat	____bow	____fall	____water
8	____fall	____stairs	____town	____wards

Dictionaries

These three words are in alphabetical order, as they would appear in a dictionary. The second one has not been written but you have its meaning to help you to work out what it must be.

EXAMPLE: ANIMAL ANKLE (where your leg joins your foot) ANNIVERSARY

1 VERSE ______ (standing up straight) VERY
2 SOLID ______ (a performance by one person) SOLVE
3 GAIN ______ (a strong wind) GALLERY
4 COMMIT ______ (ordinary) COMMUNICATE
5 EXTERNAL ______ (dead/wiped out) EXTRA
6 LINE ______ (bond/connection) LION
7 WHISKER ______ (say softly) WHISTLE
8 PUDDING ______ (small pool) PUSH
9 GLOVE ______ (shine softly) GLUE
10 RHINO ______ (beat/movement) RIB

You can use a dictionary to check your answers.

9 TELLING STORIES

INTRODUCTION AND VOCABULARY

1 **Explain the difference between these different kinds of writing. Give examples of each one, written in your own language or in English, if you can.**

biography novel play poem prose script
short story sketch tale verse

2 **Now match eight of the words in activity 1 with the following definitions.**

1 a piece of writing using beautiful or unusual language arranged in fixed lines
2 a story about imaginary events or people, possibly a story that people don't believe
3 a piece of writing intended to be performed by actors in a theatre or on television
4 a short piece of fiction
5 a book containing a long written story about imaginary or partly imaginary events
6 the written words of a play, film or television programme
7 a short, usually funny scene, usually performed within a longer show
8 the story of someone's life

3 **Find the two words that are not defined in activity 2. Define these words in a sentence using the following words:**

______ means ______ whereas ______ refers to ______ .

4 **Work in small groups. Discuss the following question. Imagine that you were about to take a long day-time journey by train, boat or plane. What would you take with you to help you pass the time? Put the following items in your personal order of preference.**

- a Walkman, Discman or mini-disk player
- a portable electronic game
- a magazine (which subject? Eg music, film, etc)
- a novel or book of short stories
- a book of poetry
- a study book (which type?)

5 **Put the items in the order of preference of the whole group. Then compare your preferences with the rest of the class.**

6 **The following texts are from short stories. Before you read the complete texts, look at the words in italics. They are all verbs of movement. Check the meanings in a dictionary and then define them.**

7 **Read the texts and discuss what might happen next.**

A Tom saw the parcel floating in the water as he was *strolling* home along the riverbank. He *waded* into the water and managed to catch it. He put it down on the path, a little worried about the contents. He asked a passer-by if she had a mobile phone he could borrow. 'Why?' she asked. 'I need to call the police,' Tom replied.

B As I *strode* out of the building, exhausted but pleased with the day, it started to rain. I decided to go back and wait in Martha's office for a while, so I *hurried* back into the building. When I got to the lift, a young man I didn't know was standing there, some keys in his hand and looking a little nervous. The lift arrived and we both stepped in. Neither of us said a word. I pressed the button for the fifth floor, he pressed for the eleventh – the executive suite. That surprised me. I was about to ask him who he was visiting, when the elevator suddenly stopped with a jerk.

C Henry played the last few notes of the Chopin concerto, took his hands from the keys and felt a moment of complete elation. He had played the piece beautifully and the audience rose from their seats, applauding wildly. Henry took a moment to calm himself, then he stood, faced the audience and bowed slightly. Suddenly, out of the corner of his eye, he saw the concert hall manager *rushing* towards him.

8 **The following paragraphs are from later in the same stories. Match them with the paragraphs above.**

D The president of the company shook hands and breathed a sigh of relief. 'I want to thank you for what you did,' he said. 'My son has a real problem with claustrophobia. If you hadn't been there, I hate to think what might have happened.'

E The inspector came out of the station and faced the crowd of reporters. 'I am here to tell you that the mystery of the missing diamonds has been solved. And I have to thank this young man for his help in the matter.'

F The police officer walked up to him and faced him closely. 'How can you prove that you weren't at Sir Arthur's house when the robbery took place?' he asked. Sarah laughed. 'He doesn't need to,' she said. 'There are three thousand people who can tell you that he was in London that night.'

Introduction

Charles Dickens, Wilkie Collins and Arthur Conan Doyle were three of the greatest story-tellers of the late nineteenth century. Many of their novels and short stories were published in instalments in literary magazines. All three authors were experts at writing 'cliff-hangers' – stories where the instalment or chapter ended with the reader left in suspense, desperate to find out what happened next. Collins referred to these books as 'Make them cry, make them laugh, make them wait' books.

Charles Dickens

Charles Dickens (1812-70) was one of the most prolific and successful novelists in the history of English literature. He spent his early years in Chatham, which is situated on the estuary of the River Thames near London. However, after a happy childhood there, he then moved with his family to London, where his life became one of intense misery. At the age of 12, he was sent to work in a dirty, depressing warehouse. When Dickens' father was imprisoned for debt, the family was forced to live in prison with him. Dickens' writing is coloured by these experiences.

Wilkie Collins

Wilkie Collins was one of the best known, best loved and best paid of Victorian fiction writers, and has been called the inventor of the sensation novel. He was born in 1824. He wrote 25 novels, more than 50 short stories, at least 15 plays, and more than 100 works of non-fiction. He was a close friend of Dickens, who was a big influence on him, and who encouraged him to write full-time. His best-known works, immensely popular in the mid-nineteenth century, are *The Woman in White* (1860) and *The Moonstone* (1867). After his death, his reputation declined but Collins's work is currently enjoying a critical revival.

Arthur Conan Doyle

Arthur Conan Doyle was born in Edinburgh on the 22nd of May 1859. The Conan Doyle family was a large one (Arthur was one of ten children) and life was hard. Even so, Arthur managed to study medicine at Edinburgh University from 1876 to 1881. Besides providing him with a medical degree, Edinburgh University also brought Conan Doyle into contact with Dr Joseph Bell, whose amazing deductions concerning the history of his patients were to provide the ideas behind the deductive skills of Sherlock Holmes, the most brilliant detective in the history of literature.

9 The above texts contain information about three great story-tellers, British novelists of the nineteenth century.

Read the introduction and discuss the following questions:

- What do you think a 'cliff-hanger' is?
- Why do you think we use the expression 'cliff-hanger'?
- Are there any magazines or TV programmes that you know which specialise in cliff-hangers?

10 Now read the paragraph about each writer. These paragraphs give biographical details about the three men. Scan the texts and see which of the following information is in it. Tick ✔ the box if the information is in the text, and put a cross ✘ if it isn't. The first one has been done for you as an example.

	Dickens	Collins	Conan Doyle
Date of birth	✘	✘	✔
Year of birth			
Place of birth			
Year of death			
Title(s) of novel(s)			
People who influenced them			

1 READING

1 **The extracts on these pages are from the first chapters of novels written by Charles Dickens, Wilkie Collins and Arthur Conan Doyle. Scan the three quickly and find the following information.**

1 Which extract tells the reader which season it is?
2 Which one starts with the narrator walking in a London street?
3 In which extract do we discover the name of the narrator?
4 In which extract does the narrator meet a young girl?
5 In which one does the narrator meet someone he knows in the street?
6 In which one does the narrator meet someone he knows at his mother's house?

2 **Before you read the complete extract from *The Old Curiosity Shop*, scan the text and find five adverbs ending in *-ly*. What actions do they describe?**

3 **Complete the following sentences, using one of the adverbs from the text.**

1 I was really tired and I got up very … when the alarm went off.
2 'You can't go the concert – that's my final word,' he said … .
3 Can you keep a secret?' he asked … .
4 The child approached the lion … .
5 When the fire started, we left the house … .

4 **Find the following words and choose the more likely meaning.**

Line 1: roaming – **a** walking to a particular place **b** walking around
Line 29: a slight figure – **a** a large person **b** a small person
Line 38: deceiving her – **a** telling lies **b** telling the truth
Line 56: at length – **a** immediately **b** eventually

5 **Now read the complete extract and find phrases that mean more or less the same as the following.**

1 Someone asked me something and I stopped walking.
2 The question and the way it was asked had an effect on me.
3 It felt as if she had known me all her life.
4 She occasionally looked at me.
5 I was as interested in her as she was interested in me.

6 **Before you read the complete extract from *The Woman In White*, scan the text and find words and expressions describing late summer. What impression do they give of life in the city during this period?**

7 **Look at the following expressions from the text. Can you think of an alternative single word to describe the feelings?**

out of health   out of spirits   out of money

8 **Here are some other expressions with *out of*. What do they describe? Make a sentence for each to show what they mean.**

out of order   out of stock   out of sight   out of date

9 **Now read the complete extract and answer these questions.**

1 Does summer in your country draw to a close at the same time as a London summer?
2 What do you find out about the narrator's financial situation?
3 He described the evening as *still*. What does this mean? What else can *still* mean?
4 Do you think the book he was reading was exciting or dull? How do you know?
5 Explain the sentence which begins: *The quiet twilight* … What does it tell you about time and place?
6 What do you know about the position and location of his mother's cottage?

10 **Before you read the complete extract from *A Study in Scarlet*, scan the text and work out who the narrator is.**

11 **Explain the meaning of the words *comfortless* and *meaningless*. Can you think of words with the same suffix that mean the following?**

1 Having no value
2 Not in motion
3 Possibly dangerous because of not taking care
4 Without power
5 Of no use to anybody

If you want to revise suffixes, return to Unit 3 page 27.

12 **Now read the complete extract. Think of more modern ways to say the following:**

1 I had neither kith nor kin in England.
2 I naturally gravitated to London.
3 I must make a complete alteration to my lifestyle.
4 I made up my mind to take up quarters in some less expensive domicile.
5 The sight of a friendly face … is a pleasant thing indeed to a lonely man.
6 Stamford had never been a particular crony of mine.

The Old Curiosity Shop by Charles Dickens

One night I was roaming through the City, walking slowly in my usual way, when I was arrested by an inquiry in a soft sweet voice. I turned hastily round and found at my elbow a pretty little girl, who begged to be directed to a certain street at a considerable distance, and indeed in quite another quarter of the town.

'It is a very long way from here, my child,' said I.

'I know that, sir,' she replied, timidly. 'For I came from there tonight.'

'Alone?' said I, in some surprise.

'Oh, yes, I don't mind that, but I am a little frightened now, for I have lost my way.'

'And what made you ask it of me? Suppose I should tell you wrong?'

'I am sure you will not do that,' said the little creature, ' you are such a very old gentleman, and walk so slowly yourself.'

I cannot describe how much I was impressed by this appeal and the energy with which it was made, which brought a tear into the child's clear eye, and made her slight figure tremble as she looked up into my face.

'Come,' said I, 'I'll take you there.'

She put her hand in mind as confidingly as if she had known me from her cradle, and we trudged away together. I observed that every now and then she stole a curious look at my face, as if to make quite sure that I was not deceiving her, and that these glances seemed to increase her confidence at every repetition.

For my part, my curiosity and interest were at least equal to the child's.

'Who has sent you so far by yourself?' said I.

'Someone who is very kind to me, sir.'

'And what have you been doing?'

'That, I must not tell,' said the child firmly.

Clapping her hands with pleasure and running on before me for a short distance, my little acquaintance stopped at a door. When she had knocked twice, there was a noise as if some person were moving inside, and at length someone opened the door. It was an old man with long grey hair.

The Woman in White by Wilkie Collins

It was the last day of July. The long hot summer was drawing to a close and we Londoners were beginning to think of the cloud-shadows on the corn-fields, and the autumn breezes on the sea-shore.

For my own poor part, the fading summer left me out of health, out of spirits, and, if the truth must be told, out of money as well. During the past year, I had not managed my professional resources as carefully as usual; and my extravagance now limited me to the prospect of spending the autumn economically between my mother's cottage at Hampstead and my own rooms in town.

The evening, I remember, was still and cloudy. The London air was at its heaviest; the distant hum of the street-traffic was at its faintest. I roused myself from the book which I was dreaming over rather than reading, and left my rooms to meet the cool night air in the suburbs. It was one of the two evenings in every week which I was accustomed to spend with my mother and my sister. So I turned my steps northward in the direction of Hampstead.

The quiet twilight was still trembling on the topmost ridges of the heath; and the view of London below me had sunk into a black gulf in the shadow of the cloudy night, when I stood before the gate of my mother's cottage. I had hardly rung the bell before the house door was opened violently; my Italian friend Professor Pesca appeared and darted out joyously to welcome me.

A Study in Scarlet by Arthur Conan Doyle

I had neither kith nor kin in England, and was therefore as free as air, or as free as an income of eleven shillings and sixpence a day will permit a man to be. Under such circumstances I naturally gravitated to London. There I stayed for some time at a private hotel in the Strand, leading a comfortless, meaningless existence, and spending such money as I had. I soon realized that I must either leave the metropolis or I must make a complete alteration in my style of living. Choosing the latter alternative, I began by making up my mind to leave the hotel, and take up quarters in some less expensive domicile.

On the very day that I had come to this conclusion, I was standing in the street when someone tapped me on the shoulder. Turning round, I recognized young Stamford. The sight of a friendly face in the great wilderness of London is a pleasant thing indeed to a lonely man. In the old days, Stamford had never been a particular crony of mine, but now I hailed him with enthusiasm, and he appeared to be delighted to see me.

'What are you up to, Watson?' he asked.

'Looking for lodgings,' I answered. 'Trying to solve the problem as to whether it is possible to get comfortable rooms at a reasonable price.'

'That's a strange thing,' remarked my companion; 'you are the second man today that has used that expression to me.'

'And who was the first?' I asked.

13 **Speculate on what happened next in the story. Discuss the following:**

1 Who do you think Stamford had also talked to about lodgings?
2 What do you think will happen next?

14 **Now discuss the following questions.**

1 Which extract makes most use of dialogue?
2 Which extract gives most information about characters?
3 Which extract gives most information about place?

1 Compound and complex sentences
2 Conjunctions

Important – read this!

We form **compound sentences** when we join two or more simple sentences (see Grammar Reference, section 10). We can do this with **coordinating conjunctions** such as *and, but, or, so, yet*. There are also paired coordinating conjunctions: *either ...or, both ... and, not only ... but also*, etc.

The sentences we join in this way can exist independently: 'Dickens not only wrote very popular novels, but was also a brilliant lecturer.' Or we could write: 'Dickens wrote very popular novels. He was a brilliant lecturer.' Note that if the subject of the two clauses is the same, it may be omitted in the second clause; but not if there are two sentences.

1 Join the following pairs of sentences with paired conjunctions.

1 Perhaps Arthur Conan Doyle wrote the book. Perhaps Wilkie Collins wrote it. (I'm sure it was one of the two.)
2 Dickens was born in the first quarter of the 19th century. Collins was born in the first quarter of the 19th century.
3 Dickens didn't survive until the 20th century. Collins didn't survive until the 20th century.

Important – read this!

We form **complex sentences** by combining a simple sentence with a **subordinate** clause. We do this with **subordinating conjunctions**, such as *although, if, as soon as* (introducing adverbial clauses); *who, which, whose* (introducing adjectival clauses) and *that, what* (introducing noun clauses).

A subordinate clause cannot exist independently: *'As soon as they arrived'* is incomplete.

NOTE: There are no paired subordinating conjunctions and it is not possible to emphasise a subordinating conjunction with a coordinating one: This is incorrect: *Although it is cold, but it is not so cold as yesterday.*

2 Connect with a suitable subordinating conjunction.

1 In *A Study in Scarlet*, Conan Doyle wrote .... Holmes lived at 221B Baker St.
2 This is an address .... has since become world-famous.
3 .... it doesn't really exist, many people still try to find it.
4 They are often very disappointed .... they are told it never really existed.
5 Of course, Sherlock Holmes is someone .... never really existed either.
6 .... the address would become so well-known is something Conan Doyle would never have imagined.

3 Explain to Helmut when you can and can't leave out the subject.

There you are, Ali. Did you buy the tickets?
Yes, I bought the tickets and got us drinks.
'And I got us drinks', Ali. You must include the subject!
Well, it's possible but not necessary.
Really? Well I didn't buy a programme because don't have enough money.
!?
Sorry, Helmut. You have to say 'because I don't have enough money'.

All kinds of strange things happen in Harry Potter novels and films – there are diaries that write you a reply, paintings that come alive and owls that carry letters. The books are the most successful stories ever. Sales are already in the hundreds of millions. They tell the imaginary story of an orphaned boy called Harry Potter. Harry goes to a boarding school for young wizards and witches. There he does battle against an evil wizard. Harry always wins in the end, but not until he's had a lot of very exciting adventures.

The author of the Harry Potter books, JK Rowling, is now one of the richest women in Britain. Joanne Rowling was born in England in 1965. She wrote her first story, called 'Rabbit', at the age of six. She studied French at Exeter University. She then worked as a bilingual secretary, but describes herself as 'the worst secretary ever'. By the time she moved to Edinburgh in Scotland, she had the outline for seven Harry Potter novels, and she wrote much of the first one in a café, while her little daughter slept beside her. She describes the moment when the book was accepted for publication as the happiest moment of her life.

What is it that makes these books so extraordinarily successful? Humour is an important key – the books are very funny. They are also a wonderfully imaginative example of the fantasy genre. Children can do all the things in the fantasy genre that they can't do in real life – for example, fly, and defeat evil wizards. We all want to forget about the real world from time to time and the Harry Potter stories enable us to dream and laugh. It's a wonderful combination.

1 **The poster above is taken from a well-known film. Do you know anything about this film?**

(See page 75 for the answer.)

2 **Read the article quickly and answer these questions:**

Which paragraph …

1. gives biographical information about the author?
2. discusses why the Harry Potter books are so successful?
3. describes the Harry Potter books?

3 **Read the article again and make a note of words or phrases that you don't know. Ask the teacher and other students to help you find the meaning of the words. If there are any of these words you still don't know, use a dictionary to find the meaning.**

4 **Work in pairs. A number of the sentences in the article are simple sentences. Rewrite them as complex sentences, using the words in brackets.**

1. The books are the most successful stories ever. Sales are already in the hundreds of millions. (of which)
2. Harry goes to a boarding school for young wizards and witches. There he does battle against an evil wizard. (where)
3. Joanne Rowling was born in England in 1965. She wrote her first story, called 'Rabbit', at the age of six. (First word: born)
4. She studied French at Exeter University. She then worked as a bilingual secretary, but describes herself as 'the worst secretary ever'. (after)
5. They are also a wonderfully imaginative example of the fantasy genre. Children can do all the things in the fantasy genre that they can't do in real life. (in which)

5 **Write an article about a famous writer from your country whom you admire. Write about 150 words. Try and use complex sentences.**

- FIRST PARAGRAPH: Think of an interesting way to begin the article. Describe the type of books written by the author.
- SECOND PARAGRAPH: Give biographical information about the author.
- FINAL PARAGRAPH: Discuss what makes the books successful. Finish with a reference to the author again.

6 **Optional writing task. Write a For and Against essay entitled *Stories provide entertainment and nothing more*. Write 150 words. Turn to page 33 for help with writing a For and Against essay.**

4 LISTENING AND SPEAKING

The bridge at Medicine Bow

1 **Look at the pictures above. Answer these questions.**

1 Why has the train stopped. What is the problem?
2 In which century do you think this scene takes place?

2 **Describe the scene in the picture, using these words.**

signal steam train gorge swollen river engine driver conductor passenger railway track dilapidated unsafe

3 **Read the following information and then answer the questions.**

In 1873 the popular French novelist, Jules Verne, wrote his best-known work, *Around the World in Eighty Days*. Published in weekly magazine episodes, each episode ended in an exciting cliff-hanger. The novel concerns an English gentleman called Phileas Fogg's attempts to prove to his friends that he can travel around the world in eighty days. With his French servant, Passepartout, Fogg travels by land and sea and has many exciting adventures. In the extract that you will hear, Fogg and Passepartout are travelling by train through the Rocky Mountains in North America.

1 How is *Around the World in Eighty Days* similar to some of the stories written by Charles Dickens, Wilkie Collins and Arthur Conan Doyle?
2 Where does the scene in the illustration on this page take place?

4 **Read the list of options that the train passengers have. Which option do you think is the riskiest and why?**

1 To cross the river at Medicine Bow by boat.
2 To wade across the river at Medicine Bow.
3 To walk ten miles north to another crossing point.
4 To drive the train at high speed over the bridge with the passengers inside.
5 To take the train back to the nearest main town and go another route.
6 To cross the bridge on foot and have the train follow afterwards.

5 **Listen to the first part of the extract. Answer these questions.**

1 Which of the options in activity 4 are suggested?
2 Which option is finally agreed on?

6 **Read this short extract from the text and underline the most important words in each sentence. These are the words that should be stressed.**

Most of the passengers found the plan a very good one.
'We have a fifty per cent chance of getting over,' said one.
'Eighty! Ninety!' said another.
Passepartout was astonished.

7 **Listen to the sentences. Did you stress the right words?**

8 **Listen to the second part of the extract. Answer these questions.**

1 What does the train driver do before attempting to cross the bridge?
2 Does the train succeed in crossing the bridge?
3 What happens next?

9 **Work in small groups. Discuss the following:**

The train drivers and passengers in the extract you have just heard took a big risk. How would you have reacted if you had been a passenger on the train? What would you have felt? For example, would you have remained on the train?

10 **Work in pairs. Look at the list of activities below. They all involve risks. For each activity, say whether you would consider doing it and explain your reasons.**

sky-diving skiing deep-sea diving mountaineering learning to fly fencing

EXAMPLE: I'd never go sky-diving. It's much too dangerous. I've heard stories of people being killed because their parachute doesn't open.

Word watch – Masculine and feminine

1 **Some words have distinct male and female forms. Fill in the missing terms.**

Masculine	Feminine	Feminine	Masculine
mayor	___________	bride	___________
nephew	___________	queen	___________
lion	___________	widow	___________
uncle	___________	cow	___________

2 **Now underline all the terms which can refer equally to a male or a female.**

cousin mate ram princess doctor
husband child politician leader president
sir lad winner ghost cat passenger lady

3 **Many names of jobs now have one form to include both men and women. Complete the sentences by solving the anagrams.**

1 Policemen and policewomen are now called ___________ CEOPIL RIFOESCF

2 Firemen and firewomen are now called ___________ RIEF GSEIFTHR

3 Headmistresses and headmasters are now called ___________ AHDE HRETASCE

Do you know the rule for animals? These examples may help.

Spot is like a member of the family. We've had him since he was a puppy.
I could see a dog in the distance. It was barking at some sheep.

How can we avoid writing *he/she*? For example in the sentence: *Every student must make sure he/she is on time for lessons.*
Easy! Use the plural form: *Students must make sure they are on time for lessons.*

Lessons in logic

1 The last Wednesday of the month was on the 24th and the last day of the month was four days later. Which month was it? ___________

On which day did the month end? ___________

2 Does it make any difference if the year was 2000? ___________

3 Christmas Day was on the last Thursday of the month.
On which day did the month begin? ___________
On which day did it end? ___________

4 Guy Fawkes' Day (November 5th) was on the first Tuesday of the month.
On which day did the month end? ___________

Pronunciation and rhyme

The way words are spelt in English is not always a good guide to how they are pronounced. Be careful to learn how to say each word correctly.

In each of the following groups of four words, one word does not rhyme with the others. Underline the odd one out.

1 show how brown now
2 two new sew true
3 enough rough tough bough
4 give hive drive arrive
5 late eight ate might
6 bear near deer fear
7 reign main sign vein
8 caught thought nought doubt
9 here there where square
10 bird door word work

Now find the word that is similar in meaning to the word in capitals and that rhymes with the second word.

EXAMPLE: UNUSUAL wear rare

1 ALL pole ___________
2 FRIEND wait ___________
3 SLIM win ___________
4 EDUCATE teach ___________
5 DAMAGE farm ___________
6 TIMID fly ___________
7 GANG bribe ___________
8 PALE paint ___________
9 PLUNGE live ___________
10 HINT new ___________

ANSWER TO ACTIVITY 1 PAGE 73
The film is called Harry Potter and the Philosopher's Stone. *It is about a boy who goes to a school for wizards and witches.*

TRAINS, BOATS AND PLANES

INTRODUCTION AND VOCABULARY

1 Work in groups. Brainstorm words about the items in the photographs. Make a list of at least 20 words related to them.

2 **Now make a list of other words relating to travel. Think of words in the following categories:**

- people – eg pilot, passenger, check-in clerk
- places – eg railway station, terminal building, level crossing
- things – eg luggage, seat belt, life belt

3 **Compare your lists with other groups. Make a list on the board of words from the whole class.**

4 **Complete these sentences and say who is most likely to say them.**

1 Will all passengers please fasten their … in preparation for take-off?
2 First of all, we flew to Barbados and then we went on a … on a luxury liner round the Caribbean.
3 The plane was diverted because both the … at Moscow airport were covered with snow.
4 Please have your passports and … ready before you get on the plane.
6 A woman fell overboard from a ferry and was saved from drowning because they threw a … to her.
7 Which … does the train to Liverpool leave from?
8 There are four … at Heathrow Airport and they are building a fifth.

5 **Work in small groups. Write another five gap sentences, where the missing word is one of the words you thought of in activity 2. Exchange your new exercise with another group.**

6 **Work in pairs. Complete the following dialogue.**

CHECK-IN-CLERK: Good morning, sir.
PASSENGER: …
CHECK-IN-CLERK: May I see your …, please?
PASSENGER: …
CHECK-IN-CLERK: Thank you, Mister Smith. So, you're flying to …
PASSENGER: That's right.
CHECK-IN-CLERK: Oh … there's a problem here.
PASSENGER: A problem? What kind of problem?
CHECK-IN-CLERK: This ticket is for yesterday's …
PASSENGER: What?!?
CHECK-IN-CLERK: I'm sorry, you should have …
PASSENGER: OK, never mind. I can …
CHECK-IN-CLERK: I'm afraid you can't. Today's flight is …
PASSENGER: What?!? This is terrible. I have to …

7 **Now add some more lines of conversation to solve the problem. Act out your conversation for the rest of the class.**

8 **Read the extract from a novel called *Scoop* by Evelyn Waugh and answer these questions.**

1 When do you think the novel was written?
2 What do you think the following things are used for?
 - the rug
 - the wad of cotton wool
 - the flask of smelling salts
 - the paper bag
3 Do any of the actions of the crew surprise you?

9 **Now answer the questions about some of the words and expressions in the text.**

1 The propellers were *thundering* – does this mean they were making a lot of noise?
2 The pilot *adjusted* his helmet – did he put his helmet on or was he already wearing it?
3 The ground staff *fell back* – does this mean that they moved towards the plane or away from it?
4 The machine *hurtled and bumped across the rough turf* – was it a smooth take-off?
5 The *track of a steamer* – does this refer to a train or a boat?

The propellers were thundering; the pilot threw away his cigarette and adjusted his helmet; the steward wrapped a rug round William's feet and tenderly laid in his lap a wad of cotton wool, a flask of smelling salts and an empty paper bag. The door was shut. The ground staff fell back. The machine moved forward, gathered speed, hurtled and bumped across the rough turf, ceased to bump, floated clear of the earth, mounted and wheeled above the smoke and the traffic, and very soon hung, it seemed motionless, above the Channel, where the track of a steamer, far below them, lay in the bright water like a line of smoke on a still morning.

From Scoop *by Evelyn Waugh*

1 READING

1 **Look at the map of the south-eastern part of the United States. Can you pronounce the names of the states? Here is an indication of where the main stress is. Which is the odd one out?**

LouisiANa
MissisSIPPi
AlaBAMa
GEORGia
North/South CaroLINa

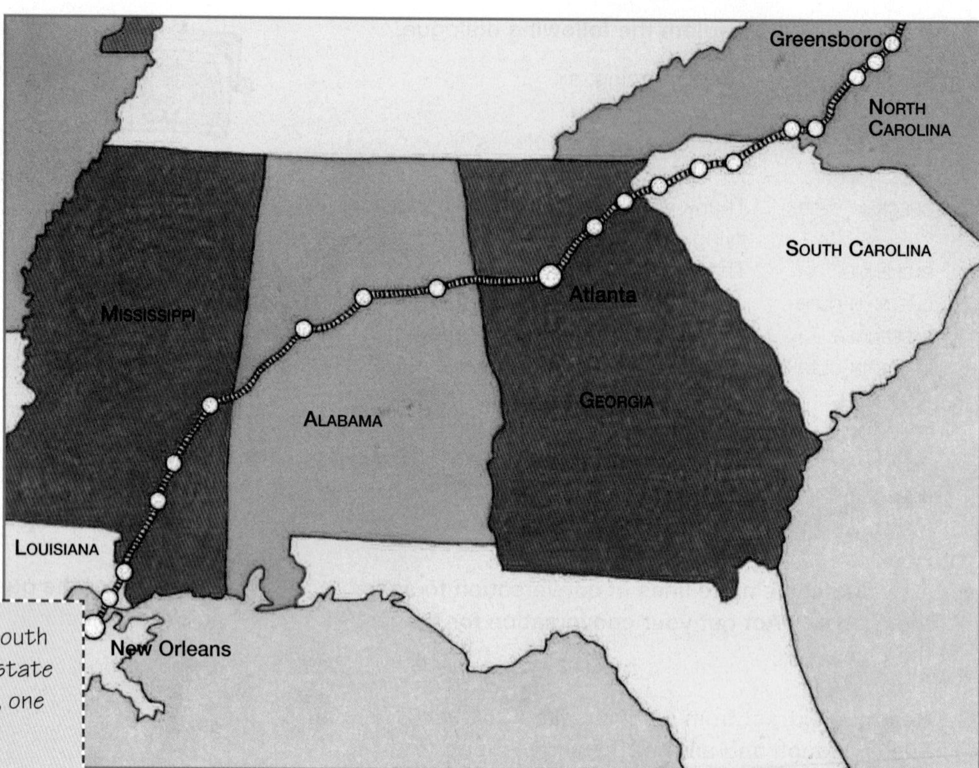

2 **Read the following information about the six states.**

> The six states are all in the south of the USA. Louisiana is the state where New Orleans is located, one of the most popular tourist destinations in the country. Mississippi is also the name of the longest river in North America. The 1996 Olympics were held in Atlanta, Georgia. Carolina, which became two states in 1710, was one of the original 13 states and was one of the cotton-producing states which used slave labour.

But how did they get their names? Some (but not all) American states get their names from native American (Indian) words. Try to work out the origins of the names from the following clues:

1. One was named in honour of King George the Second of England, who ruled from 1727 to 1760.
2. One is a Native American word meaning 'Father of Waters'.
3. Two of them were named in honour of King Charles the First of England, who ruled from 1625 until his execution in 1649.
4. One was named in honour of the French king, Louis the Fourteenth (1638-1715).
5. One is a native American word meaning people who gather vegetation.

The answers are at the bottom of page 83.

3 **Work in small groups. What else do you know about the south-eastern part of the United States? Write down any information you have and share it with the rest of the group.**

4 **The following is an advertisement for the Crescent train, which runs from New York City to New Orleans. Read the text and answer the questions.**

Crescent

New York City, NY - Atlanta, GA - New Orleans, LA

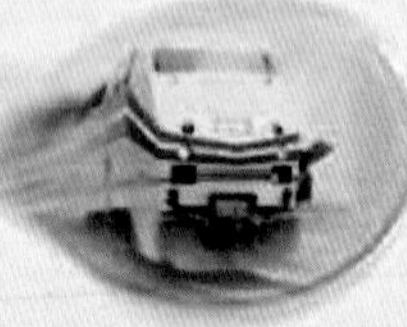

The Crescent takes you from the Big Apple to the Big Easy. As the vibrant cityscapes of the north east fade into the foothills of the Blue Ridge mountains, pine forests and sprawling farms signal your entry into the Deep South. Trees drip with Spanish moss as you travel throught the state of Louisiana. When you get to New Orleans, you'll have lots to do. Take a streetcar tor of the French Quarter or listen to the street musicians in Royal Street.

1. What do you think the letters NY, GA and LA refer to?
2. Why do you think the train is called the Crescent?
3. The Big Apple and the Big Easy are nicknames. Which places do they refer to?
4. What are foothills, and what do you think you would see near them?
5. Is a 'sprawling' farm big or small?

My Year of Meat

The train crossed Lake Pontchartrain on a low, narrow bridge. The tracks were so close to the blue water, and the water was so vast on either side, stretching as far as she could see, that Akiko felt she was riding on a magic carpet, skipping across the surface of the ocean.

Leaving Louisiana, the train headed north into Mississippi, Alabama, Georgia, the Carolinas. As she stared out of the window, she whispered the names of the Deep South to herself, matching their syllables to the rhythms of the train. No wonder people sang songs about these places; deep-blue swamplands, enormous fields of tobacco and cotton and wheat, forming horizons, bigger and more American than anything Akiko had ever seen before.

As the train approached the small towns, wooden shanties lined the tracks, where men and women sat outside on crooked porches and children played in the yard. Sometimes she caught sight of a chicken in a yard, pecking in the gravel by the skeletal wreck of a car. The cars parked along the streets were old and rusty too, as were many of those she actually saw driving down the dirt roads. Akiko had never seen a rusty car, and she realised with a shock that the people who lived there were poor. She'd never thought of Americans as poor. Maybe in the past or in the movies but not now. Not these days. Not in real life.

Many of the towns were too small to have stations, but the trains stopped in the larger ones. Most of the passengers who got on and off were black. Families hauling huge bags and suitcases with broken latches and lots of children. There were some single men and women, travelling home or away from a home perhaps. Akiko tried to imagine it. Like herself, they were on the road …

5 **Before you read the extract from *My Year of Meat* by Ruth Ozeki, find the following words and phrases and try to work out what kind of things they refer to from the context. Then check the meanings in a dictionary.**

Line 8: skipping
Line 18: swamplands
Line 25: shanties
Line 27: crooked porches
Line 30: pecking in the gravel
Line 31: skeletal wreck
Line 48: broken latches

6 **Now scan the extract from *My Year of Meat* and find the following information.**

1. Is the main character an American?
2. What means of transport is she travelling on or in?
3. Where does her journey start and which direction does she travel?

7 **Read the text more carefully and find adjectives which describe the following:**

1. the bridge she crosses
2. the water she crosses
3. the farm fields she passes
4. the cars she sees
5. the luggage carried by her fellow passengers

8 **Answer these *Yes-No* questions about the text. Quote from the text to support your answers.**

1. Was the train travelling alongside a lake?
2. Did Akiko feel happy at the start of the journey?
3. Did she say the names of the states aloud?
4. Was she surprised that people sang songs about these places?
5. Had she ever visited places like this before?
6. Did she see houses of rich people on her journey?
7. Do people in Akiko's home country drive cars like the ones she saw?
8. Was she surprised to see cars like this?
9. Did she know that there were poor people in the United States?
10. Did Akiko's feelings change as the journey progressed?

9 **Discuss these questions.**

1. What images did you have of the USA before you read this extract?
2. What were those images based on?
3. Has your opinion changed after reading the extract?

2 GRAMMAR PRACTICE

1 Complete these conditional sentences about situations in this unit.

1 If the passenger had arrived at the airport on the correct day, ______________________________ ______________________________.

2 If your ears hurt, William, ______________________________ ______________________________.

3 If I were in their position, thought Akiko about the poor Americans she saw, ______________________________ ______________________________.

4 If you take the Crescent from New York City to New Orleans tomorrow, ______________________________ ______________________________.

5 If the aeroplane had not been invented, the world today ______________________________ ______________________________.

2a Circle the subject and underline the complete verb form in these conditional clauses.

1 Were the writer to travel in a modern plane …
2 Should you take the Crescent from the Big Easy to the Big Apple …
3 Had they not built extra terminals at Heathrow …

2b Match the three conditional clauses above with the result clauses below.

A … you will arrive relaxed and ready for the excitement of New York.
B … the situation would have become impossible years ago.
C … he would find things very different.

1 _____ 2 _____ 3 _____

2c Write out the three sentences using other conditional forms having the same meaning as those in 2a.

3 Underline the (subordinate) adverbial clauses. Then write the correct letter from the key to show what type each clause is.

KEY: **A** manner **B** reason **C** result **D** place **E** purpose **F** time **G** concession

EXAMPLE: The water was very high and near the train <u>so that Akiko imagined they were floating on it.</u>

1 As soon as he was ready to take off the pilot threw his cigarette away. C
2 These days you can find an airport almost anywhere you go. ___
3 Because she thought all Americans were rich, Akiko was surprised to see a lot of poor people on the train. ___
4 Arrive early at the airport so that you can get a good seat on the plane. ___
5 Akiko noticed that some of the passengers were moving as if they were exhausted. ___
6 Although Waugh's plane made a lot of noise, it didn't travel very fast by modern standards. ___

4 What is Ali going to say to Helmut? What does Ali mean with 'That's right'? What does Helmut think he means?

This sentence starts 'Should you take the Crescent' but it doesn't have a question mark!
That's right, Helmut.
No, Helmut. The book is right.
Of course it's right. I have the book in front of me. And here's another mistake: 'Were the writer to travel in a modern aeroplane' but no question mark!
Don't be silly, Ali. And here's another question without a question mark. It starts: 'Had they not built extra terminals'. Verb first and then the subject.
But …

1 **Answer these questions. Give reasons for your answers.**

1 Would you like to study abroad?
2 If you decided to study abroad, what would you want to study?
3 Where would you want to study?

2 **Check the meaning of the following words. Then answer the questions below.**

to apply for   to enclose
to recommend   to look forward to
to be keen (on)   fee   degree   grant
result   certificate

1 What kind of thing might a student apply for?
2 If you were sending an application letter, what might you enclose in an envelope?
3 Which holiday resort in your country would you recommend and why?
4 What are you looking forward to doing in the next few months?
5 Who might you pay a fee to?
6 Which sport are you keen on?
7 Where would a person study for a degree?
8 What results did you get in your last exams?
9 In what circumstances might you receive a certificate?
10 Why might you apply for a grant?

Flat 7
39 Moharam Shawky Street
Alexandria
Egypt

Ms Angela Harrison
Study Grants International
271 Carlton Hill
Cambridge CB1 5B2

25 October 2004

Dear Ms Harrison,

I am writing this letter (1)__________ for a grant (2)__________ study for a three-year undergraduate degree at University College, London.

I am an eighteen-year-old student and have just completed my final year at the Alexandria International School, Egypt. The (3)__________ my final exams were as follows: Arabic, English, Physics, Chemistry, Mathematics, French and History (98% overall).
I have applied to University College (4)__________ a BSc* degree in Physics and my application (5)__________ accepted.

I would very much like to accept the (6)__________ to study at University College, (7)__________ it is one of the best places in Europe to do Aeronautics. My family is keen that I should do so. This is the (8)__________ I am applying for a grant.

I (9)__________ letters of recommendation from my teachers, my exam certificates, and also the letter from University College accepting my (10)__________.

I hope you will look favourably on my application, and I look forward (11)__________ from you.

Yours sincerely,

Ali Khatami

* Bachelor of Science (BSc): an undergraduate degree that takes three or four years.

3 **You're going to read an application letter for a study grant. The student who is applying for the grant writes five paragraphs, described below. Number the paragraphs in the order you think they should appear in the letter.**

a This paragraph says that Ali hopes to receive an answer to his application soon.
b This paragraph lists the documents that Ali is enclosing.
c In this paragraph, Ali gives relevant information about himself.
d In this paragraph, Ali explains why he wants to study abroad, and why he needs the travel grant.
e This paragraph briefly explains the reason for writing.

4 **Complete the gaps in the letter with one or two suitable words.**

5 **Now read the complete letter again. Were you right about the order of the paragraphs?**

6 **Imagine that you have completed your end-of-school examinations and are applying to study abroad at a college or university. Write a letter of application for a study grant. Give relevant information about yourself and say:**

- what you want to study
- where you want to study and for how long
- why you want to study in this place

7 **Optional writing task. Write a narrative describing a trip, perhaps imaginary, which you took by train, boat or plane. Write 150 words.** **Turn to page 17 for help with writing a narrative.**

LISTENING AND SPEAKING

The inside of a passenger aircraft

1 **Look at the picture above. Can you identify the following items and people?**

passenger seat belt hand luggage overhead locker tray table headset sign captain seat in upright position cabin crew exit stewardess

2 **The words and phrases below are all used in connection with flying. Match the verbs on the left with the words and phrases on the right. Some of the verbs can be used with two of these words and phrases.**

switch off	(a) seat belt
land	(a) plane
stow away	on board
catch	from a plane
fasten	at an airport
cancel	(a) mobile phone
remain	(a) flight
disembark	luggage

3 **Listen to this aircraft announcement and say if the following statements are true or false. If they are false, correct them.**

1 The plane is about to land.
2 The aircraft is stopping at London Heathrow Airport, and then going on to its final destination, Edinburgh (in Scotland).
3 The connecting flight at 2pm to Dublin (in Ireland) has been cancelled.
4 The passengers are flying with an airline called British Airways.

4 **Listen again. Answer these questions.**

1 Is the person speaking the pilot of the aircraft?
2 What things are all passengers asked to do?
3 What are passengers asked to stop doing?
4 What changes of plan are the passengers informed about?

5 **Read these questions about flying and think about your answers and the reasons for them.**

1 Have you ever flown? If so, how often and where to? If not, would you like to?
2 How do you feel about flying? Do you have a fear of flying? How does it make you feel? For example, when you think about it, do you feel frightened or excited?
3 Think of a nearby country. If you were going there on holiday, how would you prefer to travel, by plane or by some other method of transport?
4 Think of a far away country. How would you prefer to get there?
5 If a friend learnt to fly a small two-seater plane, would you fly with him/her?
6 Would you ever consider learning to fly?

6 **Work in pairs. Ask your partner the questions in activity 5. Discuss your answers together.**

7 **Imagine that you have a one-month, round-the-world air ticket. You can stop off at seven countries for as long as you want. Decide which countries you want to visit and for how long.**

Work in pairs. Tell your partner about your plans and why you have chosen these particular countries.

EXAMPLE: *The first country I intend to visit is Turkey, because I'd love to see Istanbul. I'd stay there for three days before going on to Saint Petersburg in Russia.*

8 **Work in groups. Write the script for a similar announcement to the one in activity 3. Write the script for a plane which is flying to an airport near you. Choose someone in the group to act out the announcement to the whole group.**

Word watch – Homophones

A homophone is a word which has exactly the same pronunciation as another word although the spelling and meaning are different.

1 **Complete the chart by writing a homophone for each of the following words.**

two	___________	write	___________
war	___________	waste	___________
meet	___________	wear	___________
so	___________	hole	___________
wait	___________	blue	___________
eye	___________	pear	___________
heard	___________	here	___________
rain	___________	nose	___________

Do you know any other English homophones?

2 **Choose the correct word to complete each sentence.**

1 The gold *miners/minors* worked in very hard conditions.
2 The chairman began to *praise/prays* the good work done by his predecessor.
3 It's convenient to *higher/hire* a car when you're on business abroad.
4 The audience was so *bored/board* that some of them walked out.
5 It can be very rude to *stare/stair* at somebody.
6 The box was made of *steel/steal* and was very strong.
7 Let's go for a *sale/sail* around the harbour.
8 I don't like to be *idol/idle* and need to be active every day.

Lessons in logic

Use your skills in logical thinking and close reading.

J, K, L, M and N are books. L and M are not for children but the others are. K and M are not paperbacks but the rest are. J and L are fiction but the remainder aren't.

So, which paperback book is a children's story book?

Is there a children's paperback non-fiction book? ___

Which hardback book is a non-fiction adult book? ___

Which adult paperback is fiction? ___

Is there an adult fiction hardback book? ___

Vocabulary – Find the words

1 **Find the missing four-letter word which must be added to the letters in capitals to make a new word. The new word will complete the sentence sensibly.**

EXAMPLE: She was an agile and GFUL dancer. RACE (to make the word GRACEFUL)

1 The twins were IICAL and looked exactly the same. ___________
2 The new computer was CAP of processing information at high speed. ___________
3 It was a very CY day so I took my umbrella to work ___________
4 The exhibits were beautifully DISED in glass cabinets ___________
5 We thought we had PY of time but in fact we ended up being late ___________
6 We had to wait in the DEURE lounge as the plane was delayed. ___________

2 **Find the hidden four letter words in these sentences. The word is hidden at the end of one word and the beginning of the next and the letters are in the correct order.**

EXAMPLE: We ha<u>ve</u> <u>to</u> hand in our homework today.
The hidden word is veto.

1 There were cakes and biscuits on sale in the café. ___________
2 The class collected money for the school magazine. ___________
3 'Just one more question to go,' said Julian. ___________
4 The men left the pitch and went into the changing room. ___________
5 I bought a birthday present for my mother. ___________
6 Many articles in this store are bargains. ___________

You might like to make up some of these for your friends to do!

ANSWERS TO ACTIVITY 2 PAGE 78
1 Georgia
2 Mississippi
3 North and South Carolina
4 Louisiana
5 Alabama

11 DEEP SECRETS

INTRODUCTION AND VOCABULARY

How much do you know about the oceans?

1 How much of the earth's surface is covered by water?
a 30%
b 50%
c 70%
d 90%

2 Which is the largest ocean in the world?
a The Atlantic Ocean
b The Indian Ocean
c The Pacific Ocean
d The Arctic Ocean

3 How deep is the deepest part of the ocean?
a more than 2,000 metres
b more than 5,000 metres
c more than 7,000 metres
d more than 10,000 metres

4 How many planets in the solar system have oceans?
a all of them
b half of them
c one of them
d none of them

5 Where did the water in the oceans come from?
a volcanic steam
b ice from outer space
c underground lakes
d prehistoric rivers

1 **Quick quiz. Answer the multiple-choice questions. Discuss your answers with other students. Don't worry if you don't know all the answers – you will find them later.**

2 **Now read this extract from an interview with an expert on the oceans. Find a place for the following words:**

deadly deeper fascinating heard higher unique

INTERVIEWER: What is it about the oceans that you find so (1)_______ ?

EXPERT: Well, first of all, our oceans are (2)_______! No other planet in the solar system has them. And secondly, life started in the oceans, and maybe the oceans contain the answers to some of the world's problems.

INTERVIEWER: Such as what?

EXPERT: Well, it's possible that the oceans contain cures to some of our most (3)_______ diseases. We just haven't found them yet.

INTERVIEWER: But the sea isn't as interesting as dry land. I mean, we have beautiful mountain ranges and ...

EXPERT: And so do the oceans! In some places, the ocean is (4)_______ than the height of Mount Everest – and just as interesting to look at.

INTERVIEWER: Really?

EXPERT: Yes! Parts of the Pacific Ocean, which is of course the largest ocean on the planet, are more than10,000 metres deep.

INTERVIEWER: Wow!

EXPERT: Yes! And then there's Maune Kea.

INTERVIEWER: Maune what?

EXPERT: Maune Kea – it's an island in Hawaii. Actually, it's a mountain that's 10,203 metres high. It's (5)_______ than Mount Everest, Everest is less than 9,000 metres high.

INTERVIEWER: Maune Kea is the highest mountain in the world???

EXPERT: Technically, yes.

INTERVIEWER: So why have I never (6)_______ of Maune Kea?

EXPERT: Because only 4,000 metres of Maune Kea is above sea level.

INTERVIEWER: I see.

3 **How many answers to the quick quiz questions can you find?**

4 **Look at the cross-section of the ocean and discuss the following questions.**

- How do you think marine life changes as the ocean gets deeper?
- What do you think the deepest part of the ocean looks like?
- How can we find out what is at the bottom of the ocean?

5 **Scan *Mysteries of the deep*. Which of the following topics are mentioned?**

1 the topography of the ocean floor
2 a machine that enables scientists to examine the deep ocean
3 unusual life forms that live in the deep ocean
4 a missing hydrogen bomb
5 how the oceans were formed

6 **Read the text more carefully and answer the following questions.**

1 What effect did volcanoes have on the formation of the oceans?
2 What word is used to describe the deep part of the ocean? Have you heard this word before?
3 What is *the largest single topographical feature on Earth*?
4 How did a hydrogen bomb end up at the bottom of the Mediterranean Sea?
5 What caused ALVIN to sink to the bottom of the Atlantic Ocean?

7 **In groups. Check the answers to the quick quiz at the bottom of page 91 and then discuss the following:**

- what did you learn from the information on these pages?
- what did you read that you already knew?
- if you knew some of this information, where did you learn it?

Mysteries of the deep

Covering two-thirds of the Earth's surface, oceans are where life began and are crucial for our survival. They regulate our climate, provide us with resources like fish and minerals and potentially offer us cures for disease. And yet we know more about the moon than we do about the deep ocean.

Millions of years ago, there were no oceans. The surface of the Earth was so hot that water simply boiled away. Eventually, volcanoes poured huge amounts of steam into the atmosphere and, as the Earth cooled down, the steam turned to water vapour that condensed and began to fall as rain. This downpour lasted for thousands of years, forming the world's first seas.

Eight per cent of the ocean floor is less than 200 metres below the surface of the water, gently sloping areas called continental shelves. The continental shelves end at the steeper continental slopes, which lead down to the deepest parts of the ocean, the abyss. The abyss contains spectacular mountains and long mountain ranges (called ocean ridges), and active volcanoes. The deepest parts of the ocean could easily swallow up the tallest mountains on land.

The ocean ridges form a great mountain range, almost 64,000 kilometres long, that weaves its way through the major oceans. It is the largest single topographical feature on Earth. In the centre of some ocean ridges are long rift valleys, where earthquakes and volcanic eruptions are common. Some volcanoes that rise from the ridges appear above the surface as islands.

A job for ALVIN

Nowadays, researchers can explore the ocean depths in deep submergence vessels (DSVs). They are small submarines that can manoeuvre underwater more easily than larger submarines. They are equipped with windows, searchlights, mechanical arms, cameras and scientific instruments for recording data. The most famous submersible is ALVIN, a three-person DSV that made its first descent into the deep in 1964.

Since then, ALVIN has made more than 3,200 dives, between 150 and 200 a year. One of its most memorable missions was to find a 20-megaton bomb lost in the Mediterranean Sea off the Spanish coast after two military planes collided. ALVIN located the bomb 230 metres under the sea.

In August 1968, as the ALVIN was being placed into the water a few hundred kilometres off the US coast, a cable broke and the DSV sank 1,500 metres to the bottom of the Atlantic. Luckily, the men inside were able to escape through an open hatch. The submersible was located by sonar and rescued 11 months later. It was repaired and working again before the end of 1970.

1 READING

1 Look at the photos and titles of the two reading texts on these pages and discuss these questions.

1 Which article do you think will describe valuable work being done under the sea?
2 Which article may contain information about the destruction of our environment?
3 Which article may contain good news and which may contain bad news?

2 Skim through *Swimming with sphinxes* and find words and expressions which mean more or less the following:

1 in front of
2 compete with
3 very big
4 top
5 permission
6 light (noun)

3 Now read the text more carefully and explain these references.

Line 4: brilliantly coloured fish swim among them – *swim among what?*
Line 10: the idea was originally that of his father – *what idea?*
Line 18: in such a state of ruin that it was impossible to enter – *enter what?*
Line 31: they have found more than 2,000 pieces of the lighthouse – *who are they?*
Line 34: some were broken into two or three pieces – *some of what?*

4 Find words in the text beginning with *m* or *r* to complete these sentences.

1 I read a story about a ________ warrior.
2 The view from the hotel balcony across the lake was absolutely ________ .
3 Mount Everest rises ________ above the city of Kathmandu.
4 We visited the ________ of an old castle in Wales.
5 You can see the ________ of an old fortress next to the new palace.
6 It was impossible to ________ the wreck of the *Titanic* from the bottom of the Atlantic.
7 She's trying hard to ________ the painting to its former state.
8 The government wants to ________ as much of the gold as possible from the eighteenth-century Spanish galleon at the bottom of the sea.

Swimming with sphinxes

Diving down six or eight metres into the waters around Pharos, off the coast of Alexandria, you find yourself face to face with sphinxes and colossal statues of men and women. Brilliantly coloured fish swim among them. These are the remains of the seventh wonder of the world, the Alexandria Lighthouse, and could soon rival the pyramids as a tourist attraction – underwater!

The story of Pharos began 2,300 years ago, when Ptolemy the Second ordered the building of a magnificent lighthouse, although the idea was originally that of his father, Ptolemy the First. It was a kind of courtyard of colonnades on a square base, rising majestically to a height of about 100 metres. At its summit, there was a lantern crowned with a statue of Poseidon, the Greek god of the sea. Over the next fifteen hundred years, however, the mighty structure was destroyed by a series of earthquakes. When the Arab traveller Ibn Battuta visited Pharos in 1349, he found it 'in such a state of ruin that it was impossible to enter'. It's ironic that Poseidon was also the god of earthquakes!

In the 1990s, work began to retrieve the remains of the lighthouse. While shooting underwater scenes for a film on Alexandria, the Egyptian director Asmaa El-Bakri noticed that a concrete dyke was being built to protect nearby Fort Qait Bey. Worried that this would harm the ruins, El-Bakri alerted a journalist friend about the problem. The subsequent press campaign led to work being suspended and the green light was given to a group of archaeologists to examine the underwater treasure.

Since 1994, under the direction of Jean-Yves Empereur, head of the Alexandria Study Centre, they have found more than 2,000 pieces of the lighthouse. The most exciting discoveries are a series of heavy blocks of granite – weighing between 49 to 69 tonnes. The fact that some were broken into two or three pieces indicates that they fell from a great height. Several dozen pieces have already been raised and restored, and are currently on view in the open-air amphitheatre of Kom el Dikka, in Alexandria.

Stop killing the reefs!

A coral is a form of animal life. A baby coral looks like a tiny jellyfish and it floats around in the water until it finds a hard place to attach to, usually a coral reef. Then it lands and starts to build itself a shell, shaped like a round vase.

Coral reefs start small and grow about a centimetre a year and, if undisturbed by man, they can grow to be enormous. The Great Barrier Reef off the northeast coast of Australia is 150 kilometres wide and 2,000 kilometres long.

Coral reefs are incredibly important to Earth's fragile eco-system and are among the most beautiful natural ocean feature on the planet, but already TEN PER CENT of the world's reefs have been completely destroyed. In the Philippines, the location of the world's worst coral reef destruction, nearly three-quarters of coral reefs have been destroyed and only five per cent are in good condition. The activity of humans is almost entirely responsible for this destruction.

Coral reefs are important! They provide protection and shelter for many different species of fish. Without coral reefs, these fish are left homeless with nowhere to live and reproduce. Not only do these fish increase the diversity of our world, but also reef fish and molluscs provide food for between thirty and forty million people every year.

The direct way in which humans destroy coral reefs is by physically killing them. All over the world, but especially in the Philippines, divers catch the fish that live in and around coral reefs. They sell these fish to restaurants in Asia and to pet stores in the United States. This would be OK if the divers caught the fish carefully with nets and didn't hurt the reefs or take too many fish. But the divers want lots of fish and most of them are not very well trained at fish catching. Often they use explosives to blow up a coral reef and then catch all the stunned fish swimming around. This completely destroys the reefs, as well as many of the plants and animals that call it home. And the creatures that do survive are left homeless.

1

2

5 **Before you read *Stop killing the reefs!*, read this information:**

- An eco-system is the combination of all the plants and animals in a particular area, and the way they depend on each other.
- Fuels such as coal or oil are described as fossil fuels, because they are the decayed material of plants and animals that died many thousands of years ago.

6 **Now read the first four paragraphs and complete these answers and questions.**

1 How much ______________? Ten per cent.
2 How much ______________? Five per cent.
3 What ______________? The actions of humans.
4 What ______________ like? A tiny jellyfish.
5 What happens when ______________? It starts to build a shell.
6 How long ______________? 2,000 kilometres.
7 How many ______________? Up to forty million.

7 **Read the whole text and decide if the following sentences are true or false. If they are false, explain why.**

1 The worst coral reef destruction is in the western part of the Pacific Ocean.
2 Baby coral are like tiny floating jellyfish with a shell.
3 Coral reefs can grow very big as long as humans leave them alone.
4 Many fish would have no home if coral reefs disappeared.
5 People in Asia and the United States eat fish caught on coral reefs.

2 GRAMMAR PRACTICE

1 Participle clauses
2 Other linkers

1 Rewrite these sentences, replacing the participle clauses in italics with complete clauses.

EXAMPLES: *Before leaving the party,* the chairman thanked everyone present.
Before he left the party, the chairman thanked everyone present.
This pen will last for years *if used carefully.*
This pen will last for years if it is used carefully.

1 The Pharos was built on a small island *lying about 1.5 kilometres from the coast.*

2 *Although once standing in the Caesarium,* the two obelisks are now in distant countries.

3 *Having been destroyed by fire 1,700 years ago,* both the Library and the Museum are lost to us.

4 *Having travelled a long way to see the Pharos,* Ibn Battuta found he couldn't even get into the site.

2 Rewrite as single sentences beginning with the participles indicated.

EXAMPLE: The oceans are where life began. They cover two-thirds of the Earth's surface.
Covering two-thirds of the Earth's surface, the oceans are where life began.

1 The downpour lasted for thousands of years. It filled great hollows in the land and formed the first seas.
Filling

2 Some volcanoes that rise from the undersea ridges appear above the surface as islands.
Rising

3 DSVs are actually small submarines that are equipped with windows, searchlights and scientific instruments.
Equipped

4 El Bakri alerted a journalist friend about the problem because he was worried about the ruins.
Worried

Important – read this!

Linking adverbs (mostly in written English) can also be used to connect clauses. Unlike conjunctions, they are usually separated from the rest of the sentence, often by commas.

3 Rewrite the following sentences with a linking adverb from the box

EXAMPLE: **Because** coral reefs are very important, they need special protection.
Coral reefs are very important; consequently, they need special protection.

however moreover otherwise therefore

1 **Although** we are beginning to protect the reefs, we are not doing enough.

2 The Great Barrier Reef is 2,000 km long **and** it is 150 km wide.

3 **As** the reefs offer homes to fish and molluscs, we need them for biodiversity.

4 We must protect the coral reefs better **or** we may lose them for ever.

4 Can you find a linking adverb, a coordinating conjuction and a subordinating conjunction in this note?

We wanted to see you
but there wasn't enough
time. However, we'll be
back soon – although we
don't know when.
Ali

1 **Match the following words and phrases with the definitions below.**

1 species
2 to overfish
3 global warming
4 natural resource
5 extinct (*adj.*)
6 ocean current

a the continuous movement of the sea in a particular direction
b describing animals or plants which no longer exist
c the slow increase in the temperature of the earth, partly caused by pollution
d too much commercial fishing
e a group of animals or plants of the same kind
f something from the planet that humans can use

2 **The following sentences indicate a cause and an effect.**

- **For each sentence, identify (a) the cause (b) the effect (if the effect is described).**
- **Underline the words used to talk about cause and effect.**
- **Rewrite each sentence, using the words in brackets.**

1 The temperature of the planet is rising due to global warming. (*because of*)
2 As a result of global warming, the temperature of the planet is rising. (*due to*)
3 What is the effect of global warming on ocean currents? (*affect*)
4 Many scientists believe that global warming is causing the ice in the Antarctic to melt. (*making*)
5 Many species are becoming extinct because of pollution. (*causing*)
6 How do ocean currents affect the climate? (*what/effect of*)

3 **Below are some notes on the oceans and their resources. Sort them into the following categories:**

- Global warming and its effects
- Pollution and its effects
- General information about the oceans
- Overfishing and its effects

1 Huge quantities of toxic chemicals are dumped into the oceans every year.
2 In the Mediterranean, overfishing has reduced fish by 20% in some areas.
3 80 million tons of fish are caught all over the world each year.
4 Coral reefs contain enormous numbers of species. It is estimated that pollution has caused the death of 5-10% of the world's coral reefs.
5 The movement of ocean currents has changed as a result of global warming. Europe could become much colder, with a climate similar to Alaska's.
6 The oceans contain half of the world's species. New species are found in the ocean almost daily.
7 Many ocean species may become extinct due to pollution. But these species may contain cures for disease. For example, it is believed that the sea cucumber may cure illnesses such as cancer.
8 In the North-East Atlantic, 40 out of 60 commercial species have been overfished.

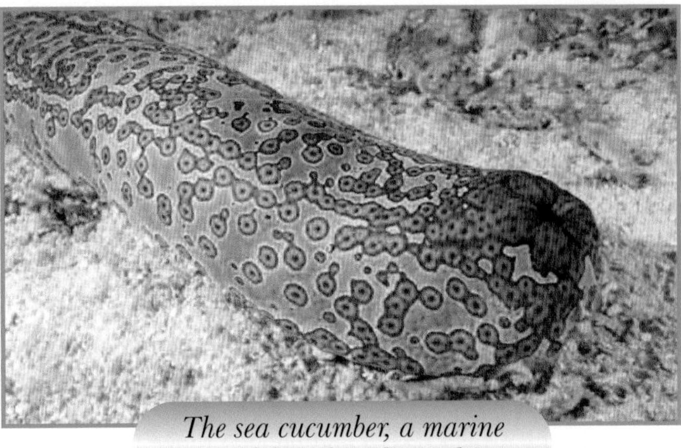

The sea cucumber, a marine animal found in the Red Sea

4 **Write an opinion essay on the statement below. In pairs or small groups, discuss whether you agree or disagree with this idea. Give reasons for your opinion, using information that you have learnt in this unit.**

We are endangering the oceans and our own survival.

5 **Plan your essay. Turn to pages 57–8 for help with writing an opinion essay and to page 33 for help with useful expressions.**

INTRODUCTORY PARAGRAPH: Give one or two general facts about the oceans.
PARAGRAPHS 2/3/4: Begin paragraph 2 with some more general facts before going on to give reasons for your opinion. Try and use some of the cause and effect language that you have practised in this lesson.
FINAL PARAGRAPHS: Summarise the reasons for your opinion and restate your opinion.

Here are some ways of expressing your opinion:

I believe/think (that) …
It is my belief that …
It seems to me that …
In my view/opinion, …
I strongly believe …

6 **Optional writing task. Write a summary of the reading text *Stop killing the reefs!* on page 87 of this unit. Write about 100 words. Turn to page 25 for help with writing a summary.**

The wreck of a French ship called the *Deliverance*

1 **Look at the picture above. Match the words and phrases below with the items in the picture:**

cargo chest gold coins diamond earrings silver pieces gold bars gems

2 **Close your book and describe as much of the picture as you can remember.**

3 **Read the article below and answer these questions:**

1 Where and when did the *Deliverance* sink?
2 Which country chartered the *Deliverance*?
3 Why might an international row soon begin?

Legal fight over sunken treasure

An international legal row may soon begin between the Spanish government, the French government and an American sea salvage company over a valuable shipwreck.

The salvage company believes it has found the shipwreck of a French ship called the *Deliverance*, which sank in a storm 60 kilometres off Florida in 1755. The ship was chartered by Spain to carry treasure taken from Mexico, Peru and Colombia. Its cargo of gold bars, gems, coins and silver is thought to be worth an enormous amount of money. The Spanish government, the French government and the salvage company may all claim that the sunken treasure belongs to them.

4 **Listen to a news item about the *Deliverance's* cargo. Complete the chart with the correct figures.**

length of ship	________ metres
value of cargo	________ dollars
gold bars	437 kilos
gold coins	________
chests with gems	6
silver pieces	________

5 **Work in groups of three.**

STUDENT A: You represent the Spanish government.
STUDENT B: You represent the French government.
STUDENT C: You represent the American sea salvage company, Sub Sea Research.

Listen to the second part of the news item. Each student must then state the reasons why their government or company believes that the sunken treasure is their property.

6 **Work in the same groups of three. You must come to an agreement about the treasure.**

Useful phrases
It's our government's/company's opinion that …
I suggest that we should …
I (don't) think we should consider (dividing) …
I'm sorry, but I cannot agree (to these conditions/to your suggestion).
One possibility would be to …

7 **Pronunciation. Listen to these phrases, and look at the words in bold. For each sentence, say which sounds links these words. These sounds are not written down, but if you listen carefully you will hear them.**

1 On **the other** hand
2 The ship belonged **to a** French company
3 **Why are** you saying this?
4 There is **no answer**
5 It will **be a** long fight
6 **You are** wrong

Can you work out a rule for the sounds that link the words?

Word watch – Avoiding confusion

1 **Here are 12 pairs of words that are easily confused. Match the words and the definitions.**

compliment ___________	complement ___________
(to give praise / to go together well)	
lastly ___________	at last ___________
(final result / final item in a list)	
unknown ___________	infamous ___________
(not known / known for something bad)	
goal ___________	gaol ___________
(prison / a score in sport or an aim)	
historic ___________	historical ___________
(used to exist in the past / important in history)	
misused ___________	disused ___________
(no longer used / used in a wrong way)	
certainly ___________	surely ___________
(definitely / expressing surprise)	
dairy ___________	diary ___________
(relating to milk products / a record of events)	
desert ___________	dessert ___________
(a dish served at the end of a meal / an area of dry land)	
council ___________	counsel ___________
(to advise / local government)	
uninterested ___________	disinterested ___________
(not interested in something / not favouring any side)	
enquiry ___________	inquiry ___________
(formal investigation / a request for information)	

2 **Are these sentences correct? If not, cross out the mistake and write in the correction.**

1 Certainly you can't have lost your bag – it was here a second ago.

2 I really enjoy historical novels, especially set in the eighteenth century.

3 Martin finally achieved his goal and became a doctor.

4 He waited for an hour and lastly a taxi came.

5 The people were so disinterested in the election that many did not vote.

ANSWERS TO ACTIVITY 1 PAGE 85
1d *2c* *3d* *4c (Earth)* *5a*

Lessons in logic

1 Thomas and Julian went fishing together Thomas caught two more carp than Julian while Julian caught four more trout than Thomas did. If the total number of carp caught was twelve and the total number of trout caught was ten, who caught the most fish? ___________ How many did he catch? ___________

2 Amy has more pocket money than Claire but less than Emma and Jemma. Jemma has less than Mary. Claire receives less than Amy but more than Susie. How many girls have less pocket money than Amy?

____

Who receives the most pocket money?

____

Spelling

Test your own spelling with these exercises. Then check your work in a dictionary.

1 **Add *-ING***

EXAMPLE: plan + ing = planning

hop + ing = ________	upset + ing = ________
develop + ing = ________	hope + ing = ________
try + ing = ________	ski + ing = ________
die + ing = ________	see + ing = ________
marry + ing = ________	refer + ing = ________

2 ***–ABLE* or *–IBLE***

Write each of these words with either the *–able* or *–ible* suffix.

advise ________	reason ________
imagine ________	sense ________
recycle ________	like ________
flex ________	respond ________
agree ________	believe ________

3 ***– ARY, -ERY* or *-ORY***

Add the correct ending to each word:

Mem ________	extraordin ________
Vict ________	Diction ________
discov ________	sal ________
Deliv ________	necess ________

4 **IE or EI**

Insert the letters in the correct order to complete these words.

REC_ _VE	F_ _LD	C_ _LING	BEL_ _VE
V_ _L	FOR_ _GN	CH_ _F	S_ _Z_

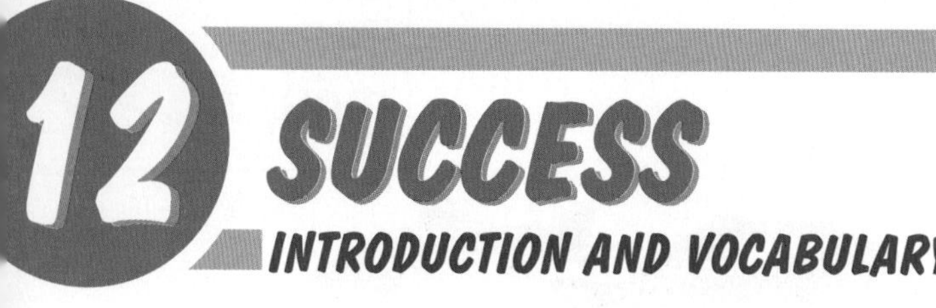

I will SUCCEED today

I am receptive and READY TO LEARN

Today I will overcome ALL OBSTACLES

If we work together, we can achieve ANYTHING WE WANT

Our greatest advantage is our ability to LEARN

Learning is fun, enjoyable and WORTHWHILE

1 **Read the above 'affirmative messages', which are designed to put you in the right mood to be successful in class. Then discuss the questions with the rest of the class.**

1 Do you think affirmative messages like these can help you succeed in class?
2 Which of the affirmative messages appeals to you most?
3 Can you think of a better affirmative message or slogan to put on the wall?

2 **Whole class. Discuss the following questions.**

1 What, for each of you, constitutes a 'successful' day?
2 What would you like to have done by the end of this school year to call it a successful year?
3 Looking ten years into the future, what would you like to have done to call these years a success?

3 **You are going to read a series of quotations in activity 5 from famous people about success. Before you read them, look at the names of the people at the end of each quote. Do you know who they are? What do you know about them? Discuss what you know with the rest of the class.**

4 **Try to match the people and these short biographies.**

1 He studied medicine and raised money to establish a hospital in French Equatorial Africa. Over the years, tens of thousands of Africans benefited from his work.
2 He was the author of *Huckleberry Finn*, a classic of American literature.
3 He built the first mass-produced car.
4 Born in St Petersburg, Russia, she was one of the finest ballerinas of all time.
5 The electric light, the record player and the movie camera are three of the things that he is credited as the inventor of.
6 One of the finest artists in history, he was born in Holland and spent most of his creative years in the south of France.

Check your answers at the bottom of page 99.

5 **Now read the quotations. Decide which is your favourite one and say why. Discuss your choice with the rest of the class.**

How to be a success – quotes from successful people

★ *If you hear a voice within you say 'you cannot paint,' then paint, and that voice will be silenced.* VINCENT VAN GOGH (1853-1890)

★ *Keep away from people who try to belittle your ambitions. Small people always do that, but the really great make you feel that you, too, can become great.* MARK TWAIN (1835-1910)

★ *Whether you think you can or you think you can't - you are right.* HENRY FORD (1863–1947)

★ *Success is not the key to happiness. Happiness is the key to success. If you love what you are doing, you will be successful.* ALBERT SCHWEITZER (1875–1965)

★ *To follow one aim, without stopping. That's the secret of success.* ANNA PAVLOVA (1885-1931)

★ *Genius is one per cent inspiration, ninety-nine per cent perspiration.* THOMAS EDISON (1847-1931)

6 **Before you read the texts on this page, check the following:**

- the four most important professional tennis tournaments in the world are in Australia, France, the USA and Britain. These tournaments are referred to as Grand Slam tournaments
- the US Grand Slam tournament is called the US Open
- Ladies' Doubles is a tennis match with women playing in teams of two
- the Premiership is England's top football (soccer) league
- Everton is a soccer club situated in the city of Liverpool
- a friendly international soccer game is a game between two countries that is not part of the World Cup or other international competition
- 'slam dunk' is a basketball expression, which refers to the habit of tall basketball players jumping and placing the basketball directly into the basket
- the basket rim is the metal ring that holds the string basket in a basketball game

7 **Work in groups of three and follow these instructions.**

- Each student chooses one of the mini-biographies on this page and reads it.
- Then close your books.
- Tell the other students in your group what you remember from the mini-biography.
- Open your books and read the other two mini-biographies.
- Tell your partners what they missed in the summaries.

8 **Read all three summaries and answer the following questions. You may have to give an opinion or work out the answer. If the answer is yes/no, give reasons.**

1. Are most of the Williams sisters great tennis players?
2. How old was Serena Williams when she won her first Grand Slam title?
3. How old was Wayne Rooney when he first played for England?
4. Is it likely that Wayne and John Rooney will ever play in the same team?
5. Does Lebron James always throw the ball into the basket to score points?

9 **Discuss the following questions.**

1. Do you know a young person with a special sporting talent?
2. What kind of people are successful at such a young age?
3. Do you think competition with a brother or sister is important?

Young, gifted – and rich!

Serena Williams

born 26th September 1981

Serena's father was very keen on his daughters becoming professional tennis players, and encouraged them to start playing from an early age. Serena was four and a half when she played in her first tournament and won 46 of the next 49 tournaments she entered as a junior. She turned professional at the age of 14 and made her debut in Quebec, Canada in 1995. Four years later, she won her first Grand Slam tournament, the Australian Open and then on 11th September 1999, she won the US Open after dominating the tournament. The next day, she won the Ladies' Doubles with her sister Venus.

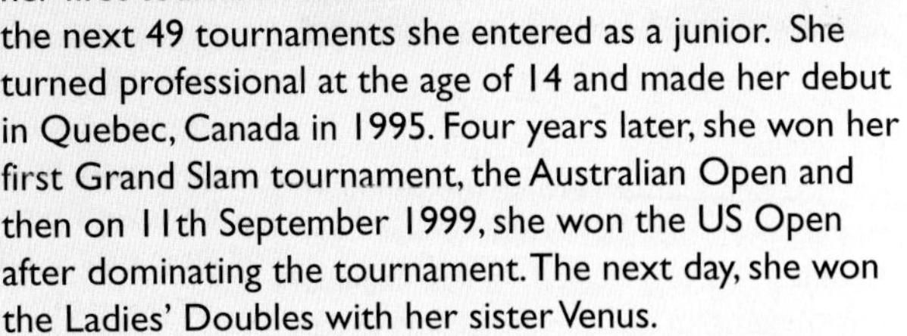

Serena is the youngest of five sisters. Her sister Venus is also a world-class tennis player.

Wayne Rooney

born 24th October 1985

Wayne Rooney was signed by English Premiership soccer club Everton when he was seven and scored 99 goals in a season when he played for the under-10s team. He was in Everton's first team squad by the time he was 16, and at the age of 16 years and 360 days, he became the youngest-ever scorer in the English Premiership. In February 2003, he became the youngest England player of all time when he played in a friendly international against Australia. In April 2003, he won a place in the England starting line-up. He had started fewer than ten Premiership games for Everton.

Wayne has two younger brothers, Graeme, a talented boxer, and John, who is six years younger than Wayne and plays for Everton Juniors.

Lebron James

born 30th December 1984

Two-metre tall Lebron James is the basketball sensation of his generation. He has so much physical power that he regularly breaks the basket rims when he scores with a 'slam-dunk'. He hit the headlines in 2003, when he was 18 and still at high school in Akron, Ohio. After a year when he led his school team to 27 victories in 27 games, he was offered a nine million dollar contract to play in Italy, which he turned down. Almost immediately, an athletic shoe and clothing maker signed him on a seven-year contract worth more than ninety million dollars.

Lebron has a younger brother, who is not involved in sport.

READING

Seb Clover

In January 2003, an English teenager called Seb Clover became the youngest person ever to sail solo across the Atlantic, having sailed single-handed from Tenerife in the Canary Islands to the Caribbean island of Antigua, a distance of more than 4,300 kilometres. The trip took him 25 days to complete. Moreover, he was neck and neck with another boat all the way. **(1)** ____________________

Father and son set out on the voyage from Tenerife in identical yachts on the 19th December 2002. During the race both were followed by killer whales and Seb had to contend with broken rigging. Although his father won the race, Seb had the last laugh. **(2)** ____________________

Sailing triumphantly into English Harbour, Antigua, the teenager admitted that there had been times when sailing alone across the Atlantic had been frightening, **(3)** ____________________

Seb said he was delighted to be back on dry land and with his family. 'Sailing is nice when it all stops and the longer the trip, the better it is when it stops. This is absolutely brilliant!' he added. Describing his lowest point, he said: 'You can't have three meals a day on a boat – you run on snacks – **(4)** ____________________

Asked if it might be an anticlimax to return to school, he said: **(5)** ____________________

Ted Grey, secretary of the Young Explorers Trust, believes that the growth of youth exploration is directly related to schemes such as Operation Drake and Operation Raleigh [see below], which sparked off a yearning for adventure amongst a generation of young people in Britain and other countries. At the beginning, such schemes were once almost entirely the preserve of boys, **(6)** ____________________

Mr Grey added: 'The British are an island nation. **(7)** ____________________. Also, I think adventure runs in the veins of British people – we have it fed to us in children's books and on television.'

Ted said that the exploits of Ellen MacArthur were also an inspiration to other young people. Ellen became the fastest woman and the fastest Briton ever to circumnavigate the globe by sea at the age of 24 in February 2001. **(8)** ____________________. She is currently preparing for a new world record attempt, hoping to go round the world in less than 64 days.

Ellen MacArthur

1 **Scan the article about Seb Clover and choose the best headline from this list.**

Father and son argue after race

Success for 15-year-old Atlantic sailor

Killer whales spoil Seb's triumph

Single-handed teenage sailor reaches Europe

2 **Choose the most likely meaning of these phrases from the text.**

Line 9: he was neck and neck with another boat
- **a** the two boats took almost the same time to complete the race
- **b** the two boats were right next to each other during the race

Line 14: Seb had to contend with broken rigging
- **a** he was required to compete in the race with broken ropes
- **b** he had a problem with the ropes holding his sails

Line 16: Seb had the last laugh
- **a** he was the real winner
- **b** he didn't understand the joke

Line 28: Describing his lowest point
- **a** explaining when he felt most tired and depressed
- **b** talking about the bottom of the boat

Line 30: 'you run on snacks'
- **a** eating snacks helps you run faster
- **b** you survive by eating small amounts of food

Line 39: Operation Drake … sparked off a yearning for adventure
- **a** Operation Drake created the desire for adventure
- **b** Operation Drake stopped the desire for adventure

Line 44: such schemes were once almost entirely the preserve of boys
- **a** boys were the only ones who remembered these schemes
- **b** only boys were involved in the schemes

Line 49: adventure runs in the veins of British people
- **a** adventure makes British people happy
- **b** adventure is a natural thing for British people

Line 50: we have it fed to us in children's books and on television
- **a** we become aware of it through books and television
- **b** we read books and watch television while we're eating

3 **Read the text about Seb Clover and find a place for these sentences and phrases.**

- **a** The other boat was being sailed by his father Ian.
- **b** 'so when I ran out of chocolate I wasn't too pleased.'
- **c** 'He doesn't walk away with the world record and I do,' he said.
- **d** 'It might be a bit dull but I think I'll be pleased to get back and see my friends.'
- **e** but nowadays, boys are outnumbered by girls on expeditions.
- **f** We've always had to cross the water to go anywhere.
- **g** Having battled against icy seas, storms, rigging failures and exhaustion, she became an immediate celebrity.
- **h** but that he had 'still enjoyed every moment'.

4 **Now read the complete text again and decide whether the following sentences are true or false.**

1. Seb Clover's voyage started on an island and finished on an island.
2. He and his father were sailing in the same boat.
3. Seb had a problem with his sails during the race.
4. His journey took him exactly three weeks.
5. He was very happy when he finally got off the boat.
6. He agreed that there was nothing to look forward to on his return to school.
7. His supply of chocolate didn't last for the entire voyage.
8. Operation Drake and Operation Raleigh are responsible for the increase in young people doing exciting and interesting things.
9. There has been a change in the kind of young people who do these things.
10. Ellen MacArthur is hoping to break a world record sometime in the future.

5 **Read the information about Operation Drake and Operation Raleigh.**

You will find out more about Operation Raleigh on page 98.

6 **Discussion. Talk about the following aspects of the kind of challenges described on these pages.**

1. What is the point of sailing single-handed across the ocean?
2. Is it dangerous to allow a 15-year-old boy to do this?
3. What is the value of sailing round the world and becoming involved in 'land-based projects'?

7 **Class survey. How many people would like to do these things? Vote with a show of hands, give your opinions, work out the percentages, and write a report on the findings.**

Who would like to ...

- sail single-handed across the ocean?
- sail across the ocean with school friends?
- sail across the ocean on a boat with an experienced crew?
- travel round the world on a boat with 400 other students?
- work on building and other projects in far-off countries?

In 1978, Prince Charles, the son of the British Queen, launched a two-year, round-the-world youth expedition to commemorate the 400th anniversary of Sir Francis Drake's circumnavigation of the globe. Operation Drake enabled a group of young people to sail round the world and get involved in useful community projects in different countries along the way.

The aim was to help young people develop self-confidence and leadership through their participation in adventure, scientific exploration and community service, accompanied by some of the world's foremost explorers, scientists and geographers. During the two-year project, 414 people participated in the round-the-world voyage on a ship called *The Eye of the Wind*, which followed Sir Francis Drake's route and worked on land-based projects in 16 different countries.

Operation Drake was an outstanding success, surpassing all expectations. This inspired the organizers to launch a much larger and more ambitious programme.

Operation Raleigh, now called Raleigh International, was launched in 1984 and is a youth development charity which inspires people from all backgrounds and nationalities to discover their full potential by working together on challenging environmental and community projects, such as building hospitals, around the world.

Expeditions last for three months and there is a programme of training weekends and workshops beforehand, concentrating on personal development, cultural awareness and global issues. There are eleven expeditions a year to Chile, Costa Rica, Nicaragua, Ghana, Namibia and Borneo. Participants, aged between 17 and 25, have to raise their own funds to finance their trips before they start and many of them look for sponsorship.

1 Phrasal and prepositional verbs
2 Prepositions in final position

Important – read this!

Phrasal verbs are **separable**, that is, a direct object may come (and if it is a pronoun, must come) between the two parts: *Albert Schweizer* ***set a big hospital up/set up a big hospital****. He set it up in French Equatorial Africa.*

Note that some phrasal verbs may be intransitive: *Bob Dylan said you're a success if you can* ***get up*** *and do what you want.*

Prepositional verbs may look like phrasal verbs, but they are **inseparable**: *Schweizer's hospital* ***looked after*** *people suffering from leprosy and it* ***looked after*** *them well.*

All verbs of this kind must have an object, which can be the object of a relative clause: *The people they* ***looked after*** *were very poor.*

All **three-word verbs** belong to this type: *Edison suggested that he didn't* ***come up with*** *his ideas by accident.*

1 Underline the phrasal verbs and circle the prepositional verbs.

1 Can affirmative messages help you get on in class, and do you come across them in your own classrooms?
2 Do you find it easy to live up to your parents' expectations and how would you sum these up?
3 When Henry Ford came out with his revolutionary Model T in 1912, he didn't realise that nearly all later cars would take after it in terms of production system.
4 When JK Rowling's publishers brought it out, the first Harry Potter book was a huge success, but many other publishers had previously turned the book down.
5 Many nineteenth-century artists never sold a painting and Van Gogh certainly took after them in that, but he never gave up and now prices for his work run into millions.

2 Give reasons for your decisions in exercise 1.

3 Use the clues in brackets to complete these sentences.

1 Everton is the team Wayne Rooney ______. (play)
2 I'm not sure which state high school Lebron James ______. (go)
3 Venus, this is a fantastic CD I'm ______! (listen)
4 The company Lebron James ______ makes sports clothing. (pay $90 million)
5 Serena is lucky because she has her sister Venus ______. (practise)
6 Who did Rooney play ______? (first international)

4 Match these descriptions with the sentences above to explain uses of prepositions in final position.

A With the passive ___
B With exclamations ___
C With a question word ___
D With relative clauses ___
E With an infinitive structure ___
F With an indirect structure (noun clause) ___

5 Explain what the object of *come across* is in Ali's first sentence.

That looks interesting. What is it, Ali?
Oh, it's something I've just come across.
Wrong, Ali! It says here that 'come across' is inseparable, so it must have an object!
Why is that, Helmut?
Because 'across' is a preposition!
That's good, Helmut! You're making progress. But it has got an object.

1 **Read the information below. Then explain how the following figures relate to the information:**

$75 $100,000   50 hours   21   grade 12   17   25 hours

Karl Hummel is a seventeen-year-old San Diego teenager who has been running his own computer consultancy business for the past year and a half. He charges $75 an hour and spends at least 50 hours a week online. Most of the time, he's earning money. 'Money is my main motivation,' said Hummel. 'There are teenagers out there who are already millionaires. I want to be a millionaire before I'm 21.'

A grade 12 student at Foxwood High School, Hummel says that his main interest is web design. At the moment, he's developing a website for Nautilus Finance, a company which provides financial advice. Hummel works on his website project for about 25 hours a week.

How much does he earn? His consultancy fees are $75 an hour, and he expects to make more than the US average annual income (about $60,000) on the Nautilus website project.

'That's the job I do during school time,' he said. 'During the summer vacation, I worked on three or four other projects as well. I expect to make more than $100,000 this year.'

2 **In the dialogue below, a journalist interviews Karl. Read the dialogue and find two factual mistakes.**

JOURNALIST: What do you do in your spare time, Karl?
KARL: I run a computer consultancy business.
JOURNALIST: Tell me more.
KARL: I design websites.
JOURNALIST: What are you doing at the moment?
KARL: I'm developing a website for a company called Nautilus Finance.
JOURNALIST: How many hours a week do you work, apart from your schoolwork?
KARL: About 25.
JOURNALIST: How much do you charge?
KARL: $75 an hour.
JOURNALIST: That's a lot for a seventeen-year-old! What's making you do all this?
KARL: I want to be a millionaire.
JOURNALIST: How much do you earn?
KARL: This year I expect to earn about $60,000.
JOURNALIST: That sounds good. Well, thanks for the talk.
KARL: Thanks.

3 **Indirect questions are a way of asking questions more politely. Rewrite the questions in the dialogue above as indirect questions. Choose from the initial phrases below:**

I'd love to know/hear about
I wonder
Would you mind telling me
(Could you) tell me
I'm interested in

EXAMPLE: What do you do in your spare time, Karl?
Tell me what you do in your spare time, Karl.

4 **The journalist in the dialogue in activity 2 needs to show more interest. One way to do this is to use echo questions. Write echo questions for the sentences below.**

EXAMPLE: I run a computer consultancy business.
Do you?

1 I've been working hard.
2 Everyone should work hard.
3 He could have made a lot of money.
4 He didn't enjoy it.
5 I never do that.

5 **Find places in the dialogue where the following expressions would be appropriate:**

It's been my pleasure.
Quite a bit.
I get a real kick out of it.
I've heard so much about you.
I'm sure you'll be a great success/do brilliantly.
Good luck for the future!
I'm aiming high.
It's a real challenge.

6 **The dialogue in activity 2 is rather boring. Karl gives very little information and the journalist needs to comment more and show more interest. Rewrite the dialogue, using the suggestions below.**

- Use some indirect questions and echo questions.
- Use the information about Karl in activity 1 to make his answers more interesting, informative and livelier. Change Karl's answers as much as you want.

  EXAMPLE: What do you do in your spare time, Karl?
  I run a computer consultancy business. I've been doing it for a year and a half now. It's a real challenge.
- Use exclamations to show that the journalist is interested in Karl's replies. Below are some phrases you can use:
  That's amazing!
  Really? That sounds fascinating!
  Goodness! What a (lot of money)!
- Use interjections, eg *well, actually, I see.*
- Think about the kind of comments the journalist might make in answer to Karl's replies.

  EXAMPLE: I design websites.
  You're very young to do something so difficult. I'm fascinated. Tell me more.

7 **Optional writing task. Write a For and Against essay on the following subject. Write about 150 words. Turn to page 33 for help in writing a For and Against essay.**

Happiness is the key to success.

4 LISTENING AND SPEAKING

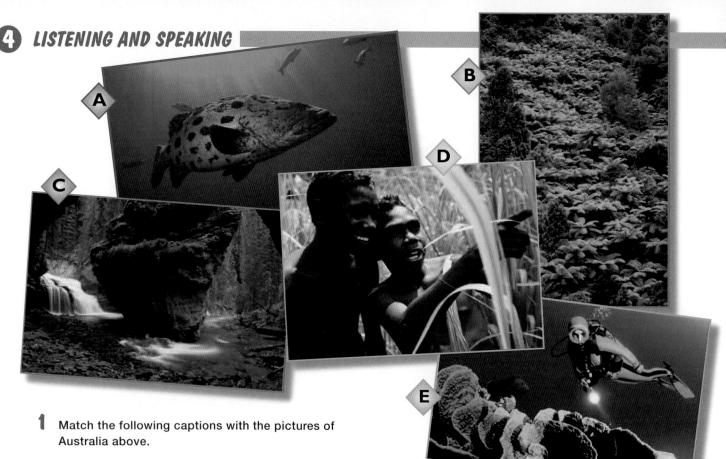

1 **Match the following captions with the pictures of Australia above.**

1 Aborigines following tracks in the Australian bush
2 An area of dense vegetation in the Australian rainforest
3 A diver exploring the Lizard Island coral reef
4 Potato Cod fish in the Great Barrier Reef
5 Johnston Gorge in the Cape York Peninsula

2 **In the reading text on page 95, activity 5, there is information about a youth organisation called Raleigh International. Say what you remember about it. If you have not read the text, turn to page 95 and read it now.**

Would you like to go on one of Raleigh International's expeditions? Say why/why not.

3 **Divide the following words into groups. Explain your reasons for doing so.**

axe rat shovel to clear starfish crowbar leech to renovate octopus

4 **Nineteen-year-old New Zealander Adam Horden recently spent three months working on a Raleigh International expedition. The young people who went on the trip were called 'venturers'. You will hear him talk about his experiences. Listen and number the pictures above in the order that you hear the topics mentioned.**

'Venturer' Adam Horden

5 **Listen again. Answer these questions:**

1 How many parts were there to the expedition?
2 How long did each part last?
3 How did the venturers reach the Johnston Gorge?
4 Why was the experience in the gorge uncomfortable in some ways?
5 What kind of creatures did the divers see in the coral reef?
6 How long were the Potato Cod fish in Cod Hole?
7 During the third month, who did the venturers spend a lot of time with?

6 **Work in small groups. Your task is to plan a youth project that would:**

- attract young people aged 17-25
- give them a sense of real achievement
- be enjoyable and challenging
- help the community in some way

Decide on:

- the location of the project
- the aims of the project
- the length of the project
- what the work would consist of

Present your project to the class. Each student will then vote for the project they would most like to join. The project that receives the most votes is the winner.

Word watch – Measurements

1 **Which unit of measurement would you use to talk about the following? Choose from those in the box. Then add the abbreviation in brackets. The first one has been done for you.**

litres millilitres metres millimetres
centimetres kilometres seconds hours
days ~~months~~ degrees kilogrammes

A baby's age	*months (mths)*
A walk in the country	
The weight of a man	
An amount of petrol for a car	
The temperature	
The length of an exam	
The height of a television	
By how much a race is won or lost in the Olympic Games	
The thickness of a piece of paper	
A long train journey	
The size of a room	
A dose of medicine	

2 **Sometimes it can be tricky to know whether to use a singular or plural form with quantities and amounts. Choose the correct answer each time.**

1 Ten kilometres is/are a long way go walk to school.
2 More than one person are/is going to be eliminated.
3 He gave me a ten-pound/ten-pounds note.
4 Eight pounds are/is a lot to pay for a cinema ticket.
5 One and a half litres of water is/are enough to carry with you.
6 We had a five-day/five-days camping expedition in the mountains.
7 There is/are a man and two women waiting to see you.
8 There is/are three girls and their grandmother sitting outside.

ANSWERS TO ACTIVITY 4 PAGE 92

1 *Albert Schweitzer*	2 *Mark Twain*
3 *Henry Ford*	4 *Anna Pavlova*
5 *Thomas Edison*	6 *Vincent Van Gogh*

Lessons in logic

Read carefully and think hard.

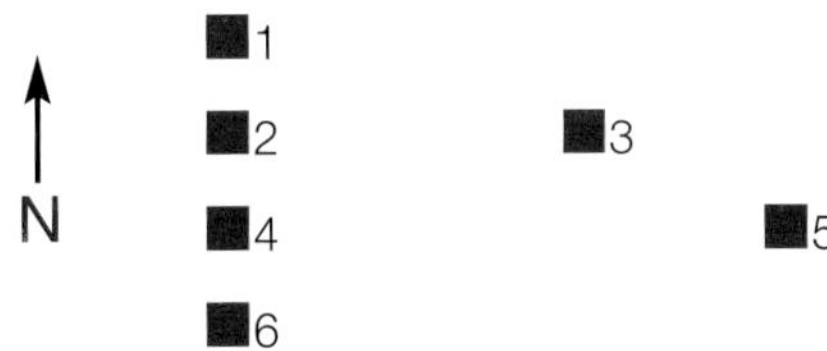

Here are six towns: Allington, Barnbury, Carnforth, Denbi, Ellish and Forecastle. Forecastle is further to the north than Ellish but is not the most northerly town. Barnbury is directly south of one town and directly west of another. Allington is south-east of Carnforth which is south-west of another town. Write the names of each town.

1 ________ 2 ________ 3 ________
4 ________ 5 ________ 6 ________

Spelling – Silent letters

Some words in English contain silent letters – this makes pronunciation difficult and you also have to remember them when it comes to writing.

1 **Underline the silent letters in these words:**

LISTEN CLIMB HANDKERCHIEF WHOSE
AUTUMN WHISTLE PSYCHOLOGY
MUSCLE WEDNESDAY KNIFE DUMB
WHO HOUR SCIENCE COMB

2 **Now add the missing silent letter to these words (be careful to put it in the right place!)**

C A M ________	W I P ________
O F E N ________	E I R ________
S A N W I C H ________	W A K ________
C A S L E ________	C L I M ________
R I T E ________	H A F ________
C O U D ________	O N E S T ________

To check if you are right, count the letters you inserted in exercise 2. There should be 4 x L, 3 x H, 2 x T, 1 x D, 1 x B and 1 x W.

Can you think of any more words yourself which have silent letters?

Write them here: ________________________

____

____

Think of your own language. Do you also have letters that are not pronounced?

13 HAVE YOU HEARD THE NEWS?

INTRODUCTION AND VOCABULARY

The big question – How does news get to your TV screen?

1 **Look at the pictures in the cartoon story. Which of the following items can you see?**

communications satellite   microphone
newsreader   news reporter   satellite telephone
TV camera   TV studio

2 **Scan the cartoon quickly and find the meaning of the following initials, abbreviations and words.**

sojo   OB   ENG   Telstar   mic

3 **Now read the cartoon strip and explain the following in your own words.**

1 a talking head
2 a camera crew
3 broadcast live
4 film footage
5 further afield
6 a communications satellite
7 a built-in mic
8 wireless satellite phone
9 beamed across the world

Note: in this story, the word live is pronounced /laɪv/, not /lɪv/.

4 **Read the cartoon strip again and answer these questions.**

1 In the early days, did television reporters broadcast from other countries?
2 Were the first outside broadcasts shown live on television?
3 What difference did Telstar and other satellites make?
4 What is different about the new ENG cameras?
5 How is it possible to have wireless news gathering technology?

How important is the news?

A recent survey suggests that 80 per cent of teenagers are only interested in reading or listening to news stories about fashion, sport and celebrities.

This questionnaire is designed to find out how true this is in YOUR class.

Tick (✓) the answers.

1 How often do you read a newspaper or news magazine?

- **a** Every day
- **b** More than once a week
- **c** Once a week
- **d** Occasionally
- **e** Never

2 How often do you listen to news programmes on the radio?

- **a** Every day
- **b** More than once a week
- **c** Once a week
- **d** Occasionally
- **e** Never

3 How often do you watch news programmes on TV?

- **a** Every day
- **b** More than once a week
- **c** Once a week
- **d** Occasionally
- **e** Never

4 What kind of news are you interested in? (Tick as many as you like)

- **a** Politics
- **b** Sports and sports people
- **c** Cinema and theatre
- **d** Music
- **e** Science and technology
- **f** Celebrity news
- **g** Other (please specify) ________

Answer either 5 or 6.

5 If you like radio and/or TV news programmes, what do you like about them?

- **a** The presenters are interesting.
- **b** The reports are dramatic.
- **c** The programmes are lively.
- **d** The news items are short.
- **e** Other (please specify) ________

6 If you don't like radio and/or TV news programmes, what don't you like?

- **a** They're boring.
- **b** They're depressing.
- **c** They're always the same.
- **d** I don't understand them.
- **e** Other (please specify) ________

5 Read the introduction to the news survey. Do you think the statistic is true for students in your class?

6 Follow these instructions:

- Write your own answers to the news survey.
- Then work in groups. Compare your answers to other people in your group. Are everyone's answers similar, or are they very different?
- Whole class. Talk about the findings of your group. Indicate the similarities and differences in your answers.

7 The following article is taken from a careers guide called *So you want to be a ...* Before you read it, check the meaning of the following adjectives.

accurate aspiring faint-hearted hard-pressed investigative on-the-spot unflagging willing

8 Now read the article and make notes (in your own words) about the characteristic talents required to be a television news reporter.

9 Discussion. Which students in your class do you think would make the best television news reporter? Give your reasons.

So you want to be a ... Television news reporter

A reporter's job is not for the faint-hearted. It requires a great deal of stamina, physical fitness and unflagging self-motivation. Aspiring television reporters must be strong on perseverance, be willing to work long hours, forget about weekend breaks and holidays and be ready to be on the road at a moment's notice.

Television reporters gather information, investigate leads and write and report stories 'live' or 'on the scene'. Occasionally, they tape their news stories, sometimes called 'packages', for a later broadcast. Reporters must be able to make accurate notes, conduct interviews, determine the focus of a story and complete it quickly.

Because of the increased pace and efficiency of electronic news-gathering techniques, reporters are sometimes hard-pressed to properly complete their stories before they are called upon to go 'live'. Reporters need a good memory, confidence in front of a camera and an ability to speak fluently and improvise.

News editors tell reporters what to do. Some reporters are given specific places that they must attend regularly, such as parliament, police stations or law courts. Others specialize in areas such as medicine, sports, science or weather. While most reporters do on-the-spot news coverage, investigative reporters usually cover stories that can take weeks of information gathering. News correspondents stationed in foreign countries must not only learn how to manoeuvre through difficult situations to locate sources of valuable information but must also overcome language and cultural barriers.

New York Times in shock as reporter's lies are uncovered

DUNCAN CAMPBELL

Los Angeles, Monday May 12, 2003

A New York Times reporter has fabricated and plagiarised dozens of stories that have appeared in the paper, according to a report published on its own front page yesterday. The 'frequent acts of journalistic fraud' committed by Jayson Blair 'represent a low point in the 152-year history of the newspaper,' it said.

Blair, 27, left the paper last week after he was found to have lifted material about a dead soldier's family from the *San Antonio News Express* and pretended to have been at the scene when he was not.

Since then, a team of the paper's reporters has been checking every one of the 673 stories that Blair had filed during his four years on the Times. Blair had often pretended to be in places where he was not and invented information from unnamed sources on major stories.

'It's a huge black eye,' said Arthur Sulzberger, the chairman of the *New York Times* Company. 'It's an abrogation of trust between the newspaper and its readers.'

Blair, who is from Virginia and started on the paper as a graduate trainee, had already been warned about his reporting. Colleagues became suspicious because he seemed to cover so much ground. One of his editors said more than a year ago that he did not believe he should be writing for the Times.

It transpired that Blair had often filed from New York while pretending to be at the scenes of big stories.

'His tools of deceit were a cell phone and a laptop computer which allowed him to blur his true whereabouts, as well as round-the-clock access to databases of news articles from which he stole,' said yesterday's report. Blair apparently looked at photos on the paper's database to glean colour for stories that he would then write as if he had been at the scene when, on some occasions, he was still in the office.

Blair has declined to assist the Times in its investigation. The paper is now examining how he was able to operate for so long when so many editors expressed misgivings.

FROM THE GUARDIAN 12TH MAY 2003

1 Look at the two headlines of the news articles on these pages. The second article appeared three weeks after the first. What can you deduce about the story from the two headlines?

2 The following verbs appear in the first article. Read them in context to find out the meaning. Can you express these sentences in your own words?

1 *fabricate* – Blair had no real information, so he fabricated it.
2 *plagiarise* – He found the story that he wanted to write in another newspaper and plagiarised it.
3 *lift material* – He read an article by someone else and lifted material from it.
4 *cover ground* – It would have been impossible for him to travel so far, to cover so much ground, in the time he had available.
5 *transpire* – When the truth came out, it transpired that he has stolen all the information.
6 *glean colour* – He wasn't there, so he had to glean colour, to add local details, by watching videos of news reports.
7 *decline* – When he was asked to give evidence, he declined – he simply said: 'I won't do it.'
8 *express misgivings* – Other journalists were suspicious of his work and many of them expressed their misgivings to the editor.

3 The first article is about Jayson Blair, a reporter on the *New York Times*, one of the most influential and respected newspapers in the US. Scan the article and find out what you can about Blair's background and work experience.

4 Read the complete article and answer the following questions.

1 Which newspaper broke the news about the activities of Jayson Blair?
2 In which year was the *New York Times* founded?
3 How did Blair write his story about the dead soldier?
4 Approximately how many stories per year did Blair write?
5 What did the chairman of the newspaper company mean by 'a huge black eye'?
6 Was this the first time that there had been suspicions about Blair?
7 What items made it quite easy for him to continue the deception?
8 Has Blair helped the investigation into his activities?

5 Find the following phrases in context and express them in your own words.

EXAMPLE: journalistic fraud

By using this expression, the speaker compares Blair's actions with someone who tells lies to gain money or some other advantage.

- a low point
- unnamed sources
- abrogation of trust
- tools of deceit
- blur his true whereabouts
- round-the-clock access

6 **Before you read the second article, look at the verbs in bold. Check their meanings, and then use them to complete these sentences. Be careful, you may have to change the tense.**

1 The outbreak of rainstorms ... many people to buy an umbrella.
2 I don't like people who ... about how much money they earn.
3 He's going to ... his apartment, so we are thinking of moving in.
4 A volcano in the south of Italy is likely to ... at any time.
5 After listening to the evidence, the judge ... that the accused man was innocent.
6 The exploratory operation on his knee ... that he had a torn ligament.

7 **Scan the article and explain what the following adjectives are used to describe.**

- embarrassing
- abrasive
- hastily arranged/highly emotional
- severe
- senior
- internal

8 **Read the article more carefully and find words and expressions that mean the following. They appear in the same order as in the headline and the article.**

1 (verb) – to voluntarily leave a job ____________
2 (noun) – when someone behaves in a dishonest way ____________
3 (adjective) – deeply respected ____________
4 (noun) – ability to do something in a satisfactory way ____________
5 (verb) – to cry noisily ____________
6 (noun) – to give someone a job ____________
7 (phrasal verb) – the same as 1 (informal) ____________
8 (noun) – someone or something that takes the place or does the job of another ____________

9 **Write a summary of the second article in less than 120 words.**

10 **Complete the chart of verbs, nouns and adjectives from the same root word. Some, but not all, of the missing words are in the text.**

Verb	Noun	Adjective
resign	______	
	competence	______
	______ *	journalistic
______	______ *	managerial/ ______
	______	emotional
conclude	______	

* Two words.

Editor resigns after scandal of reporter's plagiarism

Gary Younge

NEW YORK, 6TH JUNE 2003

The editor of America's most venerated newspaper, the *New York Times*, resigned yesterday after one of the most embarrassing journalistic scandals in American history **prompted** severe criticism of his managerial competence and abrasive style.

In a hastily arranged and highly emotional ceremony in the paper's third-floor newsroom, during which some reporters sobbed, Howell Raines, 60, announced his resignation, picked up his straw hat from the office he had just **vacated** and left the building with his wife. Mr Raines' parting words to his former staff were: 'Remember, when a great story breaks out, go like hell.'

The paper's managing editor, Gerald Boyd, 52, who was appointed by Mr Raines, also resigned.

The paper's publisher, Arthur Sulzberger, told the staff: 'Given the events of the last month, Howell and Gerald **concluded** that it was best for the *Times* that they step down. This is a day that breaks my heart.'

He thanked the pair 'for putting the interest of this newspaper, a newspaper we all love, above their own.' Mr Raines' predecessor, Joseph Lelyveld, will take over while a replacement is found.

The paper's top two editors are the most senior casualties to date of a scandal that **erupted** five weeks ago when the *Times* discovered that Jayson Blair, a 27-year-old reporter, had 'committed frequent acts of journalistic fraud'.

An internal investigation of Blair's work **revealed** plagiarism, deception and inaccuracies relating to 36 of the 73 articles he had written between October 2002 and April this year.

Blair's resignation on May 1 was followed by a front-page story detailing his fabrications. Blair later **boasted** that he had 'fooled some of the most brilliant people in journalism.'

FROM THE *GUARDIAN*

11 **Pronunciation. In which of the words in activity 10 is there a stress change?**

EXAMPLE: *resign resignation – there is a stress change*

12 **Discuss the following questions.**

1 What exactly did Jayson Blair do wrong?
2 Do you think it was right for him to lose his job?
3 Do you think it was right for the editors of the newspaper to lose their jobs?
4 What's the difference between what Jayson Blair did and downloading information from the internet to do your homework?

2 GRAMMAR PRACTICE

1 Reported speech
2 Indirect questions

When we report, for example, a conversation, a certain number of familiar changes usually occur. These happen because the report usually takes place in different circumstances from the original.

1 **Before continuing to read, list some of the changes that often occur and give examples.**

The first ever 'conversation' by telephone was famously when Alexander Graham Bell spoke to his assistant in the next room and said, 'Come here, Mr Watson, I need you.' There are a surprising number of difficulties in reporting this simple message! We might report it in the following way:

Mr Bell told Mr Watson **to** *come/go* (✔) *here* (✘) *there* (✘) *to him* (✔) **(because) he needed him**.

This exemplifies the following typical changes: verb tense (present > past); imperative form (come > **to come**); pronouns (I > he; you > him). But the trouble is particularly caused by the words connected with the ideas of 'here and now', which are often no longer here and now when reported: *come* means 'towards the speaker' and often becomes go when reported; *here* means where the speaker is, and often becomes *there* when reported.

But that only works if it is clear where *there is*! And notice the probable inclusion in the report above of *because*. That idea was obviously implied in the original; in the report it needs to be made explicit. Notice, too, the reporting verb itself. It might be *told*, or perhaps *asked*, *requested* or *ordered*; it couldn't be *said* or *advised*.

Not surprisingly, Mr Bell's words almost always appear as direct, not reported, speech!

Remember, too, that sometimes the time frame may still be the same when the report is made; in that case it is possible but not necessary to change the verb tenses; and the pronoun changes depend on who is reporting to whom. The most important thing to remember is that the changes actually make sense.

2 **Report what you said or wrote in answer to the survey 'How important is the news?' on page 101.**

Reporting direct questions often causes problems with word order. Remember only direct questions have the 'question' word order and are followed by a question mark.

3 **Report these questions, beginning as indicated.**

1 'Have you heard the news, Duncan?'
A friend asked Duncan Campbell ....
2 'What action are you going to take, Mr Sulzberger?'
Reporters demanded to know ....
3 'How does news get to your TV screen in today's world?'
The article posed the question as to ....
4 'Would you like to be a reporter, Mary?'
The teacher asked Mary ....

4 **Correct Helmut's three reports and then report his questions to Ali.**

What did you study in class today, Helmut?
We were talking about the invention of the telephone. Our teacher asked me how did Mr Bell send his message to Mr Watson?
That's wrong, Helmut.
No, it's not, Ali. And I asked the teacher did he text it?
That's wrong again, Helmut.
It was only a joke, Ali! And the teacher told me don't be silly.
And that's wrong too!
How do you know, Ali? Were you listening at the door?

A

Bizarre theft of Mercedes

A Liverpool businessman has had his new Mercedes 380SL stolen from outside his house in broad daylight. The theft took place at about 3pm yesterday, at the home of Clifford Barrett, who describes himself as an import-export specialist. Thieves managed to get his car keys by pushing a fishing rod through the letterbox of his house and hooking the keys, which were on a table in the hall, just inside the front door. The thieves then drove off in the Mercedes.

Barrett was upstairs in bed at the time of the theft, which failed to wake him up. However, his next-door neighbour, journalist Marion Hay, witnessed the crime and called the police immediately. The police arrived within minutes, but the thieves had gone and Barrett's Mercedes has not yet been recovered.

B

How dare they steal my car!

Liverpool businessman Cliff Barrett had the shock of his life yesterday, when thieves stole his brand new silver Mercedes from under his very nose!

Barrett was in bed, having an afternoon snooze, when the thieves made their move. Two men pushed a fishing rod through the letterbox of Barrett's front door. They then hooked the Mercedes car keys, which were on a table in the hall. Then they drove off in the Mercedes. Barrett, who was fast asleep, didn't hear a thing.

'How dare they!' said Barrett, when interviewed by the police. 'I only bought the Mercedes two days ago. It was a beauty. I'm heartbroken!' Police are hoping that Barrett's next-door neighbour, journalist Marion Hay, will be able to lead them to the thieves. Hay saw the men at Barrett's front door but did not realise what they were up to until too late. She then phoned the police, but they arrived too late to catch the thieves. Said Hay, 'I'm angry with myself. If only I'd reacted more quickly! But at least I was able to give the police a good description of the men.'

Police inspector James Trim, in charge of the investigation, is confident he will catch the thieves. Let's hope that Mr Barrett will soon be back driving his 'beauty'.

1 **Look at the words and phrases below. They give you clues about a crime that took place in the north of England. Use the words to work out what the crime was and how it was committed.**

fishing rod   Mercedes 380SL   letterbox   car keys   thieves   hall (of a house)

2 **Read the newspaper articles on this page. One is from a *broadsheet* newspaper, the other is from a *tabloid* newspaper. Broadsheets are more serious. Which article is which?**

3 **Read both articles again. Below is a list of the characteristics of tabloid and broadsheet writing styles. Write (T) beside a tabloid writing characteristic and (B) beside a broadsheet writing characteristic.**

This type of article:

1 often uses quotes from the people involved
2 uses more colloquial language
3 uses formal language
4 has a serious tone
5 often has a lighter tone
6 makes the facts the most important thing
7 gives a lot of information about the people involved

4 **Find colloquial words and phrases in the second article that mean:**

1 very sad
2 a short sleep
3 something/someone very beautiful
4 they were doing something wrong or secret
5 started doing something to achieve an aim
6 a horrible surprise
7 a situation where you should notice something but don't

5 **Write an article for a tabloid newspaper describing a robbery that took place 'under someone's nose'. Write about 150 words. Try and use some of the colloquial phrases used in activity 4. Don't make the article too serious! Include the following:**

- A headline for the article
- Information about the person who was robbed and what was stolen
- A description of the robbery
- A witness who was able to describe the thieves
- Quotes from people involved

6 **Optional writing task. Imagine that you are businessman Cliff Barrett and that the police find your car. Write a formal letter from Barrett to police inspector James Trim, thanking him for his work. Write about 150 words.** **Turn to page 9 for help with writing a formal letter.** **Begin the letter: *Dear Inspector Trim*.**

4 LISTENING AND SPEAKING

1 **Look at the map of Australia and answer these questions.**

1 Can you name the three numbered cities? Choose from this list:
Sydney Perth Melbourne
2 The Great Barrier Reef is a coral reef. What can you remember about coral reefs from Unit 11?

2 **You are going to listen to some news reports on an Australian radio news programme. Look at the vocabulary items below and predict what each news item is about.**

1 fire-fighter bush fire casualty under control
2 Great Barrier Reef commercial fishing protect ban shipping
3 bullying victim private school sum (of money) abusive email physical violence
4 safety cliff rescue (verb and noun)

3 **Listen to the bulletin. Answer these questions:**

1 Were you right in your predictions?
2 There is one extra news item that was not included in activity 2. What is it about?

4 **Listen again. Answer these questions. The answers are all figures.**

Item 1
1 How long has the fire been raging?
2 How many people have had to leave their homes?
Item 2
3 How much does the government want to increase protected areas by?
4 What percentage of the reef is protected at present?
Item 3
5 How many pupils have been bullied?
6 How much money are parents believed to have won in recent years?
Item 4
7 How old is the man who was rescued?
8 How high was the cliff?
Item 5
9 How many dollars are paid to children who leave school early?
10 What percentage of full-time students now complete the final year?

5 **Work in pairs. The third news item was about bullying. Discuss these questions:**

1 Why do you think bullying takes place?
2 Do you have it in your schools?
3 Why do you think some people bully others?
4 What would you say to a person who has been bullied?

6 **Work in groups of three. Write a news report containing three short, different news items. Below are some suggestions for topics:**

governmental news education accidents
crime health the weather the environment
celebrity news

7 **Pronunciation. Work in the same groups. Each person in the group chooses one of the news items that the group has written. Then follow these instructions:**

- check the pronunciation of difficult words (ask the teacher, if necessary)
- decide which are the important words to stress
- practise reading the news item aloud

Each student reads out their news item. The group can then offer feedback about the reading, and ask the student to read certain sentences again.

EXAMPLE: *That was very good. But I think the second sentence could have been clearer. Why don't you read it again?*

8 **Work in the same groups.**

- Groups read their news report to the class, each person taking turns to read a news item.
- Students from other groups must then briefly say what each news topic was about.
- Finally, the class votes for the best, most interesting news bulletin.

Word watch – Writing numbers

1 **Write the following numbers and amounts in words.**

EXAMPLE: 5,031 = five thousand and thirty-one

1,101	
1/4	
0.5	
75%	
30/07/1986	
020-5340-6690	
Elizabeth II	
£3.99	
$1.35	
E2.50	

2 **Now answer these questions, writing your answer in figures.**

1 What's two hundred and two plus one hundred and eight?

2 What's nineteen take away seven?

3 What's six times twenty-one?

4 What's one hundred and forty-four divided by twelve?

5 If you drive at sixty kilometres per hour, how far will you travel in two and a half hours?

6 If membership of a club costs five pounds fifty a week, how much will it cost for a year?

Lessons in logic

There are six shops in a street, arranged like this:

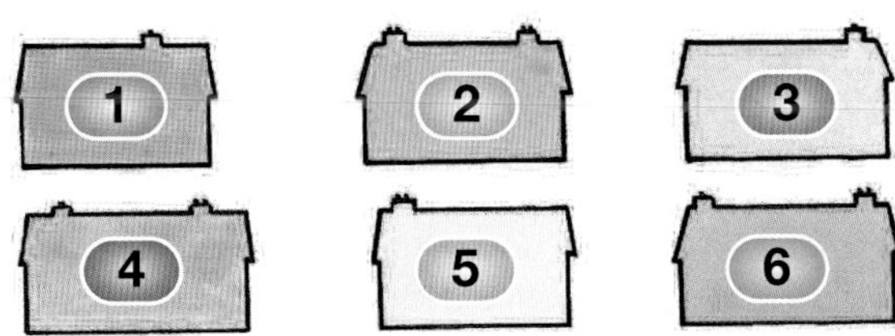

The bakery is between the newsagent's and the grocer's. The pharmacy is opposite the bakery. The bookshop is at number 2. The dry cleaner's is not opposite the grocer's.

Where is each shop?

1 ______ 2 ______
3 ______ 4 ______
5 ______ 6 ______

Talking about size – small, large and in-between

1 **Some suffixes when added to a noun make the item smaller, eg: a flatlet is a small flat. Underline any of the following that are diminutives (a word implying smallness).**

duckling hostess leaflet statuette happiness discussion booklet droplet gosling lifelike kitchenette fishmonger outermost

2 **Can you match the adult animals with their young?**

Adults: dog cat cow horse lion frog butterfly

Young: calf caterpillar cub tadpole kitten foal puppy

3 **Number these from 1 (smallest) to 5 (largest) and underline the middle in size.**

a teenager baby toddler child adult
b elephant ant rabbit goat camel
c whale sardine shark carp octopus
d motorbike tractor skateboard caravan lorry
e century millennium day year decade
f bush branch leaf tree forest
g apple melon orange strawberry banana
h violin guitar piano clarinet xylophone

Did you know? Surprising statistics

On weekdays, 81% of adults in the UK are asleep by midnight and 77% are awake by 8am.

Do people go to bed later or earlier in your country?
Do they get up later or earlier?
Why do you think different countries have different habits? (working hours/school/weather etc.)
Do you think it would be different at the weekends and why?

HEROES AND VILLAINS

INTRODUCTION AND VOCABULARY

Star Wars

The Story of Star Wars

Star Wars was the creation of film director George Lucas, but his original idea was to make a film based on a 1930s cartoon strip called *Flash Gordon*, written by Alex Raymond. In the cartoon strip, Flash battled against the evil tyrant Ming the Merciless in a world of hi-tech monsters.

Lucas couldn't get the rights to use the characters so he developed his own ideas. The *Star Wars* films contain many recognisable elements from the cartoon strip and movie versions, including the concept of a war between the Imperial Forces and the Rebels. He was also influenced by other films he had seen and books he has read.

In 1975, Lucas offered to make the film for Universal Studios, where he had already been a successful director. The studio bosses thought the idea was too complicated and silly and turned it down – a decision they have regretted ever since. Eventually, Twentieth Century Fox gave Lucas ten million dollars to film the first part. The result was possibly the most influential film in the history of cinema. The first *Star Wars* movie, which opened in May 1977, became the most successful film in North American movie history, making more than 290 million dollars in its first year.

Darth Vader is the villain of the *Star Wars* films. Standing two metres tall and dressed in flowing black robes and black body armour, Vader is the servant of the evil Emperor and the symbol of the Emperor's doctrine of rule through fear and terror.

The hero of the early *Star Wars* films is Luke Skywalker, a humble farm boy who rises to become commander in the Alliance forces against the Empire. One of his first assignments is to rescue Princess Leia, the leader of the Rebels and Darth Vader's prisoner. Astonishingly, the villainous Darth Vader turns out to be the father of both the heroic Luke Skywalker and the strong Princess Leia. Not only that, but Luke and Princess Leia are twins!

1 Which of the following words describe heroes and which describe villains?

bold brave courageous evil gallant heroic infamous tyrannical valiant villainous wicked

2 Work in small groups. Look at the photo of fictional heroes and a villain. Do you know anything about them? Discuss what you know or can imagine about them. Try to use words from activity 1 when you describe them. Tell the rest of the class what you discussed in your group.

3 Whole class. Compare the characters on these pages to fictional heroes and villains from your culture.

4 Discuss the following questions.

1. Why do stories need heroes?
2. Do good stories also need villains?
3. What kind of things do heroes do?
4. What kind of things do villains do?

5 Look at *The Story of Star Wars* on the previous page. Which of the illustrated characters on the page do you expect to read about in it?

6 Read the complete text and explain the following references.

1. *Lucas couldn't get the rights to use the characters* – which characters?
2. *The Star Wars films contain many recognisable elements from the cartoon strip* – which cartoon strip?
3. *a decision they have regretted ever since* – what decision?
4. *The studio bosses thought the idea was too complicated* – which studio bosses?
5. *One of his first assignments is to rescue Princess Leia* – whose assignment?

7 Read *How do they make films like Star Wars?* and answer these questions.

1. What kind of things are possible with special effects?
2. Why is it necessary to build miniatures?
3. What is the advantage of using the blue screen technique?
4. Has George Lucas's special effects company only worked on the *Star Wars* films?

8 Work in pairs and follow these instructions.

- Write down the name of a film you have seen where there were good special effects.
- Show the name of the film to your partner.
- If you know the film that your partner has written down, discuss the special effects in the film.
- If you don't know the film, ask your partner to describe the special effect.
- Describe the special effect you have discussed to the rest of the class.

How do they make films like *Star Wars*?

To make a movie like *Star Wars*, you need special effects and visual effects. 'Special effects' refers to things that are done to a scene as it is filmed. This includes weather effects (wind, rain, snow, fog, etc.) and other special techniques like rear projection and miniatures.

What does rear projection mean?

Rear projection involves projecting a picture onto a screen while live action is filmed in front of it. Both the background on the screen and foreground action are combined into a single image in the film. In *Star Wars*, this is used every time you see someone flying a space ship, for example.

What are miniatures?

Miniatures are scale models of things which cannot be built in their real size, either because the technology doesn't exist or because it would too expensive. An example would be the large animal-shaped tanks in *Star Wars*. There are also some excellent miniatures in films like *Men in Black*.

What's the difference between special effects and visual effects?

Visual effects are added after the scene has been shot. Often this is achieved by a technique called 'blue screen'. With blue screen, actors and miniatures can be filmed in totally imaginary situations – in space ships, hanging on a rope over a cliff, flying through the air like Superman. The technique is also used when there is a fire or explosion in the film – something that the actors don't want to be near!

Who makes all these things possible?

There were no special effects workshops when they started filming *Star Wars*, so George Lucas started his own – a company called Industrial Light and Magic (ILM). ILM has created effects for almost every fantasy film made since then, including *Jurassic Park* and *Harry Potter*. The technicians at companies like ILM can now create completely artificial animated characters and settings, which appear in almost every major film we see today.

1 **Read the background information about *The Arabian Nights.***

The tales of the Arabian Nights

The tales contained in *The Arabian Nights* probably originated from travellers and traders who travelled the silk route, which extended from northern China to the Middle East. These travellers would break their journeys in caravanserais. Caravanserais were large inns which could accommodate caravans – companies of traders who travelled together through the desert with camels. There, the travellers would tell stories to entertain each other. The stories were kept alive by professional story tellers, who would perform in coffee houses in Persia, Arabia and Egypt.

The first identifiable written version of *The Arabian Nights* seems to have been a book of Persian tales called *Hazar Afsanah* (A Thousand Legends), translated into Arabic about 1,200 years ago. A fragment of paper dating from the ninth century and containing the opening lines of one of the main stories was discovered in the Egyptian desert in the late 1940s.

The stories reflect the enormous and highly civilised trading world of the ninth to thirteenth centuries, stretching from Spain across North Africa to Cairo, across the Arabian peninsula, up to Damascus and Baghdad, further north to Samarkand, across what is now Afghanistan, down into India and beyond. Part of the success of the stories was based on the fact that many of the people in the region shared a language, the Arabic of the Koran.

2 **Before you read *The Adventures of Sindbad the Sailor*, check the meaning of the following verbs. Then answer the questions.**

squander stroll plunge cling float drift perish

1 Which verb means *die*?
2 Which ones have something to do with water?
3 Which one means *waste*?
4 Which one means *walk*? Does it mean fast or slow walking?
5 Which one means *hold*?

3 **Read part 1 of the text. Work out the meaning of the following expressions and express them in simpler English.**

1 I had squandered it recklessly.
2 We found ourselves becalmed close to a small island.
3 We sat down to enjoy the repast which we had brought with us.

4 **Do the following sentences mean the same or the opposite of phrases and sentences in the text?**

1 The wind got stronger and our boat moved very quickly.
2 The captain allowed those who wanted to to go onto the island.
3 I was one of the people who did that.
4 As soon as we got onto the island, we lit a fire.

5 **Read part 2 and answer these questions.**

1 Did the people on the 'island' expect the sudden and violent trembling?
2 What caused the trembling?
3 What did the people on the 'island' do?
4 Why wasn't Sindbad able to do the same thing?

6 **Decide if these sentences are true or false.**

1 Sindbad was able to control his movement in the water.
2 He was in the water all day and all night.
3 He rested when he reached the top of the cliff.
4 The man he met was the king of the island.

7 **Find words in part 3 of the text which mean the following:**

start a journey tell look for approach

8 **Now read the whole of part 3 and answer these questions.**

1 What sort of welcome did Sindbad get from the king?
2 What kind of people did Sindbad look for?
3 How long had the ship that he saw been in port?
4 What did he see written on some of the packages?
5 What did he ask the captain?

9 **Read part 4 of the text and match the words and expressions from the text on the left, with their meanings on the right.**

1	merchandise
2	resolve
3	drown
4	audacity
5	just
6	for the sake of
7	invent
8	falsehood

a	nerve
b	honest
c	goods
d	in order to
e	decide
f	lie
g	die in the water
h	make up

The Adventures of Sindbad the Sailor

1 I had inherited considerable wealth from my parents and, being young and foolish, I at first squandered it recklessly, but then I resolved to live a more sensible life and joined a company of merchants who traded by sea, embarking with them at Balsora. We set sail towards the East Indies by way of the Persian Gulf. From time to time, we went on land and sold or exchanged our merchandise.

One day, the wind dropped suddenly and we found ourselves becalmed close to a small island, which rose only slightly above the surface of the water. The captain gave permission to all who wished to go onto the island and amuse themselves. I was among the number, and after strolling about for some time, we lit a fire and sat down to enjoy the repast which we had brought with us.

2 Suddenly, we were startled by a sudden and violent trembling of the island. We realised to our horror that it was no island – it was the back of a sleeping whale! Those who were nearest to the boat threw themselves onto it, others jumped into the sea, but before I could save myself, the whale plunged suddenly into the depths of the ocean, leaving me clinging to a piece of the wood which we had brought to make our fire.

I was left at the mercy of the waves. All that day, I floated up and down and when night fell, I despaired for my life. I clung to the piece of wood and great was my joy when the morning light showed me that I had drifted close to an island. The cliffs were high and steep, but I was able to climb up. At the top of the cliffs, I lay on the ground, more dead than alive, till the sun was high in the heavens. Suddenly, I heard voices, and in a moment a man appeared who asked me how I came upon the island. I told him my adventures, and heard in return that he was a servant of Mihrage, the king of the island.

3 Early the next morning we set off and when we reached the capital, I was graciously received by the king, to whom I related my adventures. He ordered that I should be well cared for and provided with such things as I needed. Being a merchant, I sought out men of my own profession, and particularly those who came from foreign countries, as I hoped in this way to hear news from Baghdad and find out some means of returning there.

One day, down at the quay, I saw a ship which had just cast anchor, and was discharging her cargo, while the merchants to whom it belonged were busily directing the removal of it to their warehouses. Drawing nearer, I noticed that my own name was marked upon some of the packages, and after having carefully examined them, I felt sure that they were indeed those which I had put on board our ship at Balsora. I then recognised the captain of the vessel, but as I was certain that he believed me to be dead, I went up to him and asked who owned the packages that I was looking at.

4 'There was on board my ship,' he replied, 'a merchant of Baghdad named Sindbad. One day he and several of my other passengers landed upon what we supposed to be an island, but which was really an enormous whale floating asleep upon the waves. When the passengers lit a fire, the whale plunged into the depths of the sea. Several of the people who were upon it perished in the waters, including the unlucky Sindbad. This merchandise is his, but I have resolved to dispose of it for the benefit of his family if I should ever chance to meet with them.'

'Captain!' said I, 'I am that Sindbad whom you believe to be dead, and these are my possessions!' When the captain heard these words he cried out in amazement, 'What is the world coming to? In these days, there is not an honest man to be met with. Did I not with my own eyes see Sindbad drown, and now you have the audacity to tell me that you are he! I should have taken you to be a just man, and yet for the sake of obtaining that which does not belong to you, you are ready to invent this horrible falsehood.'

10 Now read the complete passage and answer these questions.

1 Re-state in your own words the story of the tragic events as told by the captain.
2 Does the captain give a truthful account of the events?
3 What is the captain's reaction when Sindbad says who he is?
4 Is Sindbad a hero?
5 If he's a hero, is there a villain in the story?

11 Work in groups. Devise an ending for the story. Follow these instructions.

- Decide if it is a happy ending or a sad ending.
- Write the continuation of the conversation between Sindbad and the captain.
- Introduce at least one other character.
- Act out your ending of the story for the rest of the class.

2 GRAMMAR PRACTICE

1 Relative clauses
2 Adjectives as nouns

1 Match 1-8 with a-h to form eight sentences with relative clauses (note the punctuation).

1 The people who ___
2 Sindbad the Sailor is a character ___
3 A Flash Gordon adaptation was the film that ___
4 *Men in Black*, which ___
5 The *Hasan Alsanah*, whose ___
6 Darth Vader was the villain ___
7 The special effects company whose ___
8 Travellers on the Silk Route, who ___

a also used miniatures, was another popular film.
b founder was George Lucas, is called ILM.
c many Europeans know and love.
d would stop at caravanserais, loved listening to stories.
e kept the tales alive were often professional storytellers.
f was George Lucas's original project.
g title means 'A thousand legends', was a book of Persian tales.
h everyone hated.

2 Write eight more sentences with the same constructions as in exercise 1.

It is possible to use some adjectives as nouns. They take the definite article (*the*), refer to all those in the group and have a plural verb: *In this country the elderly are usually looked after by their families, but an elderly person without a family may find life more difficult.* Note that adjectives cannot be used to represent a singular noun.

3 Complete these sentences with words from the box and adding any extra articles or nouns needed.

old blind rich poor sick

1 ___ have many advantages but ___ is not always a happy one.
2 How old are ___? I know ___ of 85 and she still seems young!
3 That ___ over there is John Jones and he spends a lot of time collecting money for ___ even though he is blind himself.
4 This hospital offers treatment for ___ whether they are rich or poor, but especially for ___, who have nowhere else to go for help.

4 Re-arrange these sentences paying special attention to the order of adjectives. (See Grammar Reference, section 17 for help with the order of adjectives.)

1 a/building/white/is/small/this/wonderful/stone/.
___.
2 South African/stamps/have/triangular/any/you/postage/do/? ___.
3 like/Chinese/you/brooch/jade/beautiful/this/do/tiny/? ___.
4 Brazilian/visited/they/incredible/stadium/Maracana/football/enormous//the/called/.
___.

5 Correct two of Helmut's sentences. Explain *you do, they do*. What do you think *out of order* means?

1 **Explain the meaning of these proverbs. Which two proverbs have more or less the same meaning?**

EXAMPLE: There's no smoke without fire.
This means that if there is gossip about someone, it may be true, because there must be some reason for the gossip.

1 All that glitters is not gold.
2 A stitch in time saves nine.
3 You can't judge a book by its cover.
4 It never rains but it pours.

2 **Read the story below, narrated by Matthew, a thirteen-year-old Australian boy. Answer these questions.**

1 What is Matthew's opinion of his uncle, Joe, before the event he describes?
2 What does Matthew learn about Joe?
3 Which of the proverbs in activity 1 is the last line of the story closest in meaning to?
4 This is a true story. What is your reaction on learning this?

Until last summer, everyone regarded my father, a highly successful businessman, as the 'special one' in the family. Uncle Joe, my dad's younger brother, didn't seem to mind. Joe is an engineer, and a good one, but like many Australians, it's the outdoor life that Joe loves most, and when he isn't working, Joe lives a peaceful life, barbecuing, swimming, surfing, playing with his kids, and just generally lazing around.

Our two families have always been very close, and last December, as usual, we went on holiday together. One afternoon, Joe, myself and my eleven-year-old brother Mike, were at the beach. Mike had gone for a swim and Joe and I were playing a fast game of volleyball. Suddenly we heard terrible screams. Turning to look at the sea, we saw the thing that every Australian fears most – a black shark's fin only a few metres from the shore. And it was attacking Mike, who was flailing desperately around. My legs turned to jelly and I almost fainted. But the next thing I knew, Joe was running into the sea and swimming incredibly fast towards Mike. There were splashes, and shouts, then Joe started heading towards the shore with Mike in his arms. As soon as people had seen what was happening, they had called the emergency service, and Mike, who was covered in blood, was rushed to hospital.

To everyone's astonishment, Mike survived. When we asked Joe how he had done it, he said that he had kept punching the shark really hard until it moved away. When we asked him why he had done it, he said, 'I got angry.' I realised then that you should never judge people by appearances.

3 **Explain in what way the story illustrates the last line.**

4 **When we tell a story, we need to:**

1 Start with a first sentence that interests the reader. *Why is the first sentence interesting?*
2 Set the scene. *How does the writer set the scene?*
3 Describe the main event in detail. *Which details in the second paragraph do you find the most interesting?*
4 Have one or two surprises in the story. *What are the surprises in the story?*
5 Write a conclusion. It can say something general that the writer has learnt or surprise the reader in some way. *Which does this story do?*

5 **In order to narrate a story and make it interesting, we can use the following language items. Find examples of each of these items of language in the story.**

Time words and phrases (eg *when, after*)
Present participles (eg *leaving*)
Direct speech (eg *'Where are you going?' he asked.*)
Indirect speech (eg *He asked where I was going.*)

6 **Choose the correct word or phrase from the underlined words.**

1 The moment/Immediate my parents heard the news we rushed to the hospital.
2 My uncle went with Mike to the hospital. Meanwhile/While, I had phoned my parents and told them the news.
3 Sharks sometimes come close to the shore while/during the summer months.
4 It was not for/until a week later that Mike regained consciousness.
5 First/At first he could only walk a few steps at a time. But he slowly began to improve.
6 I've known him since/for years and years.
7 My parents came as soon as/as they heard the news.
8 Before leave/leaving the house we had been laughing and joking.
9 When/While people saw what was happening, they started screaming.
10 The Doctor left. After that/Then he came back in again.

7 **Write another story of about 150 words, ending with the last sentence of the story in activity 2.**

I realised then that you should never judge someone by appearances.

- Plan your story: spend the first five minutes writing any ideas that come into your head.
- Write down the main things that you want to include.
- Write the story.

8 **Optional writing task. Write a summary of *The Adventures of Sindbad the Sailor*, texts 1 and 2, on page 111 of this book. Write about 100 words. Turn to page 25 for help with writing a summary.**

1 **The picture on this page shows a scene from a story in *The Arabian Nights*. Describe the picture using the following words to help you.**

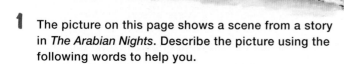

genie fisherman seashore nets vase

Do you recognise the story? What is it about?

2 **Read this story from *The Arabian Nights*. Try to complete the missing sentence in each section.**

1 Once upon a time there was an old fisherman who was extremely poor. Early one morning he threw his nets and as he pulled them in he felt a great weight. But ______________________________

2 The old man threw his nets out twice more, but with no success. Then he threw his nets for the fourth time and pulled in a heavy yellow vase which was sealed with lead. He took his knife and opened the seal. A ______________________________

3 'Tell me why you have been shut up in that vase,' the terrified fisherman cried. The genie told him that the king of the genies had shut him up in the vase for three hundred years in order to punish him. The genie became so angry that he vowed to kill the person who released him. The fisherman ______________________________

4 Then the fisherman had a clever idea. 'I really can't believe you were in that vase,' he said. 'You're much too big. I can't believe it unless I see you go back inside the vase.' The genie ______________________________

5 The fisherman quickly took the lid and placed it on the vase so that the genie could not escape again. 'If you take off the lid,' the genie cried, 'I will repay you. 'No,' answered the fisherman. 'I ______________________________

3 **Listen to the complete story. As you listen, write down the missing sentence(s) in each section. You will hear each of the missing sentences twice.**

Compare the missing sentences from the complete story with the sentences you wrote in activity 3. Were your sentences similar to the sentences in the listening passage?

4 **Listen to four extracts from the story. Say which section each extract is from.**

5 **Work in small groups. Take turns to tell part of the story you have just heard.**

6 **Work in small groups. Think of another traditional story. Look up any new vocabulary you need or ask your teacher for help. Then take turns to tell the story.**

Word watch – Sounds

Onomatopoeia (pronounced ON-O-MAT-O-PAY-A) means using words which sound like the noise they are describing. Match each of these examples with the correct item.

BUZZ HISS RAT-A-TAT-TAT
MIAOW PLOP BANG ZZZZ

1 A cat waiting to be fed will ______________.
2 When someone falls asleep and starts snoring, we can hear ______________.
3 An insect flying around you will ______________.
4 If a door closes very violently, you will hear ______________
5 A snake when it is agitated will ______________.
6 A hat floating over a lake will land on the water with a ______________.
7 If someone knocks loudly on a door, you'll hear ______________.

A noisy world

1 What noise do these objects make? Link the two words together.

clocks	patters
stairs	rings
coins	creaks
rain drops	slams
doors	ticks
telephones	jingles

2 And these people?

Someone with a bad cold	sob
Someone who is crying	cheer
Someone who is out of breath	sniff
Someone who is amused	pant
Someone who is amazed	chuckles
Someone who has really enjoyed something	gasp

Lessons in logic

1 Vincent and Victor have both been to see five films during the past month. Victor saw two films that Vincent had already seen.

How many different films did they see altogether? ______

2 To get to the cinema, Vincent has a 10-minute walk to the station and he then gets straight onto a train to the centre of town where he then has just a five-minute walk to the cinema. One evening the train was 15 minutes late and he missed the beginning of the film. If he left home at 6.15 and got to the cinema at 7.03 pm, how long was the train journey when there were no delays? ______

How long was the whole journey door to door usually? ______

Abbreviations

An abbreviation is a short form of a word or phrase make by leaving out some of the letters of the word or by using only the first letters. Abbreviations are very commonly used in English to save time and space when speaking and writing.

1 Do you know these abbreviations connected with times? Write the full form.

mins	yrs
Mon	Sun
Nov	Aug
am	pm

2 And these connected with places? Write the full form.

N	W	SE
St	UK	US

3 Now write the abbreviation yourself. All these concern people.

female ______ male ______ Prime Minister ______
Member of Parliament ______ Doctor ______
Doctor of Philosophy ______ Junior ______
senior ______ Very Important Person ______

4 Choose from these abbreviations to complete the sentences.

BA SOS HQ BBC asap PTO

1 The company's __________ was in Cairo.
2 She wrote __________ at the end of her letter as she had written a final point on the other side.
3 Their __________ was picked up by the coastguard's radio and they were all rescued.
4 I hope to pass my __________ exams and graduate from university next summer.
5 The students were able to listen to the __________ World Service to do research into current affairs.
6 Please reply __________ as I need to know numbers.

SEVEN THOUSAND LANGUAGES

INTRODUCTION AND VOCABULARY

1 Look at the illustration. The slogan connects the diversity of language and the unity of the planet we live on. Can you think of another slogan for a similar badge?

2 Look at the list of the ten most widely spoken languages in the world on these pages. Complete the text, using these languages. You may also have to add the name of a country.

Arabic French Mandarin Chinese Portuguese Russian Spanish

3 Read all the information about languages and answer these questions. Use your own words in your answers, don't just quote from the text.

1 How did Mandarin Chinese get its name?
2 Does the number of speakers of English include people like you, learning the language at school?
3 Why is it unlikely that Hindustani will overtake Mandarin as the world's most spoken language?
4 What is the difference between Latin America and South America?
5 What is the 'Mother Country' and what is its capital city?
6 Why are there speakers of Arabic in non-Arabic countries?
7 What percentage of Bengali speakers live in Bangla Desh?
8 How did Portuguese spread round the world?
9 Are Malay and Indonesian different languages?
10 Is French the language of diplomacy?

4 The following list of languages didn't make into the Top Ten, but are spoken widely in the world. Say what you know about the languages themselves and/or the places where they are spoken. Don't worry if you've never heard of some of them!

German Japanese Urdu Korean Tamil Marathi Cantonese Vietnamese Javanese Italian Turkish Tagalog Thai

There is information about some of the languages at the bottom of page 123.

The world's top ten languages

1 ______________ – More than one billion speakers

The language with the most native speakers in the world is spoken in the most populated country in the world. ______________ is spoken by more than 70 per cent of the population of ______________. Before the twentieth century, ______________ was referred as *guan hua*, which means 'speech of the officials'. Westerners named it ______________, because it as the language used by the imperial magistrates, who were called ______________s. In Hong Kong and other areas of the south of the country, the language of education and formal speech remains Cantonese, although ______________ is becoming increasing influential.

2 English – 750 million speakers

It is estimated that more than 375 million people speak English as their first language, with possibly another 375 million speaking it as a second language. This does not include the people who speak it as a foreign language.

The United States has the largest number of native English speakers – more than 226 million Americans speak the language as a mother tongue. More than 80 per cent of the world's electronically stored information is in English and two-thirds of the world's scientists read in English. Of the estimated 500 million users of the Internet, some 80 per cent currently communicate in English. It is the official language, or has special status, in more countries than any other language, more than 75 in total. Apart from Great Britain and the US, there are native speakers in countries all over the world, including Australia, South Africa, Canada, New Zealand and many islands in the Caribbean.

3 Hindustani – nearly 500 million speakers

Hindustani is India's primary language, and it includes a huge number of dialects (of which the most commonly spoken is Hindi). Many predict that the population of India could one day be more than the population of China, but the importance of English in India would prevent Hindustani from becoming the number one language of the world.

4 ________________ – 392 million speakers

As well as the European country which gives it its name, ____________ is spoken in just about every country in Latin American (South and Central America), and also Cuba, some islands in the Caribbean and by 25 million people in the US.

5 ________________ – 277 million speakers

One of the six languages in the United Nations, ____________ is spoken not only in the Mother Country, but also in nearby countries such as Belarus, Kazakhstan and Ukraine, and there are two million ____________ speakers in the US, including 600,000 in New York!

6 ________________ – 246 million speakers

____________, one of the world's oldest languages, is spoken in the Middle East, with speakers found in countries such as Saudi Arabia, Kuwait, Iraq, Syria, Jordan, Lebanon and Egypt. Furthermore, because ____________ is the language of the Qur'an, millions of Moslems in other countries speak it as well. So many people have a working knowledge of the language that it was made the sixth official language of the United Nations in 1974.

7 Bengali – 211 million speakers

Bangla Desh, with a population of about 120 million people, and West Bengal in India are the two places where Bengali is spoken as a native language. India has more than 67 million Bengali speakers, and these figures do not include Indians who reside in various other countries. For instance, the United Arab Emirates has about 70,000 Bengalis and the US and Britain have a far greater number.

8 ________________ – 191 million speakers

About 900 years ago, ____________ was only spoken in the country that gives it its name. But then the country won its independence from Spain and the use of the language expanded all over the world with the help of explorers such as Vasco da Gama and Prince Henry the Navigator, establishing itself especially in Brazil (where it's the national language), in the African nations Angola and Mozambique and the former colony of Macau in China.

9 Malay-Indonesian – 159 million speakers

Malay-Indonesian is spoken in Malaysia and Indonesia. Indonesian is actually one of many dialects of Malay, but they're all more or less based on the same root language. Indonesia is a nation made up of over 13,000 islands, the sixth most populated country in the world. Malaysia, the capital of which is Kuala Lumpur, borders on two of the larger parts of Indonesia, including the island of Borneo.

10 ________________ – 129 million speakers

Often called the most romantic language in the world, ____________ used to be the language of diplomacy. In addition to being spoken in the country that gave it its name, it is spoken in many other countries, including Belgium, Switzerland, Canada, the African nations of Rwanda and Cameroon, and some Caribbean islands, including Haiti.

1 **Look at the signs in different languages on this page. How many of them can you translate or guess the meaning of? Check your answers on page 123.**

2 **Check the meaning of the following words and expressions.**

- *genocide* – the deliberate murder of a whole race of people
- *contribute to their demise* – be one of the causes of their death or failure
- *take their toll* – have a serious effect on something
- *the outlook is particularly bleak* – the future is not good
- *a claim verified by linguists* – linguists say that the claim is true
- *rattle off* – say something easily
- *ripple-effect* (literally, the movement of water when something is thrown into it)
- *anthropologists* – scientists who study people, society and culture
- *passing away* – dying
- *grimmer* – more pessimistic

3 **Read the headline of the newspaper article on page 119 and predict the contents.**

4 **Before you read the complete article, scan it for references to the following languages. What do you find out about them?**

Udihe Eyak Arikapu Kutch Manx Ubykh

5 **Read the first three paragraphs and find five reasons which can cause the reduction in the use of a language.**

6 **Find the following numbers in the text. What do they refer to?**

6,800 2,500 100,000 30,000 100 81 3,400 6,120

7 **Now read the complete text and answer these questions.**

1 About how many languages could have disappeared by the year 2100?
2 What is the minimum number of speakers required to keep a language alive?
3 Explain what happens when a more dominant language is adopted.
4 What kind of study is adversely affected by the loss of a language?
5 What is unique about the Ubykh language?
6 Which are the two countries where the most languages are spoken?
7 'One language death in two weeks' – How many language deaths in a decade?
8 In which country did Payal Sampat grow up?

8 **Re-write the following sentences from the text, starting with the indicated word or phrase.**

1 Up to ninety per cent could be extinct by the end of the century.
The year 2100 ______________________
2 Half of all languages are spoken by fewer than two thousand five hundred people each.
Only two thousand five hundred ______________________
3 Languages need at least a hundred thousand speakers to pass from generation to generation.
A hundred thousand ______________________
4 Marie Smith says she's the last speaker of Eyak, a claim verified by linguists.
Linguists ______________________
5 Anthropologists and others lose rich sources of material for documenting a people's history.
It becomes more difficult ______________________
6 A Turkish farmer's passing away marked the end of Ubykh.
Ubykh ______________________
7 Eight countries account for more than half of all languages.
More than fifty per cent ______________________
8 Children should be encouraged to speak other languages in addition to their native tongues.
As well as speaking ______________________

Thousands of Languages Face Extinction

BY DARLENE SUPERVILLE

19th June 2001 Associated Press

Have you ever heard someone speak Udihe, Eyak or Arikapu? You probably never will. Among the world's six thousand eight hundred languages, up to ninety per cent could be extinct by the end of the century.

Half of all languages are spoken by fewer than two thousand five hundred people each, according to the Worldwatch Institute, a private organization that monitors global trends.

Languages need at least a hundred thousand speakers to pass from generation to generation, said a spokesperson from UNESCO, the United Nations Educational, Scientific and Cultural Organization. In addition, war, genocide, government bans and the adoption of more dominant languages, such as Chinese and Russian, contribute to their demise. Fatal natural disasters also take their toll – a catastrophic earthquake in western India killed an estimated thirty thousand speakers of Kutchi, a language spoken by fewer than eight hundred thousand people.

The outlook for Udihe (spoken in Siberia), Eyak (Alaska), and Arikapu (Ithe Amazon jungle) is particularly bleak. About a hundred people speak Udihe, six speak Arikapu, and Eyak is down to one. Marie Smith, 83, of Anchorage, Alaska, says she's the last speaker of Eyak. She doesn't like the distinction.

'It's horrible to be alone,' she said. 'I am the last person that can talk in our language.'

The losses ripple far beyond the affected communities. When a language dies, linguists, anthropologists and others lose rich sources of material for documenting a people's history, finding out what they knew and tracking their movements from region to region. And the world, linguistically speaking, becomes less diverse.

Manx, from the Isle of Man in the Irish Sea, disappeared in 1974 with the death of its last speaker. In 1992, a Turkish farmer's passing away marked the end of Ubykh, a language from the Caucasus region with the most consonants on record, eighty-one.

Eight countries account for more than half of all languages. They are, in order, Papua New Guinea, Indonesia, Nigeria, India, Mexico, Cameroon, Australia and Brazil.

Linguists believe between three thousand four hundred and six thousand one hundred and twenty languages could become extinct by 2100, a statistic grimmer than the widely used estimate of about one language death every two weeks.

'Governments can help by removing bans on languages, and children should be encouraged to speak other languages in addition to their native tongues,' said Payal Sampat, a Worldwatch researcher who is fluent in English, French and Spanish and grew up speaking Hindi, Marathi, Gujarati and Kutchi.

9 The following letter was written to a newspaper by someone who had read the above article. Scan it and decide which of these headings would most suit it:

Disaster is avoidable
Don't be so pessimistic!
Fewer languages – that's good!
Something must be done

10 Now read the letter and make a note of any words or expressions you don't know. Don't look anything up until you have finished the complete article. Discuss the new words and expressions with the rest of the class.

To the editor

I was interested to read Darlene Superville's article in your newspaper yesterday. Some estimates are even more pessimistic than hers. Michael Krauss, a linguist at the Native Language Centre in Alaska, estimates that only 600 of the world's languages are 'safe' from extinction, insofar as they are still being taught to children.

And to this I say: 'Hooray!' Why? Because the world's economic development is completely connected to people speaking the same languages, not different ones.

The majority of the world's books, newspapers, movies, music etc are in English or, if not English, one of the world's other main languages, such as Spanish, Chinese or Arabic. More importantly, most of the world's academic books are in English, so you have to learn to read English if you want to study.

The reduction in the number of world languages is a reason to celebrate, not to mourn. Most people who speak little-known languages don't complain if other people don't speak them! In the modern world, people are prepared to give up part of their ancestral culture in order to reap the rewards of the global economy. Speaking a little-known and little-used language excludes you from doing this.

What is more, government efforts to save dying languages are doomed to fail, partly for these same economic reasons.

When we first begin to speak, we all communicate in a unique dialect, a mixture of parental language, baby talk and inaccurate syntax. When we grow up, we leave our 'mother tongue' behind. As we get older, we move on to learn the language of our peer group. When we become grown-ups, we forget those childish things we said when we were young. And so it is with dead languages. They simply outgrow their usefulness.

Yours sincerely,

Alexander Morgan

Alexander Morgan
President
Global Trading Industries

11 Write a short summary of Mr Morgan's arguments. Refer back to page 25 for notes on how to write a summary.

Revision: Helmut's final English quiz

Rewrite the sentence. Combine the underlined words:

1 Alex Ferguson is the manager of a club that plays football in the Premier League.
Ferguson is a ________ manager.

Underline the correct answers.

2a A: You *read/are reading* my magazine!
B: Yes, I *enjoy/'m enjoying* it.

2b A: What *do you think/are you thinking* of my idea?
B: I *think/'m thinking* about it.

2c When Ranulph Fiennes *started/had started/used to start* the New York marathon on November 2nd 2003, he *finished/was finishing/had finished* six marathons in the previous six days. Even more amazingly, he *ran/was running/had run* in his seventh different country in one week!

2d I *used to/would* like watching cartoons on TV and I *would watch/had watched* them for hours, but now I *don't used to watch/ never watch* them.

Complete these sentences using the words in italics.

3a These items ________ of delicate material and they should always ________ carefully before ________ to customers. *make wrap send*

3b The manager said he wanted ________ as soon as the car ________ because he thought his briefcase ________ on the back seat. *tell bring in leave*

3c This factory was Mr Biro's; he ________ in Argentina and an American ________ while he was on holiday. *set up come across* (add *it*)

4a I don't know what else ________, so instead of ________, and ________ me calm down, I'll play again! *say talk help*

4b I hope that Ali's knowledge ________ English and his interest ________ explaining things, together with my enthusiasm ________ grammar has made you more enthusiastic ________ English and better ________ it. *about at for in of*

Underline the correct answers.

5a I *'m going to work/work* on my report this afternoon because I *will leave/ leave* for Cairo at 7 tonight. I *will meet/am meeting* Mary there for lunch.

5b After we *have eaten/will have eaten*, I promise I'*ll discuss/'m going to discuss* your ideas with her.

5c I *was going to have/was about to have* a sandwich at the theatre but the train was late and the concert *would begin/was about to begin* when I arrived.

6a By the end of this year I *had been/have been/will have been* here for three years. When I arrived, I'*d never seen/'ve never seen/'ll have never seen* anywhere like it.

6b A: You'*ve read/'ve been reading* all day! B: Yes, but I'*ve only finished/'ve only been finishing* half of it.

6c A: Where's David? B: He's *gone/been* to the cinema. A: He's always going to the cinema! How many times has he *gone/been* this week?

7a A: What's wrong? B: Well, I *taste/'m tasting* this special tea and it *doesn't taste/isn't tasting* very good.

8a A: Where's my sandwich? B: The dog *can have/must have/should have* eaten it. You *can't have/mustn't have/shouldn't have* left it on the table!

Rewrite this sentence to include these adverbs: *often, hard, extremely, last year*.

8b My friend Ali worked.

Rewrite these sentences, starting as indicated:

9 Shakespeare wrote wonderful plays and he wrote beautiful poetry.
Shakespeare wrote not ________

10a I wouldn't have started it had I known how difficult this book was.
If ________

10b If you met his parents, you would understand him better.
Were ________

11 Dinosaurs were very successful animals. They survived for 240,000,000 years.
Surviving ________

Underline the phrasal (separable) verbs; circle the prepositional (inseparable) verbs.

12 Henry Ford came up with the assembly-line production system and tried it out with the Model T Ford, which came out in 1912. This model was produced in the millions, but you would never come across it in any colour except black.

Rewrite these sentences, starting as indicated.

13a What are you laughing about, Ali?
Helmut wanted to know ________

13b Were you laughing at me?
He asked Ali ________

13c Don't forget to change the question word order, Helmut!
Ali told Helmut ________

14a The story was long and rather boring. We all knew the ending.
The story, ________

14b The shirt was made of silk. It was green in colour. It was small and very old. It was Chinese and I thought it was beautiful.
It was a ________ shirt.

1 **The task for this lesson is to write a For and Against essay with the following title:**

Everyone should be proficient in at least three languages.

Work in pairs. In preparation for writing the essay, discuss the following questions. Note down any new vocabulary that you need in order to answer the questions. Ask your teacher for help, if necessary.

1 How many languages do you speak? Are you learning any other language besides English?
2 Do you enjoy learning a foreign language? Say why/why not.
3 What do you find the hardest aspect of learning a foreign language?
4 What are the reasons for learning a foreign language? You can, if you wish, state which the most important reason is, and how important the others are.
5 Do you know anyone who is bilingual or trilingual? Would you like to be bilingual or trilingual?
6 Can you think of good arguments as to why people should not attempt to learn two languages besides their own?

2 **Read the paragraphs below. Find:**

1 two phrases that talk about advantages and disadvantages
2 a word that means the same as *as a result*
3 a phrase that is similar in meaning to *however*
4 a phrase that means *moreover*.

There are many advantages to living abroad for a period of time. Firstly, you learn a great deal about another culture. Secondly, by living in a country, you learn the language far more quickly than you would otherwise. In addition to improving your vocabulary and grammar, your pronunciation will also greatly improve. If you stay for two years, you have a good chance of becoming bilingual. Consequently, your employment prospects will improve.

On the other hand, living in a foreign country can be very lonely, especially when you first get there. It can be difficult to make friends if you don't speak a language well. One solution is to live with a host family, although the disadvantage of doing this is that if you don't like the family, you may not enjoy your stay very much or even have much conversation with them.

3 **The following words and phrases are often used when writing an essay. You have already learnt a number of them in Unit 4 (page 33). Choose from these words and phrases and complete the gaps in the sentences below.**

Adding points: furthermore, what is more, also, in addition (to this/that), in addition to (speaking)
Contrasting points: however, nonetheless, nevertheless, although, on the one hand … on the other hand, despite
Concluding: to conclude, all things considered, to sum up, in conclusion, on the whole
Talking about results: consequently, as a result, in consequence
Talking about (dis)advantages: to have an advantage, there are advantages to (speaking), an advantage of (speaking) is (that) …

1 English spelling is not phonetic. ___________, many people have problems with it.
2 ___________ speaking three languages well, he is also a talented artist.
3 ___________ being bilingual is that you can understand films in two languages.
4 ___________ studying English for three hours a week, I have never learnt to speak it well.
5 On the one hand, living abroad is interesting, ___________ it can be very lonely.
6 I have examined the good points and bad points of living abroad. ___________, it is my opinion that it is a useful thing to do.
7 ___________ grammar exercises are boring, they can be a good way to improve your language.
8 Living with a host family means that you have people to talk to. ___________, you learn a lot about the way people in that country live.

4 **Below are some useful phrases and ways of starting sentences. Write complete sentences.**

1 The ability to … is …
2 It is useful to …
3 To be proficient in three languages is …
4 In order to … you must …
5 To be able to … is …
6 Many people have difficulty …

5 **Plan and write your essay. Turn to page 33 in Unit 4 for more information about how to write a For and Against essay. Begin by writing an outline, in note form, of your essay.**

Write about 150 words. Spend at least five minutes looking through your essay for mistakes.

6 **Optional writing task. Imagine that a boy or girl of your age from another country comes to stay with your family for a week. Write a narrative describing this visit. Write about 150 words. Turn to page 17 for help with writing a narrative.**

4 LISTENING AND SPEAKING

☐ pyjamas ☐ alligator ☐ bedouin ☐ turban

☐ garage ☐ algebra ☐ cigarette ☐ forest

☐ hotel ☐ bazaar ☐ sure ☐ sheik

☐ zero ☐ kiosk ☐ chocolate

☐ tornado ☐ garden

☐ giraffe ☐ caravan

☐ tomato

1 Work in pairs. Discuss this question:

To loan means to lend something to someone. What do you think a *loan word* in a language is?

2 Work in pairs. Look at the words above. They are all *loan words* in English, and are also known as *borrowed words*. They were originally taken from French, Spanish, Arabic and Persian. Can you guess which words come from which languages? Divide the words into four groups, according to the original language.

3 Try to answer this short quiz on language. Don't worry if you don't know all the answers. You will hear the answers to most of the questions later in the lesson.

1. What language did the Romans speak?
2. Can you imagine why Spanish has words that originated in the languages of Native American tribes?
3. The Normans invaded England in 1066. What language do you think they spoke?
4. Which language do you think the word *tomato* comes from?
5. A Spanish word used in English is the word *viva*, meaning *live*. Can you guess what the phrase *Viva España!* means?

4 Work in pairs. Discuss these questions.

1. Has your language absorbed a lot of words from English? Can you quickly think of five English loan words in your language?
2. Look at the words you have just thought of. What is the original English word? Has the form of the word changed or has it remained the same?

5 Listen to a short lecture on loan words in English. Tick (✔) the topics that you hear mentioned.

Examples of Arabic loan words
Original meanings of Spanish loan words
How new words enrich the language
Problems that loan words create
Examples of French loan words
Words of Native American origin
How some loan words change their form and others don't
Examples of Chinese loan words
Past invasions of England and the result

6 Listen again. Number the words in colour above in the order that you hear them mentioned in the listening passage.

7 Most of the answers to the quiz in activity 3 are in the listening passage. Were your answers correct?

8 Listen to the lecture again. Take notes in preparation for making a presentation on loan words.

9 Work in pairs. Make notes for a presentation on loan words.

- Use the information from the lecture about loan words in English.
- Talk about loan words in your own language and give examples.
- If possible, include some information about how your language has developed.

Find another partner. Make your presentation. When you have finished, your partner can ask questions about any part of your presentation talk he/she didn't understand or wants to know more about.

Word watch – Pairs

A 'pair-phrase' consists of two words very often used together and linked by *and*, eg: *Ladies and Gentlemen*. Note that the order is very important and we never say 'Gentlemen and Ladies'.

1 Make 8 pair-phrases from these 16 words and be careful to put the right one first!

women | far | tired | tidy | knife

blood | regulations | cons | men | fork

flesh | sick | pros | rules | wide | neat

_______ and _______ _______ and _______
_______ and _______ _______ and _______
_______ and _______ _______ and _______
_______ and _______ _______ and _______

2 Now complete these sentences by finding the second part of the pair. An anagram has been given to help you.

1 If you want to give a convincing presentation to your class, you need to have all the facts and __________ (RIGUFSE) at your fingertips.
2 Hotels in Britain are expensive and many tourists prefer to stay at a bed and __________ (AKETRSBAF) establishment.
3 My grandfather had walked the length and __________ (EHADRTB) of the island and knew it like the back of his hand.
4 A popular English take-away meal is fish and __________ (SHPIC) with salt and vinegar.
5 After being lost for six days, the dog eventually returned home safe and __________ (USDON).

Lessons in logic

Five women called Anna, Beth, Carol, Diane and Ellen, all have different jobs. One is a teacher, one a doctor, one a shopkeeper, one a fashion designer and one a writer.

The tallest is the fashion designer. Anna is the next tallest. Beth is a doctor. Ellen is a writer and is the shortest. The shopkeeper is the tallest but two, being much shorter than Diane.

Who is the fashion designer? __________

Who is the shopkeeper? __________

Who is the teacher? __________

Who is the shortest but one? __________

Colourful language

There are lots of words for colours in English and lots of expressions and idioms using colour too. Test your knowledge!

1 Shades: put these words into word families.

navy olive crimson khaki golden
emerald lilac silver pearl mauve tan
turquoise charcoal scarlet ivory amber

Red shades	Blue shades	Green shades
__________	__________	__________
__________	__________	__________

Yellow shades	Brown shades	White/very pale shades
__________	__________	__________
__________	__________	__________

Purple shades	Grey shades
__________	__________
__________	__________

2 Idioms: fill in the correct colour to complete the idiomatic expression.

1 After walking in the snow, her hands were __________ with cold.
2 Angie was a great idealist and looked at the world through __________-tinted spectacles.
3 When James looked at his bank statement, he was horrified to see that he was in the __________ and owed the bank considerable sums.
4 Edward fell off his bike so many times that he was __________ and __________ all over.
5 I was __________ with envy when all my friends were on holiday while I still had exams to take.
6 Once I read the account in __________ and __________, I had to believe that it really was true.

INFORMATION ABOUT SOME OF THE LANGUAGES ON PAGE 116:
Tagalog – one of the major languages of the Philippines.
Urdu – one of the languages spoken in Pakistan – 10 million speakers.
Marathi – one of many languages spoken in India.
Javanese – spoken in parts of Java, the most populous island of the Republic of Indonesia - 75 million speakers..

ANSWERS TO ACTIVITY 1 PAGE 118
A Post Museum, B Service Desk; Meeting Room, C Private Property, D Pool Hall, E Underground Station.

GRAMMAR REFERENCE

Contents

1 Present tenses

Present simple

Use the present simple especially for:

1 **Facts** which are always or generally true:

2 **Habits** or **routines** in the present:

(Particularly when an adverb of frequency is included.)

*My brother **usually gets up** very late.*
*The weather **is sometimes** cool at night.*

(For more on adverbs, see section 19.)

Other uses include:

3 **Commentaries** on actions of short duration:

*Now I **pour** in the mixture, **add** the lemon and **stir**.*
*Beckham **crosses**, Scholes **heads** the ball on and Giggs **shoots** and **scores**!*

4 Verbs which are themselves the action:

*We **apologise**. I **swear** I didn't do it. This court **finds** you innocent.*

Present continuous

Use the present continuous for:

1 Something happening **at the moment**:

2 Something seen as **temporary**:

3 to express **complaints**:

*You're **drinking** my lemonade!*
*She's **sitting** in your mother's chair!*

NOTE

See sections 3 and 11 for future uses of these present tense forms.
See section 2 for possible past uses of these forms.

2 Past tenses

Past simple

Use the past simple for:

1 Actions and events **finished in the past**:

Japan and Korea ***hosted*** *the 2002 World Cup.*
Did *you* ***watch*** *the news on TV last night?*

And especially for a series of completed actions:

Did you **contact** Bill yesterday?

No, I **didn't**. I **telephoned** him at home, then I **called** his mobile, then I **sent** a fax to his office and an e-mail to his house, but I **didn't get** any reply.

NOTE
The past time is either given (*yesterday*) or indicated (*the Sydney Olympics*) or understood. *That was* in the following conversation shows the past is understood:

That was a really difficult test!

Yes, I **didn't do** very well.

2 For repeated past actions:

How many times **did** you **call** Bill?

Once at his home and I **called** his mobile about ten times.

Past continuous

Use the past continuous:

1 To describe (a) an **activity** or (b) a **scene** at **a moment in the past**:

a What **were** you **doing** at 8 o'clock last night?

I **was reading** a book.

b *When we arrived at the park, some boys* **were playing** *football and others* **were watching** *the game. Several children* **were riding** *bicycles and one boy* **was flying** *a kite. Then I saw Jack and waved to him.*

NOTE
What **happened**: *we arrived, I saw Jack and waved.* The other verbs describe the scene (what **was happening**) 'when we arrived'.

2 To indicate a past action interrupted by a past event:

I **was reading** my e-mails when you called.

NOTE:
For the contrast between the past tense and the past perfect see section 4.

Used to

Use *used to* to talk about past habits and to suggest that the situation is now different:

When I was younger, my mother **used to give** me and my sisters a lot of broccoli to eat. Now I love broccoli but **I didn't use to. Did** you **use to like** green vegetables?

When I was younger I ***used to read*** *a lot of comics.*
My brother ***didn't use to*** *like English but now he does.*
Did your father ***use to work*** *as a teacher?*

NOTE
There is no present tense form of this structure (*I used to go*). Do not confuse it with *I am use to going …* , which means *I am accustomed to going … .*

Would

In the 1940s most English men ***would*** *always wear a hat.*
English people ***wouldn't*** *usually travel abroad in those days.*
Would *people watch TV then? No, they* ***wouldn't****.*

Used to and would

NOTE
This use of *would* is similar in meaning to *used to* for describing past habits, but only *used to* can be used with stative verbs (see section 5). And *would* requires a past tense adverbial to indicate that the meaning is not conditional *(in those days, then*). So the second and third examples of form for *used to*, above, would not work with *would*, though the first example would work.

3 The future

There are several different ways of expressing the future in English, but they are used in different situations.

will is used to talk about the future in general, and especially for:

predictions: *I'm sure you* ***won't have*** *any problems.*
promises: *I****'ll be*** *home before nine o'clock, Dad.*
offers: *We****'ll bring*** *the food for your party.*
requests: ***Will*** *you* ***help*** *me with my homework?*

going to is used to talk about:

plans: *John****'s going to visit*** *his grandmother tomorrow.*
intentions: *What* ***are*** *you* ***going to do*** *now? I****'m going to talk*** *to Mr Smith.*
predictions: (with present evidence): *I think it****'s going to rain****. Look at those clouds!*

The present continuous tense is used to talk about:

fixed arrangements for the future:

Are *you* ***coming*** *to the concert tonight?*

No, ***I'm taking*** *my children to the circus.*

The present simple tense is used to talk about:

timetables and scheduled events:

What time ***does*** *your train* ***arrive****?*

The concert ***starts*** *at 8 o'clock.*

It is also used in:

future time and conditional clauses (see sections 10 and 11):

When you ***get*** *here, we'll talk about the plan.*

If John ***is*** *in York in April, we'll probably meet.*

The future continuous tense is used to talk about an action that will be going on at a moment in the future:

In one hour's time, **I'll be doing** the test!

It can also be used instead of the present continuous to give a strong emphasis to the future idea:

*We****'ll be seeing*** *the Smiths next week.*

The future perfect tense is used to talk about something which will be completed by a time in the future (see section 4):

By this time tomorrow I**'ll have finished** this composition.

be about to is used to emphasise that something will happen in the immediate future:

*I can't talk to you now – I****'m about to go*** *to school.*

NOTE

Like *will*, all modal verbs (see section 6) can refer to the future and may be used instead of *will* in most of the above constructions.

4 The perfect tenses

Present perfect simple/continuous

CINEMA
I **liked** that adventure film but I **have** never **liked** cowboy films.

Use the present perfect to connect the past and the present in a number of different ways (the adverbs in brackets emphasise the idea indicated in each case):

1. With the idea 'in your whole life up to now':
   *Have you (****ever****) seen an elephant?*
2. With the idea of 'so far/up to now':
   *Has John done his homework (****yet****)?*
3. With the idea of 'before now':
   *I've (****already****) read that magazine.*
4. With the idea of 'very recently:
   *Mary's (****just****) finished her exam.*
5. When no past time is indicated:
   Thank you. We've had a wonderful time!
6. When you want to indicate an effect on the present:
   I've walked 10 kilometres and ***now*** *I'm really tired.*
7. When the time period mentioned includes the present:
   How many ice-creams have you eaten ***today****?*
8. With the idea of 'this' or 'now' and an ordinal number:
   This is the third time they've come here ***this week****.*

NOTE

The present perfect, like the simple present, can be used for the future in time clauses (see sections 3, 10, 11): *We'll discuss your essay when you****'ve finished*** *it.*

The present perfect **simple** focuses more on the **completion** or the **result** of the activity (e.g. 3 above, 'so I don't want to read it now'; 5, 'and now we're leaving'; 6, 'so I'm tired'). The present perfect **continuous** focuses more on the **activity itself** and **without the idea of completion**, or on **repeated activity**. For example:

*I****'ve been reading*** *that magazine* does not suggest I've finished reading it.

*We****'ve been having*** *a wonderful time* suggests that we still are.

*You****'ve been eating*** *a lot of ice-cream lately* indicates repetition.

A connected difference is that the **simple** may indicate a **long-term situation** while the **continuous** is more likely to refer to a **short-term situation**:

*He****'d lived*** *in England for years but he****'d*** *only* ***been living*** *with us for six months when he died.*

In general, the present perfect simple may include 'how much' or 'how many', the present perfect continuous 'how long':

*They****'ve been running*** *for hours.*

I**'ve been reading** 'Great Expectations' and I'm about halfway through it.
I**'ve read** 'Great Expectations' but I didn't like it much.

The past perfect

Use the past perfect, simple and continuous, to relate to a moment in the past in the same way that the present perfect relates to the present:

*John was very excited because he **hadn't seen** an elephant before, but I'**d visited** the zoo a day earlier. I'**d been** very impressed with the elephants then but now I was an expert!*
*I **hadn't told** John about my visit because I'**d been waiting** to see his reaction.*

Also use it to show that one event in the past happened before another one:

*When we finally **reached** the bus station, our bus **had left**.* (We missed it.)
*When we finally **reached** the bus station, our bus **left**.* (It waited for us.)

NOTE
The past perfect plays an important part in reported speech (see section 13) and in some conditional sentences (see section 11).

Future perfect

Use the future perfect, simple and continuous, to relate to a moment in the future in the same way that the present perfect relates to the present:

Tomorrow **I'll have been working** here for ten years, and **I'll have replied** to thousands of letters!
COMPLAINTS DEPARTMENT
COMPLAINTS A-E
TODAY'S COMPLAINTS

5 Stative and action verbs

Verbs which describe not an action but a state are not used in the continuous form.

Examples of action and **stative** verbs:

*I'm enjoying the party and I **like** the music.*
*We're meeting John tomorrow but we **don't know** his wife.*
*Were you buying that house when we saw you or **did** you **own** it?*

Stative verbs include:

appear (=seem) believe belong consist of depend on dislike expect feel (=have an opinion) forget forgive hate have (=possess) imagine (=suppose) include know like love matter mean owe own possess prefer realise recognise remember resemble see (=understand) seem smell (=have a smell) suppose taste (=have a flavour) think (=have an opinion) understand want wish

What's John's opinion, now, about these three books?
He **thinks** he prefers the second but he still **likes** the first and he **wants** to read the next one!

Several of these verbs may be used both as stative and as action verbs. In these cases, the verb has different meanings:

I **think** that's a good idea!
Please be quiet, **I'm thinking**.

NOTES
The restriction on stative verbs with continuous forms is the same for all tenses:

*When we arrived, the cook **was tasting** the soup and it **tasted** really good.*
*We'**ll be working** at 8 o'clock and we'**ll understand** if you **don't want** to come.*

However, as with other verbs, the *-ing* form of stative verbs can be used as participles (see section 14), gerunds and as the objects of prepositions:

***Preferring** to get home early, I decided not to stay for coffee.* (participle)
***Seeing** is **believing**.* (gerunds)
*In spite of **wanting** to eat, we stayed for the speech.* (object of preposition)

6 Modal auxiliary verbs

The following are modal auxiliary verbs: *can, must, shall, should, ought to, will* and *may,* together with *could, would* and *might*.

In terms of **form**, modal verbs are different from ordinary verbs in these ways:

1. They have no *-s* on the third person singular:
   *Tom sing**s** very well but **can** he act?*
2. They form negatives and questions like other auxiliary verbs (*be, do, have*):
   *We must**n't** be late. **Should** we leave now?*
3. They have no infinitives, *-ing* forms or past participles. (**to can**, **shoulding**, **have musted** are all impossible.)
4. Like other auxiliary verbs, they appear in structures such as short answers (see section 8) and tag questions (see section 9):

They can swim, **can't** they?

Use modal auxiliaries to add different meanings to the verbs they combine with. In fact, all the modal auxiliaries can express a number of different meanings. This makes them different from the other auxiliaries (*be, do, have*), which indicate such things as tense, or passive voice.

We can take can as an example of different meanings:

***Can** you swim?*	(ability)
***Can** I swim here?*	(permission)
*You **can't** swim here.*	(prohibition)
*That **can't** be Mary!*	(inference)
*Accidents **can** happen.*	(possibility)

All modal verbs can be used to refer to the present (*You **may** leave now*) or the future (*You **may** come tomorrow*).
Three modal verbs (*can, may, will*) have past forms (*could, might, would*), but these can also be used for present and future.

NOTE
It is not possible to use two modal verbs together. In combinations of modals, use *have to* in place of *must*, and *be able to* in place of *can*:

*I can't find my key so we **may have to** get in through the window.*
*I **might be able to** help you with your homework.*

Use *have to* instead of *must* in the past tense:

*We went to be early as we **had to leave** at 4 o'clock the next morning.*

Perfect modals

Modal verbs can generally refer either to the present or the future. Modal perfects refer in some way to the past:

We **should have stopped** at those traffic lights.

Generally, they correspond directly to simple modals in this way:

*You **ought to tell** John before he **leaves**.*
*You **ought to have told** John before he **left**.*
*They **may go** there **tomorrow** but I'm not sure.*
*They **may have gone** there **yesterday** but I'm not sure.*

On the other hand, *must have* and *can't have* correspond to only one, not very common, meaning of these verbs in the present: that of inference:

*The house is completely empty – the Smiths **must have** left.*
*The lights are on in the house – the Smiths **can't have** left.*

There is also an idiomatic used of *might have*, which does not correspond with the idea of *might* but means 'I think you should have':

*You **might have** told me!*
*I think they **might have** offered us some food!*

NOTE
The perfect modal form of various modal verbs can be used in third-type conditional sentences (see section 11).

7 The passive voice

In English, we usually put new information at the end of a sentence. By changing the order, the passive allows us to change the focus.

Only transitive verbs (verbs which can have a direct object) can be used in the passive. With intransitive verbs (*arrive, die, sleep, hesitate, rain*, etc.) the passive is not possible.

Use the passive voice when you don't know, don't care or don't want to say who (or what) did something:

*John **was injured** in a car accident.*
*The driver of the car **has been arrested**.*
*He **is being interviewed** at the present time.*

On the other hand, you can give strong emphasis to the person doing the action by using the passive and including this (the 'agent'):

*France didn't win the cup. It was won **by Brazil**.*

With many verbs that take two objects (*give, tell, show, send, offer, promise, lend, pay*, etc), the personal indirect object is often preferred as the subject of a passive sentence:

*My uncle sent **me** a large parcel.* (active)
***I** was sent a large parcel by my uncle.* (passive)

With verbs of saying and believing, a passive construction can be used with *it*. This allows us to avoid saying who said or believed something, or to avoid saying whether or not we agree:

It has been said *that she may be the next prime minister.*
It was believed *that this was the oldest house in the village.*

8 Omissions after auxilary verbs

An important aspect of English is that auxiliary verbs (*be, do, have* and modal auxiliary verbs, section 6) can be used to represent longer pieces of language:

He told me to go, but I ***didn't*** *and now I* ***can't***.
(= 'didn't/can't go')
I thought I knew what he was doing, but I ***didn't***.
(= 'didn't know what he was doing')

Other common structures in which auxiliary verbs operate in this way include:

'Short answers'

These operate with all types of auxiliary, always agreeing with the auxiliary in a 'yes/no' question (see section 9):

Are *you studying Chinese calligraphy? Yes I* ***am*** (studying Chinese calligraphy).
Must *you go so early? I'm afraid we* ***must***. (go so early).

Tag questions

Again these questions operate with auxiliary verbs. Many languages have a single form to encourage a response, but in English the form depends on the auxiliary verb in, or implied in, the main clause. See also section 9:

I really ***like*** *these concerts,* ***don't*** *you* (really like these concerts)?
The game ***hadn't*** *begun when you arrived,* ***had*** *it* (begun)?

So and *neither*

(my name)

(know Paris)

The auxiliaries operating in the agreeing structures do so in a way basically similar to that in 'tag questions':

*I****'ve*** *always been fascinated by the pyramids at Giza. So,* ***have*** *I* (been fascinated by them).
They ***couldn't*** *go to the play. Neither* ***could*** *we* (go to the play).

9 Questions

Yes/No questions

(1) *Have you finished your homework?* (2) *Does Mary enjoy learning languages?* (3) *Should we go now?* (4) *Are your brothers interested in football?* (5) *Have you got a bicycle?*

Questions with a yes or no answer generally begin with an auxiliary verb. This may be a tense auxiliary (1), *do/did* in simple tenses (2), or a modal auxiliary (3). The exceptions are with *be* (4) and *have [got]* (5) as main verbs.

Answers to these questions may include the auxiliary from the question: (1) *No, I haven't.* (2) *Yes, she does.* (4) *Yes, they are.*

NOTE

The auxiliary verb form in the question cannot be contracted. When the auxiliary verb is included in the 'short' answer, that cannot be contracted either.

Information questions

(1) *Where are you going?* (2) *Which shoes did Mary buy?* (3) *When is the exam?*

These questions begin with a question word, generally followed by an auxiliary verb (1-2) or by *be* or *have [got]* as main verbs (3).

But, if the question is about the ***subject*** of the sentence (especially with the question words *who, what, which*), the auxiliary is not used in the question, but may appear in the answer. Compare these two pairs of sentences:

A: ***Which shoes*** *cost the most?*
B: ***The black ones*** *did.*

(the answer 'the black ones' corresponds to the subject)

and

A: ***Which shoes*** *did Mary buy?*
B: *She bought* ***the black ones***.

(the answer 'the black ones' corresponds to the object; she (Mary) is the subject).

Less direct questions

It is possible to make yes/no and information questions more polite by making them less direct. (*What's your name?* is very direct; *Could you tell me your name?* may be more acceptable in some situations.)

In making yes/no questions less direct, it is necessary to add *if* (or *whether*) after the opening:

Does Jane Smith *work here? > Could you tell me* ***if Jane Smith*** *works here?*
Is that *my magazine? > Do you know* ***if that*** *is my magazine?*

Tag questions

These consist of an auxiliary verb (or *be* or *have [got]* as main verbs) and a pronoun. Both refer back to the previous statement:

***Dave can** speak French quite well, **can't he**?*
***They haven't** eaten already, **have they**?*

The exception is with '*there is/are*'. In this case there is used instead of a pronoun:

***There are** a lot of interesting places to visit, **aren't there**?*

When the verb in the statement is in the present or past simple, the *do* auxiliary is used in the tag:

*Bill and Anne **got married** last month, **didn't** they?*
*Your father **works** for the Ministry, **doesn't** he?*

The pronoun corresponding to indefinite pronouns (see section 19) is *they* and the verb in the tag is plural – even if the original verb is singular:

***No one has** finished, **have they**?*

The tag following suggestions beginning with *Let's ...* is *shall we*?:

***Let's** stay in this evening and work, **shall we**?*

Reported questions

These are introduced with such expressions as '*He asked ...*' '*They wanted to know*'... . Note: These do **not** introduce a question and are not followed by a question mark. What follows therefore does not have a question word order (see section 13).

10 Compound and complex sentences

Compound sentences

There are five simple sentence patterns:

1. subject + verb *The train arrived.*
2. subject + verb + complement *My father is an architect/young.*
3. subject + verb + direct objecteg *Tom read the book.*
4. subject + verb + indirect object + direct object. *Bill sent my brother a letter.*
5. subject + verb + object + complement *They made my father captain/unhappy.*

These simple sentences can, of course have added details:

The old steam train arrived rather late.

We can join simple sentences like these together into a single compound sentence in different ways:

a **with a coordinating conjunction** (*and, but, or, yet*, etc.):
The train arrived late and Tom took a taxi home.
The company awarded him a prize yet made him redundant.

b **with a semi-colon:**
The train arrived very late; that made my father angry.

c **with a semi-colon and a connecting adverb:**
It was late; nevertheless, they decided to stay a little longer.

NOTE
If the subject of coordinate clauses is the same, it can be omitted (see the 2nd sentence in (a) above) in the second clause.

Complex sentences

These consist of a main clause and a subordinate clause (or more than one of each type). A *subordinate clause* is a clause which forms part of a **main clause**:

1 ***We*** ***explained*** *what we were doing.*
subject verb object
What we were doing is the object of *explained* and we call this type of clause a 'noun clause', because grammatically it could be replaced by a noun: *We explained **our behaviour**.*

For a very common type of noun clause see section 13.

2 ***The woman*** *who we spoke to* ***didn't understand*** ***us.***
subject (identifier) verb object
'Who we spoke to' says which woman and we call this type of clause an 'adjectival clause' because grammatically it could be replaced by an adjective: *The **old** woman.*

For more on adjectival clauses see section 12.

3 ***She*** ***understood*** ***us*** *when we spoke to her in German.*
subject verb object adverbial
'When we spoke in German' says when the woman understood and we call this an 'adverbial clause' because grammatically it could be replaced by an adverb: *She understood us **eventually**.*

Adverb clauses can be introduced by many different types of ***subordinating conjunction***, including *although* (contrast), *where* (place) *so that* (purpose), *as soon as* (time), *because* (reason), *if, unless* (condition).
For more on adverbial clauses of condition see section 11.

The subject of the three types of subordinate clause above cannot be omitted even if it is the same as the subject of the main clause:

*They agreed with the idea but (**they**) didn't vote.*

(Two main clauses because *but* is a coordinating conjunction. Subject can be omitted if it's the same as in the previous main clause.)

*They agreed with the idea although **they** didn't vote.*

(*although* is a subordinating conjunction so the subject must be included again.)

Complex sentences can also be formed with participle clauses (see section 14), mainly in written English. In these cases, a present or past participle replaces the subject and verb:

*Believing their opinion would make no difference, **they** didn't vote.*

11 Conditional sequences

1 In the **present–present** sequence, sometimes called the zero conditional, *if* has the same meaning as *when* or *whenever*. If the condition is met, the result always occurs:

*People **respond** differently if you **try** to speak their language.*
*If someone **is carrying** a metal object, the alarm **rings**.*

2 present–future

If you don't work hard, you won't pass the exam.
John will go to university if he passes his exam.

Often called the 'first conditional', this is used to talk about a future result of meeting a present, or future condition:

*If I **give** you the money* (now, tomorrow)*, **will** you **buy** me the book?* (future)
*I'**ll give** him your message* (future)*, if I **see** him.* (future)

3 past-conditional

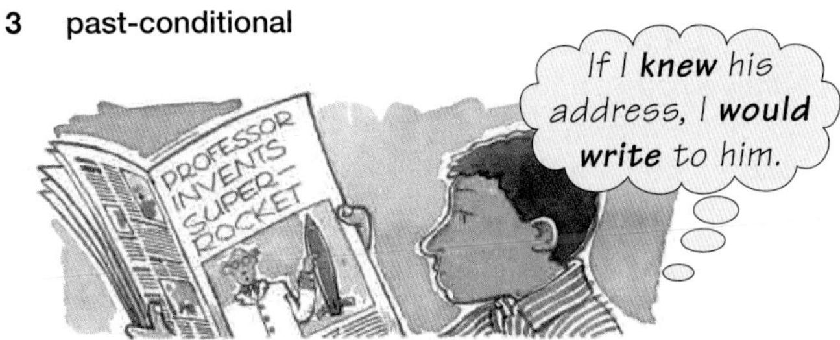

PROFESSOR INVENTS SUPER-ROCKET
If I knew his address, I would write to him.

There are two main uses of this sequence (the 'second conditional'):

a The more important use is to talk about hypothetical situations:
*If I **had** enough time, I **would help you** with your homework.* (But I don't have enough time.)

NOTE
The phrase *If I **were** you ...* is used for giving advice, and is followed by a verb in the conditional: *... I **wouldn't lend** him your book*. In this fixed phrase we use *were* instead of *was*. Other verbs do not have special conditional forms, and today it is generally acceptable to use *was*, except in fixed phrases.

b The other use is similar in meaning to the 'first conditional', but indicates that it is less probable that the condition will be met:
*If I **saw** Bill, I **would give** him your message.*

4 past perfect–conditional perfect

We use this sequence (the 'third conditional') to talk about hypothetical situations in the past: *If I **had known** you were coming, I **would have baked** a cake!* (But I didn't know, so I didn't bake a cake.)

*We **would have been** in trouble if you **hadn't helped** us.* (But you did help us so we weren't in trouble.)

5 A common variation on the previous sequence is past perfect–conditional:

TERMINAL 2
If we hadn't missed the plane last night, we wouldn't have this problem now.

Here the condition refers to the past, but the result refers to the present.

In very formal English, usually written, you may find the following variations:

***If** you **have** time ... > **Should** you have time ...* (for **if** + present)
***If** you **saw** them ... > **Were** you **to see** them ...* (for **if** + past)
***If** you **had found** it ... > **Had** you **found** it ...* (for **if** + past perfect)

Some other **conjunctions** (see Unit 10) may be used in conditional sequences, apart from *if*. The most obvious is *unless: (Unless we get more money, we will have to abandon the project)*, which basically means 'if not'; but don't use *unless* in hypothetical conditionals. The following may also be used: *provided that* (only *if*), *so long as*, *on condition that*.

12 Relative clauses

There are two types of relative clause: *defining* and *non-defining*. In the first kind, the information in the clause is part of the subject. You can't leave it out:

The play that he wrote about the Prince of Denmark is called 'Hamlet'.
THE PRINCE OF DENMARK

In the second kind, the clause gives extra information. If you leave it out, the sentence still makes sense.

'Twelfth Night', **which Shakespeare wrote in 1601**, is very enjoyable.
TWELFTH NIGHT

There are some formal differences between the two types of clause:

a Non-defining clauses are marked off by commas. Defining clauses are not.

b You can use *that* instead of *who[m]* or *which* as the relative pronoun in defining clauses, but not in non-defining ones.

c You can leave out object pronouns in defining clauses; you can't leave them out in non-defining clauses:

*The wonderful instruments (**that/which**) Stradivari made were all stringed instruments.* (Defining: the pronoun can be left out.)

*The instruments, **which** he made using special techniques, are now each worth millions of pounds.* (Non-defining: the pronoun must be included.)

NOTE

This last sentence implies that he made all his instruments using special techniques. The same sentence without commas would mean only those he made using special techniques are worth millions of pounds now.

13 Reported speech

When you report what someone said, certain changes usually occur. These include:

- **tense changes** (if the reporting verb is in the past).
- **pronoun changes**, particularly from 1st and 2nd person to 3rd person. This is because what was said is usually reported to someone who wasn't there for the original conversation. But the specific changes depend on who is reporting.
- **adverb changes**, especially to time and place adverbs (because the time and place of the original conversation have usually changed when it is reported).
- **word order changes** for grammatical reasons. This is especially true in reporting questions (where the question word order is lost):

How long will this concert last, Mary?
SUMMER CONCERT

*Bill asked Mary **how long** the concert would last.*

Have you ever eaten Indian food, Anna?

*Ray wondered **if** Anna **had** ever eaten Indian food.*

Reporting structures

The most important difference with reporting verbs is between those which report statements (*say, tell*, etc.) and those reporting questions (see above).

Say can be followed immediately (with or without *that*) by the report:

Mary: *I like the large picture.* > *Mary said (that) she liked* the large picture.

Tell, however, needs to be followed by an indirect personal object in reporting:

Mary: *I like the large picture, Mum.* > *Mary told **her mother** that she liked the large picture.*

Many verbs which report imperative forms (*tell, order, advise*, etc.) can be followed by a personal object and an infinitive. The choice of reporting verb depends on the speaker's intention:

Teacher: *Draw a house, Mary.* > *The teacher told **Mary to draw** a house.*

Doctor: *Stay in bed, Peter.* > *The doctor advised **Peter to stay** in bed.*

In reporting questions, the main difference is between yes/no questions and those which start with a question word. In reporting yes/no questions, you need *if/whether*:

Mary: *Is it too late to go?* > *Mary asked **if** it was too late to go.*

In reporting questions with question words, keep the question word:

Policeman: *What are you doing?* > *The policeman demanded to know **what** Tom was doing.*

14 Participle clauses

These clauses, formed with a present or past participle, are rather formal and occur mainly in written English. They are useful because they offer variation in style and allow us to express an idea more briefly:

__Being__ mostly underwater, Maune Kea in Hawaii doesn't appear to be as high as Mount Everest.
***Because** (of the fact that) **it is** mostly underwater, Maune Kea in Hawaii ... .*

Participle clauses have either an adverbial or an adjectival function:

	ADVERBIAL	*ADJECTIVAL*
PRESENT PARTICIPLE	***Lying off the coast**, the ruins are under several metres of water.* (= adv. clause of place)	***The work being carried out** is very important.* (= which is being ...)
PAST PARTICIPLE	***Forgotten for centuries**, the ruins are now being restored.* (= after being forgotten ...)	***Already raised and restored**, some pieces can be seen in Alexandria.* (= which have already been ...)

Participle clauses can follow a number of conjunctions, including *while, though, if, when, before, after, once:*

***Before leaving** the room, we said goodbye to everyone there.*
***If used** carefully, this product should last for years.*

The present participles of stative verbs (eg *be*, above), which are not usually found in the continuous form, can be used in the same way as other verbs. They are often the equivalent of adverbial clauses of reason:

***Thinking** he was a friend of mine, I tapped the man on the shoulder.*
***Having** children of her own, she was sympathetic with the parents' troubles.*

Participle clauses should generally have the same subject as the main clause. For example, in the two examples above, *I* thought he was a friend so *I* tapped the man on the shoulder; and *She* had children of her own so *she* was sympathetic. Do not make mistakes like this: **Driving* too quickly round the corner, a dog jumped out at us.* This means that the dog was driving too quickly!

15 Infinitives and gerunds

Infinitives

Infinitives can be used in a number of structures, including:

- as the **subject** of a sentence: ***To be** here is a great honour.*
  (Note that the gerund is more common than the infinitive here.)
- as the **object** of certain verbs: *I wanted **to jump** into the water.*
  (Note that the object of other verbs would be the gerund.)
- in order to express **purpose**: *We've come **to bring you** some good news.*
- **after** the following:
  it is* + adjective**: *It is easy **to understand.
  question words: *I didn't know what **to do** or how **to respond.***
  indefinite pronouns: *Do you have anything **to say**?*
- in the **subject–verb–object–infinitive** structure: *We wanted you **to come**.*

Gerunds

A gerund is the *-ing* form of the verb when this functions as a noun. It may be used in the following structures:

- as the **subject** of a sentence: ***Exercising** regularly is good for you.*
- as the **object** of certain verbs: *But I don't always enjoy **running**.*
  (It is necessary to learn which verbs can be followed by infinitives and which by gerunds.)
- as the verb form **object** of prepositions and after some **conjunctions**: *We found the house by **following** the map, while **taking** good care that we were not followed.*

16 Phrasal and prepositional verbs

Phrasal verbs

These consist of a verb and an adverb. Examples are *make up* (invent) and *throw out* (expel). The verb is usually a one-syllable verb and the meaning of the combination is often quite different from the meaning of the two parts. *He couldn't **put** his ideas **across*** means his couldn't explain his ideas to others.

Phrasal verbs may be **transitive**:

*They **put off** making a decision.* (postponed it)

or **intransitive**:

*I always **get up** early.*

Transitive phrasal verbs are **separable**, meaning that a **noun** object may come after the adverb:

*My sister is very good at making up **stories**.*

Or it can come between the two parts of the verb:

*She's very good at making **stories** up.*

However, if the object is a **pronoun**, it must come in the central position:

*She loves making **them** up.*

Prepositional verbs

These consist of a verb and a preposition. Again, the meaning of the combination can be quite different from the meaning of the two parts.

*I'm **looking after** my cousin today.* (taking care of my cousin)

*Where did you **come across** this book?* (find it, by chance)

Prepositions have objects so all prepositional verbs are transitive. They are **inseparable**, meaning that the object, whether a noun or pronoun, never comes between the two parts of the verb:

*This is an interesting old book. Where did you **come across it**?*

Three-word verbs

These verbs consist of a verb, an adverb and a preposition. Because of the preposition the object always comes after the verb, never between its different parts (they are **inseparable**):

*I've known John for years and I **get on with him** very well.*

Both phrasal and prepositional verbs are very common in conversational and written English. It's important to remember them in sentences which show whether the verb is separable or inseparable.

17 Adjective issues

Order of adjectives before the noun

It is possible to put more than one adjective in front of a noun. Usually there is a special order for these. Immediately before the noun comes any adjective that says what it's for (often a noun used as an adjective), e.g.: *a pocket handkerchief*. Before that comes any adjective that says what the noun is made of: *a cotton pocket handkerchief*. This may be preceded by any adjective giving information about origin: *an Egyptian cotton pocket handkerchief*. Before that comes any adjective describing colour: *a black and white Egyptian cotton pocket handkerchief*. Before these come adjectives giving information about age, size, shape, etc.: *a small black and white Egyptian cotton pocket handkerchief*. Note that all the adjectives listed so far refer to facts about the noun. A parallel example: *a large-sized grey Thai silk dinner jacket*.

Before all the above kinds of adjective come those representing opinions: *a delightful small black and white Egyptian cotton pocket handkerchief; a smart large-sized grey Thai silk dinner jacket.*

Remember, however, that it is unusual to have more than two or three adjectives before the noun.

Adjectives as nouns

While many nouns can be used as adjectives, only a very limited number of adjectives can be used as nouns. And even those which can be used in this way require a special structure: they must be used with the word *the* and the meaning is always plural – in fact, it must refer to the group of people as a whole. Thus, *the rich* means 'people who are rich', not 'some people who are rich'. Verbs used with this structure must be plural:

*The unemployed **have** to face many difficulties.*

Most adjectives need to be followed by the indefinite pronouns *one* or *ones* if a noun is not used, or repeated:

A: *Which cakes would you like, **the big ones** or the **small ones**?*

B: *I'll have two **small ones** and a **big one**, please.*

Instead of using adjectives as nouns, we can add an indefinite pronoun (*one* or *ones*):

A: *I like those shoes.*
B: *Which **ones**?*
A: *The black ones.*

A: *Would you like a cup of coffee?*
B: *Yes. I'd like a big **one**, please.*

18 Preposition issues

Prepositions consist of one (*in, since, opposite*), or more (*because of, in spite of*) words which have a noun, a noun phrase, a pronoun or a gerund as object: *according to* John (noun); *since* the early part of the century (noun phrase); *between* you and me (pronouns); *in spite of* falling, he won the race (gerund).

Note that the pronouns are in the object form and the verb in the gerund, even when the preposition is *to*: I'm not used to *doing* this.

The normal position for a preposition is before its object, but there are a number of structures where it usually comes after it, including:

in *wh-* questions:	*Where do you come **from**?*
in relative clauses:	*That's the car (which) he came **in**.*
in passive clauses:	*He was being listened **to** with great attention.*
in infinitive clauses:	*I need something to write **with**.*

Note that the relative pronoun *that* cannot follow a preposition:

*It was a book **that/which** I had read and **of which** I still had a copy.*

19 Adverb issues

Types and position

Adverbs of manner (they answer the question *how?*) come in the final position.

Adverbs of place (*where?*) come in the final position.

Adverbs of time (*when?*) come either in the initial or final position.

If there are adverbs of all three types they usually come in the above order:

John spoke ***very well at the meeting last week.***

Adverbs of frequency (*how often?*) and some other adverbs often used with the present perfect (see section 4) come in the mid-position:

I ***often*** *go to that shop but I've* ***rarely*** *seen you there.*

(Do not put the adverb between the verb and the object.)

Adverbs of degree (grading an adjective or another adverb) come immediately before the word they refer to:

It was ***terribly*** *cold and people were behaving* ***very*** *strangely.*

The only exception is *enough*, which comes after:

It was cold ***enough*** *for snow.*

Sentence adverbs (explaining how the speaker views the sentence) usually come in the initial position but can come in the others:

Sadly, *they lost the game.*

20 Linkers

Linkers, words which connect ideas in a text, may be of different types grammatically. In the following, the linkers, in bold, all indicate the idea of contrast:

In spite of *the snow, we made good time.* ***However,*** *by eight o'clock further progress was impossible and* ***although*** *we had a tent, the wind made it very difficult to put it up. We tried several times* ***but*** *did not succeed.*

In spite of is a preposition, *however* a linking adverb, *although* a subordinating conjunction (see section 10) and *but* a coordinating conjunction.

In the same way, we could indicate the idea of addition with: *in addition to* (preposition), *furthermore* (linking adverb) and *and also* (coordinating conjunction) and the idea of cause/result with *because of* (preposition), *consequently* (linking adverb), *because* (subordinating conjunction) and *and/so* (coordinating conjunction).

Macmillan Education
Between Towns Road, Oxford OX4 3PP
A division of Macmillan Publishers Limited
Companies and representatives throughout the world

ISBN 978-1-4050-1863-0

First published 2004

Designed by Ann Samuel
Illustrated by Gary Rees; Tony Morris; Terry McKenna; Martin Salisbuy; Margaret Welbank; Jim Eldridge; Roger Fereday; Pauline King; Dave Burroughs; Kay Dixey; Trevor Parkin; Linda Rogers Associates.
Cover design by Macmillan, original cover design by Wheeler and Porter
Cover photo by Getty Images

The authors and publishers would like to thank the following for permission to reproduce their material:

The Associated Press for adapted extracts from *'Many world languages on brink of extinction'* by Darlene Superville first published in **Associated Press** 19.06.01.

Nicholas Brealey Publishing for Adapted extracts from *When Cultures Collide, Managing Successfully Across Cultures* by Richard Lewis (Nicholas Brealey Publishing, London, (0207 239 0360), 1999).

Macmillan Publishers Limited for adapted extracts from *My Year of Meat* by Ruth Ozeki (Pan Books, 1999), copyright © Ruth Ozeki 1999.

PFD on behalf of the Evelyn Waugh Settlement Trust for extracts from *Scoop* by Evelyn Waugh (Penguin Books Ltd, 1938), copyright © Evelyn Waugh Settlement Trust 1938.

Printed in Malaysia

2013 2012 2011 2010 2009
10 9 8 7 6

The authors and publishers would like to thank the following for permission to reproduce photographs their photographic material:

Alamy p98 (bl), Alamy/Ali Kabas p89 (tr), Alamy /Barry Mason p14 (tr), Alamy/Imagestate p87 (tr), Alamy/Images of france p12 (tm), Alamy /Janine Wiedel Photolibrary p34 (mr), Alamy/Nordic Photos p30 (tm), Alamy/Photofusion Picture Library p97 (tl), Alamy/Popperfoto pp13 (tm, tl), p18 (tm), p92 (br, mr), p93 (tr), p69 (ml), Alamy/Robert Harding Picture Library p54 (tl), Alamy/Reinhard Dirscherl p98 (tr), Alamy/Stephen Frink Collection p98 (tl), Associated Press p94 (tl), Brian Maebius/Brian Maebius p86 (tr); Corbis pp5 (bm), 6 (bl), 7 (tl), 10 (tr), 14 (mr), 15 (tl), 17 (tl), 18 (tr), 28 (ml), 44 (br), 45 (ml, bl, tr, tl)), 58 (tr), 69 (mr, tr), 79 (tr), 95 (br), 98 (mt,tr), 109; Cut2white.com pp20 (ml,tr,mr), 22 (br,bl,bm), 26 (all), 49 (tl), 54 (ml), 73 (tl), 76 (ml, mr, tl), 116 (tr); Getty Images pp5 (br), 6 (tr, bm), 7 (bl), 13 (tr), 14 (ml), 18 (tr), 20 (ml, bl), 22 (tl), 25 (ml), 28 (tl,tr), 30 (mr), (ml), 36 (mr,ml,tr), 37 (ml,tl,bm), 39 (bl, tr,tl), 45 (mr), 46 (tl), 58 (tm), 60 (tr,ml,tl,tm), 63 (tm), 66 (tm,tl), 76 (tr, bl), 84 (bl), 93 (br, mr), 94 (mr); Hulton Archive p6 (mr); Jürgen Freund p87 (mr); Movie store collection/Moviestore Collection pp44 (tl, ml, mr); p46 (tr); MTV Europe/MTV Europe p13 (tr); Panos pictures/Mark French p6 (ml); Reuters/Kevin Lamarque p52 (tl).